WELFARE, THE FAMILY, AND REPRODUCTIVE BEHAVIOR

RESEARCH PERSPECTIVES

Robert A. Moffitt, editor

Committee on Population
Board on Children, Youth, and Families

Commission on Behavioral and Social Sciences and Education

National Research Council and Institute of Medicine

NATIONAL ACADEMY PRESS
Washington, D.C.   1998

NATIONAL ACADEMY PRESS • 2101 Constitution Avenue, N.W. • **Washington, D.C. 20418**

NOTICE: The project that is the subject of this report was approved by the Governing Board of the National Research Council, whose members are drawn from the councils of the National Academy of Sciences, the National Academy of Engineering, and the Institute of Medicine. The members of the committee responsible for the report were chosen for their special competences and with regard for appropriate balance.

This report has been reviewed by a group other than the authors according to procedures approved by a Report Review Committee consisting of members of the National Academy of Sciences, the National Academy of Engineering, and the Institute of Medicine.

Library of Congress Cataloging-in-Publication Data

Welfare, the family, and reproductive behavior : research
perspectives / Robert A. Moffitt, editor.

     p. cm.
   Includes bibliographical references and index.
   ISBN 0-309-06125-3 (pbk.)
   1. Public welfare—Government policy—United States. 2. Child
welfare—Government policy—United States. 3. Birth
control—Government policy—United States. 4. Aid to families with
dependent children programs—United States. I. Moffitt, Robert A.
(Robert Allan), 1917-
   HV91 .W478 1998
   361.973—ddc21
                        98-9099

Additional copies of this report are available from: National Academy Press, 2101 Constitution Avenue, N.W., Washington, D.C. 20418

Call 800-624-6242 or 202-334-3313 (in the Washington Metropolitan Area).

This report is also available on line at **http://www.nap.edu**

Printed in the United States of America

CONTRIBUTORS

CHRISTINE A. BACHRACH, Center for Population Research, National Institute of Child Health and Human Development

REBECCA M. BLANK, Council of Economic Advisers, Executive Office of the President

ELISABETH BOEHNEN, Institute for Research on Poverty, University of Wisconsin, Madison

TOM CORBETT, Institute for Research on Poverty and Department of Social Work, University of Wisconsin, Madison

JANET CURRIE, Department of Economics, University of California, Los Angeles

JACOB ALEX KLERMAN, RAND, Santa Monica, California

REBECCA MAYNARD, Department of Education, University of Pennsylvania

ROBERT A. MOFFITT, Department of Economics, Johns Hopkins University

JANE MOSLEY, National Center for Children in Poverty, Columbia University

GARY SANDEFUR, Department of Sociology, University of Wisconsin, Madison

This project was supported by the Annie E. Casey Foundation and the Kellogg Fund of the Governing Board of the National Academy of Sciences, the National Academy of Engineering, and the Institute of Medicine. Any opinions, findings, conclusions, or recommendations expressed in this publication are those of the authors and do not necessarily reflect the view of the organizations or agencies that provided support for the project.

Preface

Over the last decade, welfare reform has figured prominently in the policy agenda at both the state and the federal levels. One of the most important issues in the policy debate concerns the effect of welfare programs on individual demographic behavior. Some of the possibilities most frequently mentioned are that welfare programs affect labor force participation rates, living arrangements, migration patterns, and reproductive behavior, with perhaps the biggest fear being that welfare programs encourage out-of-wedlock childbearing, particularly among teenagers.

Unfortunately, there is great uncertainty regarding the scientific evidence for these and other possible effects of income support programs. The policy debate is filled with unsubstantiated claims, in both directions (that the programs have no behavioral effects or that they have extremely large behavioral effects). Faced with conflicting claims, even well-informed participants in the policy process find it difficult to distinguish whether disagreement is due to differences in data sources, analytic methods, variability in program or nonprogram factors affecting the behaviors in question, or the interpretation of results.

In an attempt to clarify some of the issues both for the policy debate and for setting research priorities, the National Research Council organized a Workshop on The Effects of Welfare on the Family and Reproductive Behavior in May 1996, which brought together experts in demographic and family studies, along with researchers and policy makers familiar with income support programs. The chapters in this volume were first presented at that workshop and cover the lessons from available research and the implications for future research.

This report is the product of the efforts of many people. The Committee on Population was very fortunate in being able to enlist the services of committee member Robert Moffitt, whose unflagging efforts in organizing the workshop and editing the resulting papers have contributed enormously to the volume. In addition, Ronald Lee, former chair of the Committee on Population, provided much thoughtful guidance at the formative stages of the project. Most importantly, the committee is deeply grateful to the various authors for all their fine work on these papers.

The committee offers appreciative thanks to the Annie E. Casey Foundation and the Kellogg Fund of the Governing Board of the National Academy of Sciences for financial support and to Michael Laracy and William O'Hare at the Casey Foundation for their encouragement and intellectual input.

Finally, the committee thanks the staff at the National Research Council. John Haaga, former director of the Committee on Population, led the initial staff work and served as a rapporteur at the workshop. Anne Bridgman, Nancy Maritato, Kristin McCue, Faith Mitchell, and Deborah Phillips provided essential input at various stages of the project. Final production took place under the guidance of Barney Cohen, director of the Committee on Population. Florence Poillon edited the volume. LaTanya Johnson prepared the papers for publication. The committee is grateful to them all.

Jane Menken, *Chair*
Committee on Population
May 1998

Contents

WELFARE, THE FAMILY, AND REPRODUCTIVE BEHAVIOR

1

Introduction

Robert A. Moffitt

Whether the U.S. welfare system has an effect on marriage, childbearing, living arrangements, and other aspects of demographic and family structure is an issue that has a long history both in the public mind and in research circles. In public and media discussions, the notions that welfare provides an incentive for women to not marry or remarry, to have children out of wedlock, and to live independently rather than at home with parents, have been prominent for over 30 years. Indeed, public attention to these issues accelerated in the 1990s as welfare reform debates in Washington and around the country became increasingly focused on "values" and as specific reform measures began to be proposed to reduce undesirable incentives (e.g., limiting the amount of welfare benefit a mother could receive by having an additional child). At the same time, in research circles, these ideas have been treated instead as hypotheses that should be made subject to test, and the research community has produced a long string of research studies examining these issues in great detail. The research literature itself has also accelerated to some degree in recent decades, with more social scientists examining the issue in the 1980s than in the 1970s, and more in the 1990s than in the 1980s. This research trend is undoubtedly a response to the shift in public attention to the issue.

In May 1996, the Committee on Population and the Board on Children, Youth, and Families of the National Academy of Sciences-National Research Council and Institute of Medicine convened a workshop on the Effects of Welfare on the Family and Reproductive Behavior. Its purpose was to assess what the research community has learned from the studies that had been conducted to date, to identify gaps, and to suggest new areas of research that would be relevant to the changing policy environment—to assess, in the words of the organizers, "what we know and what we need to know" about welfare and the family. The workshop brought together approximately 60 experts to hear a series of presentations by prominent researchers in the area and to discuss future directions. A summary of the discussion that took place at the conference is reported elsewhere (Haaga and Moffitt, 1998). This volume contains the revised and edited presentations from that conference.

This introduction first briefly summarizes each of the chapters in this volume and then discusses their implications for the welfare environment, which has changed dramatically from that in place at the time of the workshop. Just 3 months after that time, the U.S. Congress passed what is generally regarded as the most significant piece of welfare reform legislation since the Social Security Act of 1935. The legislation, titled the Personal Responsibility and Work Opportunity Reconciliation Act (PRWORA), passed Congress and was signed by the President in August 1996. The act eliminated the well-known Aid to Families with Dependent Children (AFDC) program and replaced it with the Temporary Assistance to Needy Families (TANF) program, delegated most of the programmatic and budgetary responsibility for the new program to the states, mandated new work requirement and time limit provisions for the program, and modified in major dimensions the eligibility conditions and provisions of many other welfare programs. The act could have major consequences for the demographic behavior of the low-income population. The following section discusses the relevance of the chapters in this volume for the new welfare environment.

CHAPTERS IN THIS VOLUME

Chapters 2 and 3 provide overviews of recent trends in demographic behavior and the welfare system, respectively. In Chapter 2, Christine Bachrach summarizes the changing circumstances of fertility, marriage, and out-of-wedlock childbearing since 1970. Bachrach demonstrates what most researchers in this area know but the general public often does not, which is that childbearing trends for the whole female population as well as for younger women have not exhibited drastic swings over the last 30 years. However, a major shift has occurred in the proportion of births that occur outside marriage. Bachrach develops this point further by showing that there have been much larger declines in the rate of marriage than of childbearing and that the timing of marriage has drastically shifted toward later ages. She then addresses the increasing rate of nonmarital childbearing and shows that the trend is explained by, more than any other factor, a decline in age-specific marriage rates. This is particularly true for the black population but also for the white population, although the latter has experienced significant declines in childbearing rates among unmarried women as well.

This finding has the very important research implication that it is the decline in marriage, rather than increase in desire for children, that should be the focus of further research, and the important policy implication that it is marriage, rather than childbearing, that should be the focus of any policy measures intended to address nonmarital childbearing. Bachrach also provides a useful overview of trends in sexual behavior and contraceptive use, in the acceptability of having a child outside of marriage, and with respect to socioeconomic differentials, finding that upward trends in nonmarital childbearing have been concentrated among more disadvantaged groups.

In Chapter 3, Rebecca Blank summarizes trends in the U.S. welfare system. Blank shows that the major turning point in benefits and caseloads in the system occurred in the late 1960s and early 1970s, when caseloads in the AFDC program grew dramatically and the Food Stamp and Medicaid programs were introduced. She shows that both benefits and caseloads for the programs were, however, quite stable over the rest of the 1970s and early 1980s. In the late 1980s and early 1990s, AFDC and Food Stamp costs and caseloads grew but were dwarfed by an enormous increase in Medicaid expenditures, in large part because of expansions of the eligibility pool for the program. Blank shows that this trend has put great pressure on state budgets. She then provides a detailed description of the PRWORA legislation, calling it "both less radical and more radical" than often claimed. The most radical provisions are those converting the AFDC program to a block grant, those requiring time limits on receipt of benefits in the new TANF program, and the new work requirement mandates. Blank concludes by emphasizing that the PRWORA legislation merely pushed further trends that had already been occurring for several years, including an increasing emphasis on behavioral requirements as a condition of program eligibility (with particular emphasis on work behavior), an increasing trend toward decentralization in the design of programs, and a trend toward reductions in expenditures and entitlements to welfare.

The remaining four chapters provide reviews and summaries of research findings in four specific areas: the effect of welfare on marriage and fertility; the connections between welfare and abortion; the effect of pre-PRWORA welfare reform interventions on demographic outcomes; and the effect of welfare on children.

In Chapter 4, I review the large research literature on the issue of whether the welfare system, especially the AFDC program, has discouraged marriage and encouraged childbearing. The review concentrates on behavioral research using secondary datasets and household surveys, leaving a review of demonstration research to Chapter 6 by Maynard et al. I argue that the consensus in the research community shifted over time from the 1970s, when it was generally believed that the welfare system had very little effect on marriage and childbearing, to the 1980s and 1990s, when most analysts came to believe that there is an effect. But the magnitude of any effect that is present is highly uncertain and unresolved; some researchers argue that the effect is small and others argue that it is sizable. Research has not shown the welfare system to have been the major contributor to the recent trend in nonmarital childbearing (documented in Chapter 2 by Bachrach) and, for this reason, the consensus in the research community is that other forces must have been at work in generating the trend. The chapter also goes into considerable detail on the methodologies used by different researchers to measure the existence and magnitude of welfare effects and criticizes the research community for failing to reconcile differences in findings that are reported in different studies.

In Chapter 5 on welfare and abortion, Jacob Klerman reviews several issues. One is whether reductions in the generosity of the welfare system, such as those that will result from PRWORA, are likely to affect the rate of abortions. Klerman argues that there is strong reason to believe that abortions will, if anything, increase from such a reform, although he discusses alternative perspectives that may not lead to that result. His review of the empirical studies that have been conducted leads him to conclude that there is little evidence that benefits in the AFDC program have, historically, had any significant effect on the abortion rate. However, he reviews both the data and the statistical difficulties in these studies and finds that the data have significant deficiencies and that statistical limitations reduce confidence in the results. However, Klerman does find that Medicaid restrictions on abortions have had an impact on the abortion rate, according to the research literature.

In Chapter 6, Rebecca Maynard and her coauthors turn away from the nonexperimental behavioral research to the findings of demonstration research. Maynard et al. document that there were a large number of demonstration projects mounted in the states in the 1980s and 1990s prior to PRWORA, most of which were known as "waiver" projects, that were aimed at testing various reforms in the AFDC system. The authors also document the change in the goals of the waiver demonstrations, from an emphasis on work in the 1980s to an emphasis on family structure, parenting, and socially desirable behavior in the 1990s (echoing the trend noted by Blank). Maynard et al. show that there were only two types of waiver demonstrations, however, that directly addressed demographic issues. These were waivers testing a "family cap"—a restriction on the increase in benefit payment to a welfare mother who has had an additional child—and waivers relaxing the stringent eligibility requirements in the AFDC-UP (unemployed parent) program, the program for which two-parent families are eligible (a reform that might be thought to encourage marriage). The authors find that very few evaluations of these waivers have yet reported results. From those that have, such as the family cap demonstration in New Jersey, a decidedly mixed and complex picture has resulted, possibly because of flaws in the demonstration design. The authors do review the findings of a few prior demonstrations aimed at assisting single mothers—but usually not directly aimed at their childbearing or marital behavior—and show that the findings from those demonstrations are also quite mixed, some demonstrations increasing childbearing and others decreasing it, for example. Maynard et al. conclude by reviewing the importance of good designs when conducting demonstration research and make specific recommendations to states regarding how to evaluate their PRWORA programs.

In Chapter 7, Janet Currie takes a broad look at several major welfare programs (Food Stamps, Medicaid, AFDC, housing, and several others) to assess their effects on child outcomes such as birthweight, nutrition, health care, test scores, and the like. Currie provides considerable discussion of the methodological and statistical difficulties in assessing the true effects of the programs. Nevertheless, her review of the research yields one striking finding: unrestricted transfers such as AFDC and the Earned Income Tax Credit have relatively few discernible effects on children, but transfer programs that have specific targeting on children—such as the school nutrition, WIC, and Head Start programs—are much more likely to show positive effects. This finding has clear and significant policy implications. On the other hand, Currie finds that the research literature has neglected many important issues such as the long-run effects of the programs, leading to significant gaps in our knowledge of those types of effects. In her conclusion, she lays out a series of key research questions that should be addressed in future research in this important area.

IMPLICATIONS FOR POLICY AND RESEARCH
IN THE PRWORA ERA

Chapters 4 through 7 reach conclusions that have many similarities. Most find that the majority of studies show either no significant effects of AFDC and other welfare programs, effects that are statistically significant but small in magnitude, a set of mixed effects indicating some that are favorable and some unfavorable, or effects that occur only for some specific types of programs. Although the research reviewed in these chapters does not support a finding of no effect whatsoever of welfare programs on demographic behavior, it would be difficult to argue that the research often indicates very sizable or stable effects. Whether this is a result of problems with the studies themselves, as discussed at length by the chapter authors, or whether it is the true state of affairs cannot be decided with certainty at this time. However, it is also fair to note that if there were a sizable effect of welfare on demographic behavior, it would probably be more evident with the available statistical methods than appears to be the case in the research literature. The findings reported in the chapters are, on the contrary, consistent with the existence of a small, real effect but one that is difficult to detect and sensitive to the methodology used because it is small relative to other factors determining demographic outcomes.

The wide dispersion of findings in many of the research literatures surveyed by the authors weakens the confidence one can have in this or any other conclusion. To some extent, a variance in research findings is common to all areas of investigation and is not particularly surprising. However, it does worsen the traditional conflict between the desires and needs of policy makers, who want certainty before making policy recommendations, and the research community, which is willing to accept uncertainty and thus is more accustomed to reaching tentative conclusions. Still, it would be unquestionably preferable for the amount of uncertainty to be reduced below what it is in many of these research literatures, because the impact of research on policy is, in general, in strong inverse proportion to the degree of dispersion of its findings.

In considering the implications of this research for the demographic effects of the PRWORA legislation, the clear prima facie implication is that those effects can be expected to be small. However, whether this will occur depends on whether the effects of historical programs like AFDC can be extrapolated to the findings of a much different set of state programs that will evolve in the next few years. Certainly PRWORA both requires and allows changes in the programs that are more significant than the types of variations in the AFDC program used to estimate demographic effects in past behavioral and demonstration research. The work requirements of PRWORA go considerably beyond those of the traditional AFDC programs and beyond those of the Family Support Act of 1988, as clearly do the time limits, which have been tested in the past only in waiver form.[1] Thus it is absolutely necessary to conduct rigorous evaluations of PRWORA and to include demographic outcomes (marriage, childbearing, etc.) as part of those evaluations.

Several of the chapters address the relative advantages of nonexperimental behavioral and demonstration research in studies of the past welfare system, an issue that must be addressed in evaluations of PRWORA as well. The discussions in the chapters suggest that neither type of research should be relied upon exclusively. The methodological discussions contained in various chapters make clear the difficulties of nonexperimental behavioral research, while the review of demonstration research provided by Maynard et al. shows how difficult conducting a good demonstration is as well. The chapters also provide a basis for concluding that even good demonstration research provides answers to only a narrow set of questions and that context, as well as exploration of the mechanisms by which responses occur, is more easily obtained from the analysis of nonexperimental, secondary datasets. Contextual and ethnographic perspectives also bring added information to the response of families to welfare reform that is not provided by either nonexperimental behavioral modeling or demonstration research. A balanced strategy employing a mix of all approaches, not unlike that

---

[1]It is worth noting, however, that the PRWORA legislation did not, in the end, have many provisions directly aimed at demographic outcomes. Neither family caps, significant changes in the AFDC-UP program, nor prohibitions on the provision of benefits to unmarried mothers were mandated, for example, despite the extensive legislative discussion of such provisions in the debates preceding passage of the bill. In the end, the U.S. Congress left those decisions to the states. For this reason, the major impact of PRWORA on demographic outcomes will operate indirectly from the reduction of benefits and eligibility that will result from the main provisions of the bill.

outlined by Maynard et al. in the concluding sections of Chapter 6, would appear to be the safest overall strategy toward PRWORA evaluation.

At this writing, many evaluations of PRWORA are under way, and no doubt many more will be initiated over the next few months and years. A series of demonstration projects in the individual states, many of which are funded in part or in whole by the U.S. Department of Health and Human Services, have been put in place to study state-level welfare reform and child care projects, as well as child outcomes. Some of these demonstrations are continuances of evaluations of pre-PRWORA waiver demonstrations, some of which were continued after PRWORA, and others are new evaluations. Some use experimental evaluation methods and others consist of longitudinal data collection designs (e.g., of the child welfare system). Another study has been initiated as well by the U.S. General Accounting Office to monitor welfare reform in the states as it proceeds. Many more local studies have also been begun by state agencies.

At the same time, several survey research projects have been set in motion to evaluate the effects of PRWORA by methods coming more from the tradition of nonexperimental behavioral research. The U.S. Bureau of the Census has initiated a Survey of Program Dynamics intended to follow for several more years a group of families previously interviewed under the auspices of the Survey of Income and Program Participation. The families will be interviewed on a periodic basis to ascertain responses to PRWORA. The Urban Institute has conducted one wave of a cross-sectional telephone survey of families in 13 states to ascertain welfare responses and will follow this survey up with a second wave in 2 or 3 years. Surveys of welfare recipients, former but recent welfare recipients, and nonrecipients in a set of specific cities or counties—sometimes supplemented by administrative data—have been begun by research teams centered at the Manpower Demonstration Research Corporation, Johns Hopkins University, Princeton University, and other locations. Ethnographic and contextual research is a part of several of these efforts. A project to study the administrative response to welfare reform has also been initiated by the Rockefeller Institute at the State University of New York at Albany. In addition, the research community can expect to see more traditional research studies conducted using well-known national surveys like the Current Population Survey, the Panel Study on Income Dynamics, the National Longitudinal Survey, and others, as well as using aggregate caseload data from the new welfare system. Although not all of these studies will have demographic outcomes as a major focus, many if not most will at least have them as a minor focus.

While there is no guarantee that such a decentralized and uncoordinated set of activities will produce consensus findings on the effects of PRWORA—and one of the lessons of the chapters reviewed in this volume is that the investigators conducting these studies will have to work to meet the challenge of reconciling differences in findings across studies—there are reasonable prospects that much useful information on the effects of PRWORA will be gathered.

The research surveyed in these chapters, covering studies conducted on the old system right up to the point of its demise, should provide in the years to come a statement of where we were, in terms of research knowledge, on the eve of the beginning of a new welfare era. If a similar volume comes to be produced in the future, say 10 years hence, it will be interesting to compare its reviews with those reported here in terms of the fundamental question of whether welfare affects demographic outcomes, as well as whether the research community has been any more successful in reaching consensus on what those outcomes are.

REFERENCE

John Haaga and Robert A. Moffitt, eds.
  1988   *Welfare, The Family, and Reproductive Behavior: Report of a Meeting*. Committee on
            Population and Board on Children, Youth, and Families, National Research Council and
            Institute of Medicine. Washington, D.C.: National Academy Press.

2

The Changing Circumstances of Marriage and Fertility in the United States

Christine A. Bachrach

Changes in marriage and childbearing have substantially reshaped the American family in recent decades, with consequences for the economic well-being of children, the composition and stability of families, and the complexity of family relations. Increasing rates of out-of-wedlock childbearing, especially visible among teenagers, have become a focal point of public concern and social policy debate. Some observers have suggested that these changes result in part from the effect of welfare programs—programs that, it is believed, encourage sex and childbearing outside of marriage and discourage young people from marrying and staying married. A careful assessment of scientific evidence regarding the role of welfare in stimulating out-of-wedlock childbearing or other demographic changes must begin with a thorough understanding of the nature of the changes themselves, including what demographic behaviors have changed and how, and how these changes have been distributed within our population.

This chapter provides an overview of trends in fertility, marriage, and out-of-wedlock childbearing in the United States, focusing mainly on the period since 1970. It also examines trends in the proximate factors that affect fertility, such as sexual behavior, contraception and abortion, because if welfare programs have affected fertility among unmarried women, the effects would have to be channeled through one or more of these factors. The paper concludes with a brief look at trends in out-of-wedlock childbearing among populations that vary in their reliance on welfare programs.

Several conclusions are advanced: that changes in marriage have played a central role in driving the increase in nonmarital births; that changes in marriage have included not only changes in its frequency and timing but also changes in its function of defining acceptable settings for sexual activity and childbearing; that all population groups have participated in these changes but that the changes have occurred at different rates in different groups; and that despite the ubiquitous nature of these changes, out-of-wedlock childbearing remains powerfully associated with socioeconomic disadvantage.

WHAT IS HAPPENING TO FERTILITY?

A quick glance at trends in the U.S. fertility rate (Figure 2-1) reveals that, since the early 1970s, American women in the aggregate have been bearing children at a remarkably stable rate. The fertility rate (the number of births per 1,000 women of childbearing age, 15-44) has hovered between about 65 and 70 since 1973 when it fell below 70 for the first time since the Great Depression. The intervening period from 1940 to 1970 saw, first, increasing fertility rates, culminating with the peak of the baby boom in the late 1950s, and then steadily declining rates until the early 1970s (Ventura et al., 1995a). Since then, the overall patterns have remained remarkably stable, with the exception of a slight rise at the end of the 1980s, now apparently on its way toward reversal (National Center for Health Statistics, 1996).

Beneath the surface of this demographic nontrend, however, lurk some important changes. One of these is the pattern of birth timing. Norman Ryder showed that trends in period fertility rates are a function of the number of births

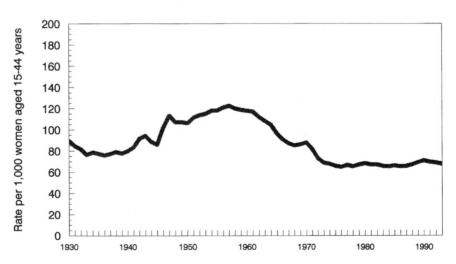

FIGURE 2-1 Fertility rates, United States: 1930-1993. NOTE: Beginning with 1959, trend lines are based on registered live births; trend lines for 1930-1959 are based on live births adjusted for underregistration. SOURCE: National Center for Health Statistics (1996).

women have and the timing of those births (Ryder, 1980). Over the past two decades, there has been little variation in the number of births women have—first and second births have accounted for about 75 percent of the total fertility rate since the mid-1970s (Morgan, 1996). However, there is much more diversity now in *when* women are having children.

Figure 2-2 contrasts the age-specific birth rates in 1972 and 1993—two years in which the total fertility rate (a function of the sum of these rates) was quite similar (2,010 and 2,046, respectively). In 1972, the likelihood of giving birth peaked in the early twenties and declined steeply after age 30. In 1993, birth rates among women under age 30 had declined relative to their 1972 levels; the peak age of childbearing had shifted to the late twenties by a slight margin, and the risks of giving birth during the thirties had increased by about one-third. The fertility of women aged 30 and older accounted for 29.2 percent of the total fertility rate in 1993, up from 22.6 percent in 1972. Despite stability in the volume of childbearing, a substantial shift toward a later and more variable pattern of birth timing had occurred.

It's worth noting that birth rates for teenagers (15-19) were stable or declining through most of the 1970s and 1980s, despite the attention given to the problem of teen childbearing during this period. Teens did participate disproportionately in the fertility "boomlet" of the late 1980s, with rates for women 15-19 rising 23 percent over a period of 3-4 years beginning in 1987, compared to 8 percent among women in their twenties. However, the most important change in

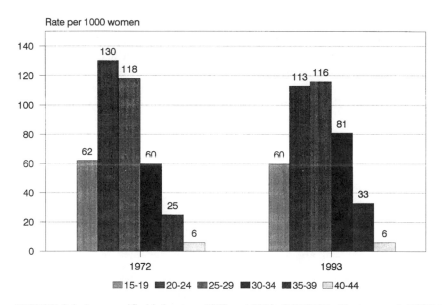

FIGURE 2-2 Age-specific birth rates: 1972 and 1993. SOURCE: Ventura et al. (1995a).

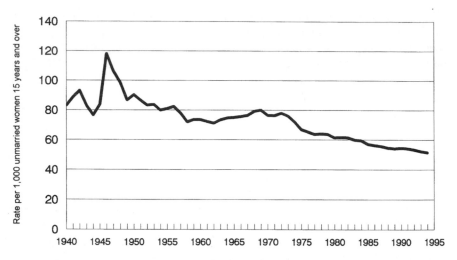

FIGURE 2-3 Marriage rates: 1940-1994. SOURCE: Clarke (1995).

teen fertility over this period is a change shared by older women as well—the increasing proportion of births that occurred outside of marriage. Trends in marriage patterns are a critical element of this change, and I turn to them next.

MARRIAGE: DELAYS AND DECLINES

U.S. marriage statistics for the past quarter century paint a grim picture of an institution that Americans continue to say they value highly. During a period when the proportion of high school seniors claiming that a good marriage is "quite or extremely important" to them held steady at over 90 percent for women and over 85 percent for men (Thornton, 1989), marriage rates appeared to be in free-fall. The marriage rate for unmarried women aged 15 and older has been declining since the early 1970s, when it had a modest resurgence following another steady decline from the postwar peak (Figure 2-3).

These overall rates tell only part of the story, however. The total first-marriage rate for women (which shows the percentage that would ever marry if subjected throughout their lives to the current year's regime of age-specific rates) declined prior to the mid-1970s but remained fairly stable between 68 percent and 72 percent from the mid-1970s to 1990, the last year for which data are available from the Vital Registration System[1] (Clarke, 1995). As in the case of fertility, what has changed most dramatically is the timing of marriage. First

---

[1]It is likely that 1990 will be one of the last years for which detailed marriage statistics are available from the Vital Registration System. After 1995, the National Center for Health Statistics plans to collect data on numbers of marriages only.

marriage rates for women aged 18-19 plummeted from 151 per 1,000 in 1970 to 53 per 1,000 in 1990 (Figure 2-4). Rates for women aged 20-24 fell from 220 per 1,000 to 93 per 1,000 during the same period. Rates for women in their late twenties and early thirties changed far less, declining during the 1970s but increasing during the 1980s. Among men, trends in marriage were roughly similar,

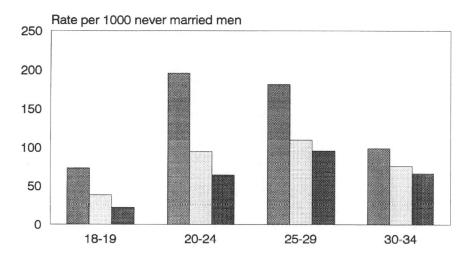

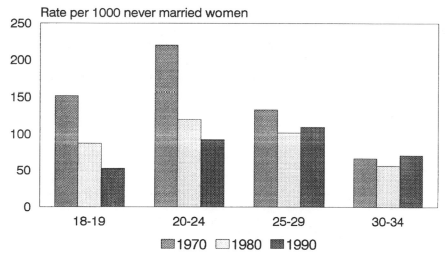

FIGURE 2-4 First-marriage rates, by age and sex: Marriage Registration Area, 1970, 1980, and 1990.

although men have shown no signs of the rebounding marriage rates observed during the 1980s among women in their late twenties and thirties.

Data from the Current Population Survey provide another view of marriage trends based on repeated surveys of large probability samples of all households in the United States.[2] In Figure 2-5, these data show that the proportions of men and women aged 18-44 who are unmarried has increased steadily in all age groups since 1970 and that increases in the percentage unmarried have been particularly steep among those in their twenties—ages at which, as we have seen previously, fertility rates are at their highest. For example, the percentage of unmarried among women aged 20-24 increased 75 percent, from 39 percent to 69 percent between 1970 and 1984; the percentage unmarried among men aged 25-29 more than doubled, from 22 percent to 55 percent (Department of Health and Human Services, 1995; Saluter, 1996).

Two qualifying observations are necessary to fill out this picture of declining marriage and increasing singlehood. First, the chosen starting point for this review of recent demographic trends, 1970, marks the end of a highly unusual period for American marriage patterns. Figure 2-6, showing the median age at first marriage from 1890 to 1994, illustrates that the pattern of early marriage in the 1950s and 1960s was an exception to a historical pattern of relatively higher ages at marriage. The median age at first marriage for men is barely higher in 1994 than in 1890; the median age for women, on the other hand, has substantially exceeded its recorded precedents (Saluter, 1996).

The second qualifying observation is that the delay in marriage does not signal a corresponding delay in the formation of marriage-like unions. Cohabitation by unmarried partners has increased dramatically over recent decades, and recent data from the second wave of the National Survey of Families and Households confirms that it is continuing to increase (Bumpass and Sweet, 1995). Bumpass and Sweet (1989) have demonstrated that increases in cohabitation substantially offset declines in marriage between cohorts of women born in 1940-1944 and 1960-1964. Thus, although only 61 percent of the later cohort married

---

[2]It is useful to examine both vital statistics and Current Population Survey data on trends in marriage because they have complementary strengths and weaknesses. Vital statistics estimates of age-specific marriage rates are based on samples of marriage records from states participating in the Marriage Registration Area (MRA). In 1989-1990, the MRA included only 86 percent of the U.S. population and excluded 8 states (Arizona, Arkansas, Nevada, New Mexico, North Dakota, Oklahoma, Texas, and Washington). Moreover, its samples did not include detailed information on the characteristics of brides and grooms obtaining nonlicensed California marriages (about 103,000 of these occurred in 1990). For this and other reasons, data from the MRA samples represent only 77 percent of the marriages that occurred during 1989-1990, and understate marriage rates for the United States as a whole (Clarke, 1995). Estimates from the Current Population Survey are based on a national probability sample of households in the United States. The advantage of this data source is thus in improved geographic coverage; disadvantages include undercoverage of men, blacks, and persons not in households and the frequent reliance on proxy reports of marital status (Saluter, 1996).

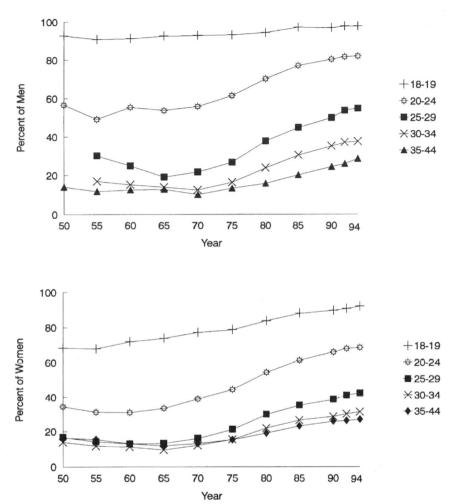

FIGURE 2-5 Percentage unmarried by age: 1910-1994. SOURCE: Department of Health and Human Services (1995).

by age 25 (compared with 82 percent of the earlier cohort), the difference in the percentage entering either a marital or a cohabitational union by age 25 was far smaller (76 percent and 83 percent, respectively).

THE UBIQUITOUS RISE OF NONMARITAL FERTILITY

At the intersection of these trends in fertility and marriage we find a phenomenon that has drawn increasing attention from policy makers and the public:

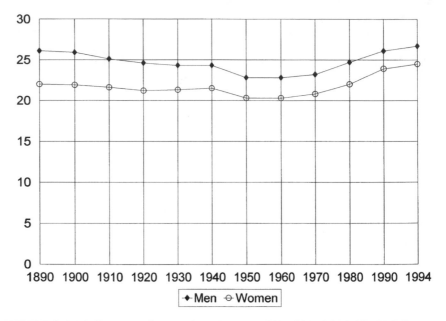

FIGURE 2-6   Median age at first marriage, by sex: 1890-1994. SOURCE: U.S. Bureau of the Census (1996).

increasing out-of-wedlock births. Since 1940, the year for which we have the earliest data, out-of-wedlock childbearing has shown an almost constant increase. This is true whether one looks at the number of nonmarital births (Figure 2-7, top panel), the rate at which unmarried women give birth (middle panel), or the nonmarital birth ratio, which shows the proportion of all births that occur to unmarried women (bottom panel). In 1993, 31 percent of births were born out-of-wedlock, up from 4 percent in 1940; and 11 percent in 1970.[3]

The simplicity and regularity of this upward trend belie considerable complexity and change in the factors that have contributed to it. Smith and Cutright (1988) have demonstrated that the increase in the nonmarital birth ratio is a function of four components: the age-specific birth rates for unmarried and for married women, the proportion of women unmarried at each age, and the age structure of the population. Since the mid-1970s,

   •   the population of reproductive age has shifted toward an older age distribution, putting slight downward pressure on the nonmarital birth ratio;
   •   the percentage of unmarried has increased at each age, as we have seen;
   •   age-specific birth rates for married women have generally increased, al-

---

[3]The increase in the percentage of births occurring outside of marriage slowed after 1993, hovering between 32 percent and 33 percent during the years 1994-1996 (Ventura et al., 1997).

Panel 1. Number of births to unmarried women

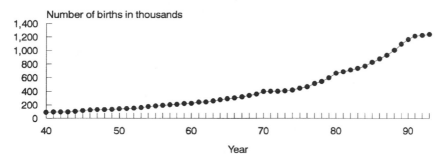

Panel 2. Birth rate for unmarried women

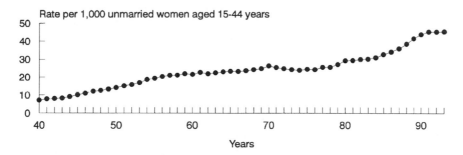

Panel 3. Proportion of births to unmarried women

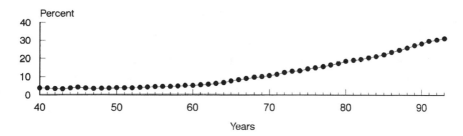

FIGURE 2-7 Trends in out-of-wedlock childbearing: 1940-1993. SOURCE: Department of Health and Human Services (1995).

though the *overall* marital birth rate has declined because the married population has become increasingly older; and

• age-specific birth rates for unmarried women increased sharply at all ages (Figure 2-8); note, however, that this was a reversal from a sharp downward trend in such rates during the preceding decade for all age groups *except* teenagers. The increase in age-specific nonmarital birth rates leveled off in the early 1990s.

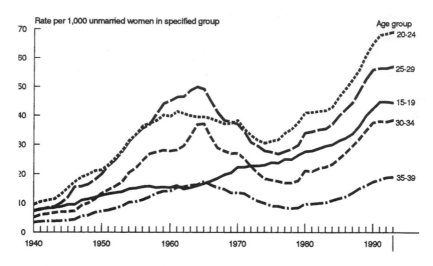

FIGURE 2-8 Birth rates for unmarried women by age: 1940-1993. SOURCE: Department of Health and Human Services (1995).

Figure 2-9 shows the results of an analysis by Smith and his colleagues showing the importance of each of these components in contributing to the upward trend in the nonmarital birth ratio for each year between 1960 and 1992. Their results are shown separately for black and white women. In these figures, the effect of each of the four components is represented by a line that has an upward slope if the component was exerting upward pressure on the ratio during the given year and a downward slope if it was exerting negative pressure. The steeper the slope of the line, the greater is the upward (or downward) pressure on the nonmarital birth ratio. The figures show that since the early 1970s, the major factor driving the increase in the nonmarital birth ratio for black women (top panel) was the increase in the proportion unmarried. For white women (bottom panel), both changes in marital status and increased rates of out-of-wedlock childbearing have been significant. Trends in marital fertility pushed the ratio up during the 1960s and early 1970s but have since exerted a slight downward pressure on the ratio (Smith et al., 1996).

To recap this overview so far, changes in the frequency and timing of marriage have been more pronounced than changes in the frequency and timing of childbearing during recent decades in the United States. Increases in out-of-wedlock childbearing have been driven primarily by changes in marriage, but also by changes in the reproductive behavior of unmarried women. In the next section, I examine the behavioral trends underlying the changing fertility of unmarried women.

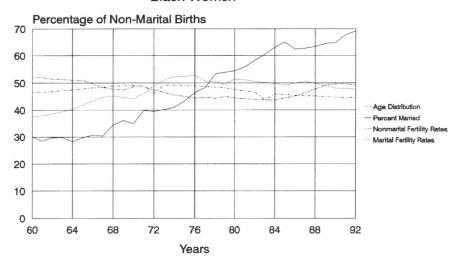

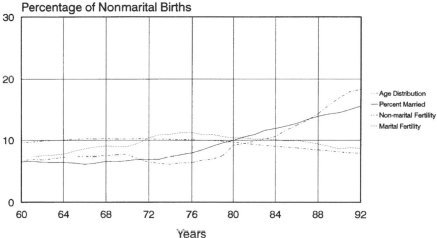

FIGURE 2-9 Standardized effects of selected factors on nonmarital birth ratios, by race: 1960-1992. SOURCE: Smith et al. (1996).

PROXIMATE FACTORS: PATHWAYS FOR THE EFFECTS OF WELFARE ON NONMARITAL FERTILITY

Births to unmarried women occur as the result of a series of behaviors and choices made by women and their partners. Figure 2-10 illustrates that choices about whether or not to have sex outside of marriage, whether to use

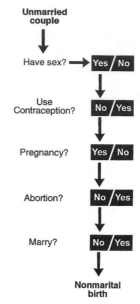

FIGURE 2-10 Path to nonmarital fertility.
SOURCE: Department of Health and Human Services (1995).

contraception consistently and effectively, whether to end a pregnancy by induced abortion, and, if carrying the pregnancy to term, whether to marry before the baby is born all contribute to increasing or decreasing the chances of out-of-wedlock childbearing. If welfare programs are to have an effect on fertility, they would have to do so through affecting one or more of these behaviors. In this section, I explore trends in these key behaviors that lead up to an out-of-wedlock birth.

Attention to these behaviors is important, because evidence suggests that the majority of births to unmarried women are unintended. Sixty-five percent of births during the preceding 5 years to women who were never married in 1988 occurred as a result of an unwanted or mistimed pregnancy; among unmarried teens, this proportion soared to 86 percent (Brown and Eisenberg, 1995). In 1987, nearly 9 in 10 pregnancies experienced by never-married women, and 7 in 10 experienced by formerly married women, were unintended (Forrest, 1994). One way that welfare programs could affect nonmarital fertility is by encouraging intentional childbearing among unmarried women. Another, more likely, way is to reduce the costs of getting "caught" with an unintended out-of-wedlock birth and therefore encourage behaviors that have childbearing as an unintended consequence, such as nonmarital sex and contraceptive risk taking.

There is no question that the sexual experience of the unmarried population has increased over recent decades. Figure 2-11, from a national survey of sexual behavior conducted by University of Chicago researchers, shows that early initiation into sexual experience has become increasingly likely for both men and

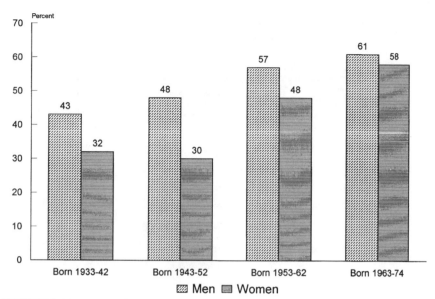

FIGURE 2-11 Percentage of adults who have had sexual intercourse by age 18, by year of birth. SOURCE: Laumann et al. (1994).

women (Laumann et al., 1994). This earlier age at sexual debut, combined with later ages at marriage, has driven up the proportions who engage in sex pre-maritally (Department of Health and Human Services, 1995). Among ever-married women aged 15-24 in 1988, 84 percent had had sexual intercourse before they married, up from 65 percent in the cohorts born 20 years earlier.

While unmarried people have sex less often, on average, than married people, most are sexually active to some degree. National data for adults 18-59 show that only 19 percent of unmarried men and 27 percent of unmarried women did not have sex at all in the past year (calculated from data in Laumann et al., 1994). Trend data on sexual activity of the unmarried population are available for women for the period 1982-1988. These data show that during this period, the percentage of never-married women who had had intercourse in the last 3 months increased from 45 percent to 49 percent; the percentage of sexually active among the formerly married declined during the period, from 68 percent to 61 percent (Forrest and Singh, 1990).

Contraceptive use by unmarried women having sexual intercourse also in-creased during the 1980s. Figure 2-12 shows that use of methods such as steril-ization, pill, and condom increased among unmarried sexually active women age 15-44 between 1982 and 1988. The percentage of these women not using a method because they were seeking pregnancy remained constant at under 3 per-cent. Nonuse of a method for other reasons by sexually active women decreased

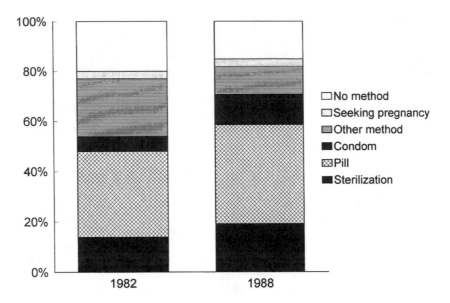

FIGURE 2-12 Contraceptive use among unmarried sexually active women 15-44: 1982 and 1988. Department of Health and Human Services (1995).

from 19 to 14 percent during the period (Department of Health and Human Services, 1995). We do not have any reliable data on trends in vigilance in contraceptive use. Yet we know that contraceptive failure rates are high, ranging from 7 percent failure during the first 12 months of use among pill users to 31 percent among users of periodic abstinence. Overall, about 16 percent of never-married contraceptors and 26 percent of formerly married contraceptors using reversible methods of contraception experience failure in the first 12 months of method use. Contraceptive failure results in part from a failure of the method and in part from inconsistent or inaccurate use of the method (Jones and Forrest, 1992).

Increased sexual activity tends to drive up pregnancy rates; improved contraceptive use tends to drive them down. Theoretically the two could balance out. In fact, pregnancy rates for unmarried women increased in recent decades. Figure 2-13 shows the trend in pregnancy rates for married and unmarried women using an approximate measure based on pregnancies ending in abortion or birth.[4] Pregnancy rates for unmarried women increased most rapidly during the 1970s,

---

[4]This measure is calculated by combining data on abortion rates by year and marital status with birth rates in which the year of "birth" is moved up by 6 months. Thus, the rates refer to a time period a few months after conceptions occurred and do not include conceptions ending in spontaneous fetal loss (Stanley Henshaw, personal communication).

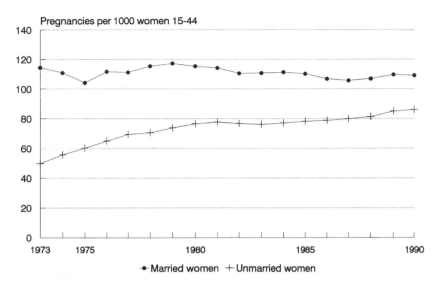

FIGURE 2-13 Estimated rates of pregnancy: 1973-1990. NOTE: Excludes pregnancies ending in miscarriage or stillbirth. Births are lagged 6 months. SOURCE: Calculated based on data in Alan Guttmacher Institute (1992).

remained level during much of the 1980s, but increased again toward the end of that decade. Pregnancy rates for 1980, 1990, and 1991 calculated by Ventura and her colleagues confirm this pattern and show that the increase during the 1980-1990 period was confined to unmarried white women: pregnancy rates for unmarried black women fell during this time (Ventura et al., 1995b).

When a pregnancy occurs, whether it is carried to term is strongly influenced by marital status. The abortion ratio, or the ratio of abortions to all pregnancies ending in either live birth or abortion, gives a rough measure of the likelihood that a pregnancy will end in abortion.[5] In 1991, the abortion ratio was 8.6 per 100 pregnancies among married women, but 51.2 among unmarried women (Figure 2-14). Abortion ratios among unmarried women increased sharply in the first few years following the 1973 Supreme Court decision, from 57 per 100 in 1973 to 66 per 100 in 1977. But since 1979, the ratio has traced a steady decline, which has accelerated in recent years. Thus, pregnancies to unmarried women have become *less* likely to end in abortion, and *more* likely to end in birth.[6]

---

[5]The missing element, spontaneous fetal loss, occurs in about 15 percent of all pregnancies.

[6]During 1980-1987, declines in the abortion ratio occurred among white women of all ages, and among black women at ages 20 and older. Abortion ratios for black teens did not decline. However, even in 1980, only 44 percent of pregnancies to black teens ended in abortion—a ratio substantially lower than that of older black women and white women of all ages (Henshaw, et al., 1985; Henshaw and Silverman, 1988; Henshaw et al., 1991).

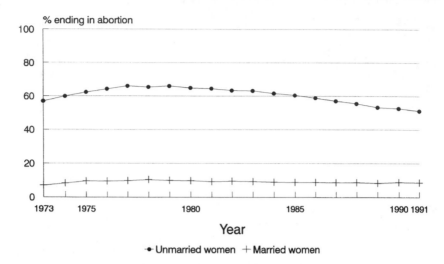

FIGURE 2-14   Percentage of pregnancies ending in abortion: married and unmarried women, 1973-1991. NOTE: % = abortions as percent of abortions+births; births lagged 6 months. SOURCE: Alan Guttmacher Institute (1992).

If an unmarried woman decides to carry a pregnancy to term, she may still avoid becoming an unwed mother by marrying before the delivery of the baby. This practice was common in previous decades but has declined steadily over time (Figure 2-15). In 1960-1964, 52 percent of first births resulting from out-of-wedlock pregnancies to women 15-34 years of age were "legitimated" before the birth by the marriage of the mother; by 1985-1989, only 27 percent were legitimated (Bachu, 1993). In a recent analysis, Morgan and his associates (1995) demonstrate that this decline in legitimation has had a substantial impact on the trend in out-of-wedlock births. Considering only those pregnancies ending in live birth, they demonstrate that the rate of nonmarital birth would have increased only marginally between the early 1960s and the mid-1980s if unmarried pregnant women had continued to marry between conception and birth at the same rate as they had in 1963.

Trends in the sexual behavior of unmarried women, and in their choice of abortion and "shotgun" marriage in response to out-of-wedlock pregnancy, reflect important changes in the meaning of marriage in our society. In the 1950s, when Davis and Blake (1956) first developed their "intermediate variables" framework, sexual activity was not included as one of the intermediate variables; marriage was. Their ability to propose marriage as a proxy for regular sexual exposure reflected the close identification of "sex" and "marriage" at that time. This identification has been seriously eroded over recent decades, as reflected in trends in public attitudes about premarital sex. The proportion of women under

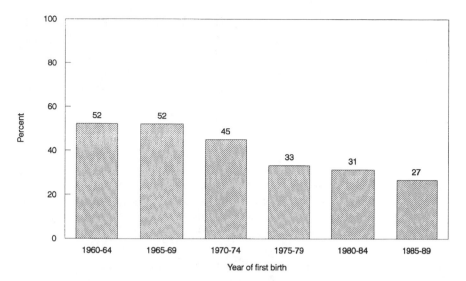

FIGURE 2-15 Percentage of women marrying between conception and birth of first child: 1960-1964 to 1985-1989. SOURCE: Bachu (1991).

30 agreeing that premarital sex is "not wrong at all" increased from about one-fifth in the mid-1960s to about half in the mid-1980s. In 1965, half of women under 30 believed that premarital sex was "always wrong" but by the late 1970s and during the 1980s, only about 13-14 percent believed this (Thornton, 1989). Attitudes towards nonmarital childbearing have shown similar changes (Pagnini and Rindfuss, 1993). Thus, as marriage has changed in its frequency and timing, it has also changed in its meaning: the consensus that it provides a normative boundary defining the acceptable settings for sex and childbearing no longer exists. Undoubtedly, these changes are mutually reinforcing: the ability to have sex and bear children outside of marriage permits marriage to be delayed or forgone; and the changing size and demographics of the unmarried and married populations contribute to marriage being seen in new ways. In this sense, change in the reproductive behaviors of unmarried women is inextricably interwoven with changes in marriage.

TRENDS BY RACE AND SOCIOECONOMIC STATUS

To this point, I have mainly focused on trends in fertility, marriage, and out-of-wedlock fertility in the U.S. population as a whole. However, since if welfare programs affect marriage and fertility they are likely to do so primarily among disadvantaged socioeconomic groups, it would be most useful to replicate these trend analyses for poor and near-poor populations. However, two basic pitfalls hinder an examination of trends by poverty status. One is a scarcity of appropriate data.[7] The source of our best data on out-of-wedlock childbearing, the vital registration system, does not collect information on family income. Data from the Current Population Survey (CPS) provide some measures, but in most years the CPS collects incomplete data on marital status and fertility. A second pitfall, which calls into question the use of cross-sectional data such as those collected by the CPS, is the endogeneity of poverty and marital and fertility behavior. The CPS measures income (and proxies such as employment, occupation, and education) as of (or close to) the survey date, whereas fertility and marital events may have occurred at any time in the past. Marriage tends to lift people out of poverty; childbearing often signals a change in living arrangements and another mouth to feed. Data linking current socioeconomic status with past or even recent fertility and marriage are therefore of doubtful value in inferring trends in poor populations.

Given these limitations, the strategy adopted here is to examine trend data according to relatively enduring characteristics that are associated with, but not identical to, poverty. The first characteristic examined is race. The advantage of race is that most trend data presented in this chapter are available by race; the disadvantage is that is it a poor proxy for income or poverty. Most black and white families are not poor even though, in 1992, poverty was three times as prevalent among black (31 percent) as among white (9 percent) families (U.S. Bureau of the Census, 1994). Differences in fertility and marriage trends among different racial groups are instructive, however, because they challenge popular stereotypes.

Table 2-1 provides a summary of some of the key trends examined elsewhere in this paper among black and white women. Although the direction of trends is frequently similar in both groups, notable differences exist in the rate at which change has taken place. The trends for which black women have experienced the greatest proportional change are all trends related to marriage. Compared with white women, black women experienced a steeper increase in the percentage unmarried among women aged 20-29 and a sharper decrease in the percentage marrying between the conception of a premarital birth and its delivery. The trends for which white women have experienced greatest change all involve reproductive behaviors outside of marriage, and in all of these areas the greater changes among white women have narrowed the differences between the racial

---

[7]Published national statistics on marriage and childbearing, and on out-of-wedlock childbearing in particular, are rarely presented by income or poverty status. My search of published statistical resources yielded no adequate trend data of this nature covering the period of interest. Trends could be analyzed using data from the Current Population Survey or (to take another approach) by attaching areal data to vital statistics data. However, such analyses would be difficult to interpret (see text) and are beyond the scope of this chapter.

TABLE 2-1 Comparison of Trends: Black and White Women, 1970s-1990s

Year	Black Women	White Women
Rate of births per 1,000 unmarried women		
1970	96	14
1993	84 (−13%)	36 (+157%)
Percentage of unmarried women 20-29		
1970	33	23
1992	70 (+112%)	45 (+96%)
Percentage of women 15-19 who had premarital sex		
1971	51	29
1988	60 (+18%)	51 (+76%)
Pregnancy rate (including fetal loss) per 1,000 unmarried women		
1980	180[a]	69
1991	174[a] (−3%)	81 (+17%)
Abortion ratio, unmarried women		
1980	52[a]	72
1987	50[a] (−4%)	62 (−14%)
Percentage married before birth: women 15-34 with premarital pregnancy resulting in first birth		
1970-1974	18	54
1985-1989	7 (−61%)	34 (−37%)

[a]Nonwhite women.
SOURCES: Nonmarital birth rates: Ventura et al. (1995a); percentage unmarried: Saluter (1996); premarital sex: Hofferth et al. (1987); pregnancy rates: Ventura et al. (1995b); abortion ratios: Henshaw et al. (1985, 1991); marriage between pregnancy and birth: Bachu (1991).

groups. Rates of teen premarital sex and out-of-wedlock pregnancy and birth rates have all increased more for whites (and in some cases decreased for blacks); abortion ratios have dropped more steeply for white than black women. If a "decoupling" of marriage and sexual/reproductive behavior occurred among black women, it had already largely occurred before 1970; since 1970, change in the function of marriage as boundary for these behaviors has primarily affected white women. Meanwhile, among both races but especially among black women, marriage itself is increasingly postponed or forgone.

Limited trend data from the Current Population Survey have been published for a second set of (relatively enduring) characteristics associated with income and poverty: occupation and education. Tables 2-2 and 2-3 present trends in several indicators of nonmarital childbearing according to these characteristics. These data show clearly that, in the period since 1982, changes in out-of-wedlock childbearing have affected all socioeconomic groups. Between 1982 and 1992, the fertility of never-married women increased at all educational levels and in managerial/professional as well as other occupations (Table 2-2). However, very

TABLE 2-2   Percentage of Never-Married Women Age 18-44 Who Had Given Birth and Children Ever Born per 1,000 Never-Married Women, by Occupation and Education: June 1982 and June 1992

	June 1982		June 1992	
Characteristic	Percent Ever Had a Birth	Children Ever Born[a]	Percent Ever Had a Birth	Children Ever Born[a]
Education				
Less than high school	35.2	746	48.4	1,089
High school	17.2	283	32.5	561
Some college	5.5	74	11.3	178
Occupation				
Managerial/professional	3.1	38	8.3	136
Other	11.2	185	17.9	296

[a]Children ever born per 1,000 never-married women.
SOURCE: U.S. Bureau of the Census (1993).

strong differentials by educational and occupational status persisted throughout the period. Between 1990 and 1994, the percentage unmarried among women who had had a child in the last year increased at all educational levels and for employed women in all occupational categories (Table 2-3). However, even though proportional increases in this crude measure of the percentage of births out of wedlock were in some cases as great or greater among higher-status women, the socioeconomic differentials remain very large. Out-of-wedlock childbearing is still much higher among members of the less advantaged educational and occupational groups.

TABLE 2-3   Percentage Unmarried at Survey Date Among Women Aged 15-44 Who Had a Child in the Past Year, by Education and Occupation of Employed Women: June 1990 and June 1994

	1990	1994	Change (%)
All women	23.3	25.9	+11.2
Education			
Less than high school	44.9	45.6	+ 1.6
High school	23.9	30.3	+26.8
Some college	11.1	13.3	+19.8
Employment			
Managerial/professional	7.8	10.1	+29.5
Technical, sales	18.3	21.1	+15.3
Service	23.4	29.3	+25.2
Operators, fabricators, laborers	26.5	33.8	+27.5

NOTE: Marital status, employment, occupation, and education measured as of time of survey.
SOURCE: U.S. Bureau of the Census (1996).

CONCLUSIONS

Out-of-wedlock childbearing has been increasing in the United States for over half a century. By most measures, the increase accelerated sharply over the past 15 years and leveled in the early 1990s. Stereotypes equating unwed births with births to black teenagers reflect the higher ratios of out-of-wedlock births in these populations, but miss the reality that fewer than one in three such births occurs to teens, and only 11 percent to black teens. Although rates and ratios of out-of-wedlock childbearing in different population subgroups have tended to move toward convergence over recent decades, sharp differentials remain. Non-marital childbearing is far more prevalent among disadvantaged populations: those with low educational attainment and those in low-status occupations.

As most people recognize, the trends in out-of-wedlock childbearing described here are shared by other industrialized countries as well. In 1992, the proportion of births to unmarried women in Canada, France, and the United Kingdom was similar to that in the United States; the proportion in both Denmark and Sweden, where social welfare policies are dissimilar from the United States, was substantially higher (Department of Health and Human Services, 1995). Out-of-wedlock childbearing has increased in all industrialized Western nations since 1960, but there are great differences among countries in the extent of change. As yet, Japan and other newly industrialized Asian countries have not experienced this change. One of the intriguing opportunities that remains to be fully explored is the possibility of careful comparative analyses of these trends across industrialized nations.

The recent focus of public concern on out-of-wedlock childbearing has tended to place emphasis on the reproductive behavior of unmarried women. Yet, as this chapter argues, changes in marriage have occupied a central, and perhaps dominant, role in this drama. The prevalence and timing of marriage have changed more dramatically over recent decades than the prevalence and timing of fertility. Further, the meaning of marriage as a boundary line for behaviors such as sexual activity, coresidential unions, pregnancy, and birth has diminished sharply. Changes in the reproductive behaviors of unmarried women have clearly contributed to the increase in out-of-wedlock births, but the changing behavior of this population may reflect in part its changing composition, since it has expanded to include many who would have married at an earlier age one or more decades ago. Women in their teens and twenties continued to give birth at the same or declining rates during the 1970s and most of the 1980s; the circumstances in which they did so were altered by the decline in marriage. Despite the central role played by marriage trends, relatively little has been invested in understanding their causes and their meaning and in ensuring the availability of data that will permit both careful demographic analysis of trends and theoretically driven analytic studies. A study of the impact of welfare programs on family and reproductive behavior would do well to attend to marriage as well as fertility, and to ways in which trends in both are interrelated.

ACKNOWLEDGMENTS

This chapter draws on materials developed by Stephanie Ventura et al., for the *Report to Congress on Out-of-Wedlock Childbearing* (Department of Health and Human Services, 1995). The author gratefully acknowledges the assistance of Stephanie Ventura, Amy Cox, and Michelle Hindin in providing and updating charts, and the comments of Sally Clarke, Stephanie Ventura, Susan Newcomer, and two anonymous reviewers.

REFERENCES

Alan Guttmacher Institute
  1992   *Abortion Factbook, 1992 edition*. New York: Alan Guttmacher Institute.
Bachu, A.
  1991   Fertility of American women: June 1990. *Current Population Reports*, Series P-20 No. (454). Washington, D.C.: U.S. Government Printing Office.
  1993   Fertility of American women: June 1992. *Current Population Reports*, Series P-20, No. (470). Washington, D.C.: U.S. Government Printing Office.
  1995   Fertility of American women: June 1994. *Current Population Reports*, Series P-20, No. (482). Washington, D.C.: U.S. Government Printing Office.
Bongaarts, J.
  1978   A framework for analyzing the proximate determinants of fertility. *Population and Development Review* 4(1):105-132.
Brown, S., and L. Eisenberg, eds.
  1995   *The Best Intentions: Unintended Pregnancy and the Well-Being of Children and Families*. Washington, D.C.: National Academy Press.
Bumpass, L., and J. Sweet
  1989   National estimates of cohabitation. *Demography* 26(4):615-630.
  1995   *Cohabitation, Marriage and Union Stability: Preliminary Findings from NSFH2*. CDE Working Paper 65. Center for Demography and Ecology, University of Wisconsin, Madison.
Clarke, S.C.
  1995   Advance report of final marriage statistics, 1989 and 1990. *Monthly Vital Statistics Report* 43(12 Suppl.). Hyattsville, Md.: National Center for Health Statistics.
Davis, K., and J. Blake
  1956   Social structure and fertility: An analytic framework. *Economic Development and Cultural Change* 4:211-235.
Department of Health and Human Services
  1995   *Report to Congress on Out-of-Wedlock Childbearing* Hyattsville, Md.: U.S. Public Health Service.
Forrest, J.
  1994   Epidemiology of unintended pregnancy and contraceptive use. *American Journal of Obstetrics and Gynecology* 170:1485-1488.
Forrest, J., and S. Singh
  1990   The sexual and reproductive behavior of American women, 1982-1988. *Family Planning Perspectives* 22(5):206-214.

Henshaw, S., and J. Silverman
1988   The characteristics and prior contraceptive use of U.S. abortion patients. *Family Planning Perspectives* 20(4):158-168.
Henshaw, S., N.J. Binkin, E. Blaine, and J.C. Smith
1985   A portrait of American women who obtain abortions. *Family Planning Perspectives* 17(2):90-96.
Henshaw, S., L.M. Koonin, and J.C. Smith
1991   Characteristics of U.S. women having abortions. *Family Planning Perspectives* 23(2):75-81.
Hofferth, S.L., J.R. Kahn, and W. Baldwin
1987   Premarital sexual activity among U.S. teenage women over the past three decades. *Family Planning Perspectives* 19(2):46-53.
Jones, E., and J. Forrest
1992   Contraceptive failure rates based on the 1988 NSFG. *Family Planning Perspectives* 24(1):12-19.
Laumann, E., J. Gagnon, R. Michael, and S. Michaels
1994   *The Social Organization of Sexuality: Sexual Practices in the United States.* Chicago, Ill.: University of Chicago Press.
Morgan, S.P.
1996   Characteristic features of modern American fertility. *Population and Development Review* 22(Suppl.):19-63.
Morgan, S.P., K. Offutt, and R.R. Rindfuss
1995   Education, Marital Status and the Changing Age Pattern of American Fertility. Paper presented at the Annual Meeting of the Population Association of America, San Francisco, April.
National Center for Health Statistics
1996   Provisional vital statistics for September 1995. *Monthly Vital Statistics Report* 44(9). Hyattsville, Md.: Public Health Service.
Pagnini, D., and R.R. Rindfuss
1993   The divorce of marriage and childbearing: Changing attitudes and behavior in the United States. *Population and Development Review* 19(2):331-347.
Ryder, N.B.
1980   Components of temporal variations in American fertility. In R.W. Hiorns, ed., *Demographic Patterns in Developed Societies.* London: Taylor and Francis.
Saluter, A.F.
1996   Marital status and living arrangements: March, 1994. *Current Population Reports*, Series P20-484. Washington, D.C.: U.S. Government Printing Office.
Smith, H.L., and P. Cutright
1988   Thinking about changes in illegitimacy ratios: United States, 1963-1983. *Demography* 25(2):235-247.
Smith, H.L., S.P. Morgan, and T. Koropeckyj-Cox
1996   A decomposition of trends in the nonmarital fertility ratios of blacks and whites in the United States, 1960-1992. *Demography* 33(2):141-151.
Thornton, A.
1989   Changing attitudes towards family issues in the United States. *Journal of Marriage and the Family* 51(4):873-893.
U.S. Bureau of the Census
1993   The fertility of American women: June 1992. *Current Population Reports,* Series P20-470. Washington, D.C.: U.S. Government Printing Office.
1994   *Statistical Abstract of the United States: 1994*, 114th Edition. Washington, D.C.: U.S. Government Printing Office.

    1996   The fertility of American women: June 1994. *Current Population Reports*, P-20-484.
            Washington, D.C.: U.S. Government Printing Office.
Ventura, S., J. Martin, S. Taffel, T. Matthews, and S. Clarke
    1995a   Advance report of final natality statistics, 1993. *Monthly Vital Statistics Report*, 44(3
            Suppl.). Hyattsville, Md.: National Center for Health Statistics.
Ventura, S., S. Taffel, W. Mosher, J. Wilson, and S. Henshaw
    1995b   Trends in Pregnancies and Pregnancy Rates: Estimates for the United States, 1980-92.
            Monthly Vital Statistics Report 43(11 Suppl.). Hyattsville, Md.: National Center for
            Health Statistics.
Ventura, S., K. Peters, J. Martin, and J. Maurer
    1997   Births and deaths: United States, 1996. *Monthly Vital Statistics Report* 46(1 Suppl. 2).
            Hyattsville, Md.: National Center for Health Statistics.

3

Trends in the Welfare System

Rebecca M. Blank

The system of public assistance in the United States is constantly evolving. In part, this is due to changing demographic and economic conditions, but even more importantly, public assistance programs have been the target of ongoing reform efforts. The most recent major legislative change occurred with the enactment of the Personal Responsibility and Work Opportunity Act of August 1996.

This chapter summarizes trends in public assistance programs over time. The first section looks at historical changes in the expenditure levels and usage of public assistance programs. The second section investigates how public assistance programs fit into state and federal budgets. The third section summarizes the recent legislative changes, and the last section discusses trends in program design and operation.

EVOLUTION OF EXPENDITURES AND PARTICIPATION IN PUBLIC ASSISTANCE PROGRAMS

For much of U.S. history, public assistance was the responsibility of local townships and counties, with states becoming more and more involved over the last half of the nineteenth and the early twentieth century. As in many other areas of social policy, the federal government's involvement did not begin until the New Deal programs of the 1930s established a precedent for federal responsibility in this area. Even so, such programs remained relatively small in the immediate decades after the 1930s, with only small numbers of recipients and small costs.

Things changed dramatically in the 1960s and 1970s. The primary cash assistance program, Aid to Families with Dependent Children (AFDC), increased dramatically due to a variety of changes that brought many more eligible single mothers and their children onto the assistance rolls.[1] The establishment of the Food Stamp program in the early 1960s resulted in major spending increases during the 1970s, when Food Stamps were expanded to every county and payment rules were simplified. The Medicaid program was established in 1965, providing health insurance to low-income families who met certain eligibility criteria. Medicaid spending levels increased steadily through the 1970s and 1980s, reflecting both increases in the eligible population and increases in medical costs. Highly variable state programs for the elderly and the disabled were moved to the federal level in the early 1970s when the Supplemental Security Income (SSI) program was created to provide uniform cash assistance to elderly, blind, and disabled individuals throughout the nation. Finally, as a supplement to low-wage workers, the Earned Income Tax Credit (EITC) program began on a small scale in 1975.[2]

Figure 3-1 shows how inflation-adjusted expenditures on public assistance programs have changed since 1965. (Medicaid is not shown in Figure 3-1, but is discussed below.) After peaking in the mid-1970s, AFDC expenditures have been largely constant. Food Stamp expenditures expanded with program expansions in the 1970s, fell during most of the 1980s, but have grown again over the past 7 years as caseloads have grown. The SSI program remained a relatively constant-expenditure program for the first 10 years of its existence, but its expenditures have recently shot upward with expanded eligibility categories. Similarly, the EITC was a small program for its first 10 years, but over the past 10 years, major benefit expansions have made the EITC program as large as AFDC, Food Stamps, or SSI.[3]

Figure 3-2 shows changes in the number of participants in income support programs. Participation in AFDC was reasonably flat throughout the 1970s and 1980s. Food Stamp participation trends mirror spending trends. In both AFDC and Food Stamps, sharp caseload increases occurred in the early 1990s. As Figure 3-2 indicates, these increases leveled off by the mid-1990s, and more recently available data indicate that caseloads have fallen substantially since 1995 in both programs. EITC participation has risen along with benefit levels. SSI participation has risen only slowly over the past decade, although costs are rising more steeply.

---

[1] As discussed later, AFDC was abolished in the 1996 legislation.

[2] These are the programs discussed in this chapter. A host of other programs can also be considered part of the public assistance system, but these are much smaller in terms of both expenditures and participation.

[3] Due to recent legislative changes in Food Stamps, AFDC, and SSI, by 1997 the EITC is expected to be the largest of these four programs.

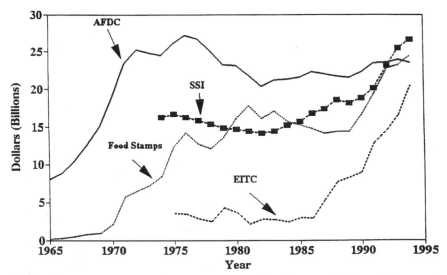

FIGURE 3-1 Dollars spent on income support (1995 dollars). NOTES: AFDC and SSI show benefit payments. Food Stamps shows coupon value. EITC shows total costs including refunds and tax expenditures. SOURCES: AFDC 1965-1993, Food Stamps 1965-1994, and SSI 1994 from Social Security Administration (1995); AFDC 1994 from U.S. Department of Health and Human Services (1995b); SSI 1974-1993 from U.S. House of Representatives (1994); EITC 1975-1982 from Internal Revenue Service (various years a); EITC 1983-1994 from Internal Revenue Service (various years b).

Figure 3-3 provides a direct comparison of inflation-adjusted benefit cost per participant in each of these programs. Per-person AFDC spending declined over time, and per-person Food Stamp spending has been largely flat. The SSI and EITC programs show increases in benefits paid per participant over time. It is also noticeable that SSI recipients receive far more assistance than participants in other programs.

In stepping away from the specific numerical trends, what are the implications of these changes over the past few decades? Cash support for nonelderly and nondisabled individuals has always been relatively limited in the United States, compared to most European nations. As a share of public assistance support, cash support has steadily declined over the past two decades. Increasingly, resources are available through in-kind programs (such as Food Stamps or Medicaid) or through behaviorally tied support programs, in which cash assistance is linked with work behavior. This is most obvious in the growth of the EITC, which is available only to families with working low-income adults. But even the AFDC program became increasingly behaviorally linked, as legislative changes over the past 15 years mandated that more AFDC recipients participate in job search and employment programs.

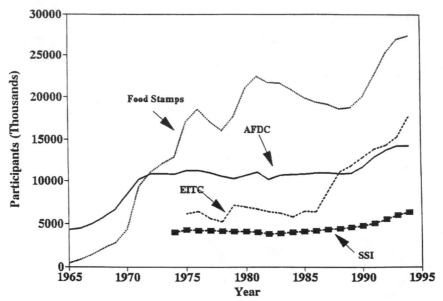

FIGURE 3-2 Participants in income support programs. NOTES: AFDC, Food Stamps, and SSI show numbers of recipients. EITC shows number of tax returns. SOURCES: AFDC 1965-1993, Food Stamps 1965-1994, and SSI 1994 from Social Security Administration (1995); AFDC 1994 from U.S. Department of Health and Human Services (1995b); SSI 1974-1993 from U.S. House of Representatives (1994); EITC 1975-1982 from Internal Revenue Service (various years a); EITC 1983-1994 from Internal Revenue Service (various years b).

The United States continues to distinguish sharply between different groups of low-income families. Elderly individuals receive far more support than families with working-age adults. Nonelderly low-income families have always been a source of frustration for the public assistance system. On the one hand, the adults in these families are viewed with some suspicion: why are they not successfully working their way out of poverty? While always applied to male-headed households, this viewpoint has also come to dominate our image of female-headed households as well, as employment among mothers has become more accepted. On the other hand, the adults in these families come attached to children, whom we view with less suspicion and want to assist. The result is a constant tension in public assistance programs between the type of requirements and limits put on assistance to families and the needs of the children in those families. Advocates of greater behavioral requirements and more limited assistance inevitably point to the adults and claim that they need to take more responsibility for their own economic well-being. Opponents of these changes inevitably point to the children and claim that they should not be hurt because of the misfortunes of their parents. Recent legislative changes have supported stronger

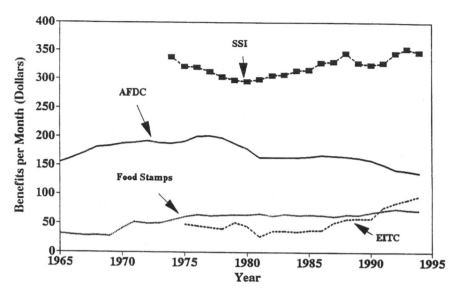

FIGURE 3-3 Average monthly benefits (1995 dollars). NOTES: AFDC, Food Stamps, and SSI show benefits per person. EITC shows benefits per tax return. SOURCES: AFDC 1965-1993, Food Stamps 1965-1994, and SSI 1994 from Social Security Administration (1995); AFDC 1994 from U.S. Department of Health and Human Services (1995b); SSI 1974-1993 from U.S. House of Representatives (1994); EITC 1975-1982 from Internal Revenue Service (various years a); EITC 1983-1994 from Internal Revenue Service (various years b).

work mandates, but this debate is far from resolved. Credible research that shows how children are affected by full-time work requirements imposed on their single-parent mothers may have a major effect on future changes in the structure of public assistance programs.

Finally, it is worth noting that the expenditure trends in these four public assistance programs are dwarfed by the growing expenditures in the Medicaid program. Figure 3-4 plots inflation-adjusted spending on Medicaid, separately showing spending on the elderly and disabled (largely those eligible for the SSI program) and spending on families with children (largely those eligible for the AFDC program.) While health expenditures rose throughout the economy, they rose faster for Medicaid, in part because Medicaid generally serves a population with greater health problems.[4] In recent years, Medicaid spending on the nonelderly, nondisabled population has leveled off, but it has continued to increase

---

[4]Figure 3-4 adjusts Medicaid dollars by the gross domestic product price deflator. Even if they are adjusted by the consumer price index for medical care, Medicaid spending still doubles between 1980 and 1995.

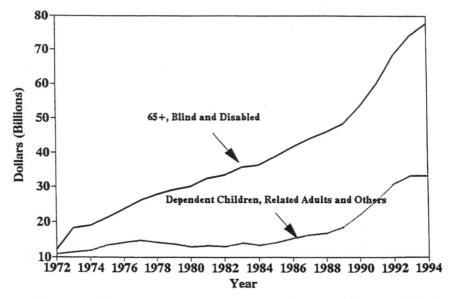

FIGURE 3-4 Dollars spent on Medicaid by eligibility category (1995 dollars). SOURCES: 1972 and 1994 from Social Security Administration (1995); 1973 from U.S. Department of Health, Education, and Welfare (1975); 1974 from U.S. Department of Health, Education, and Welfare (1976); 1975-1993 from U.S. Department of Health and Human Services (1995a).

for the elderly and disabled. Some of the biggest expenditure increases have been for the Medicaid population in long-term care facilities.

Trends in the number of Medicaid recipients look quite different from spending trends, as Figure 3-5 indicates. Until the late 1980s, the population of recipients was quite flat, despite steady increases in expenditures. Recent eligibility expansions for children in low-income families have greatly increased the number of young Medicaid recipients.[5] Slight increases in recipiency among the elderly and disabled have also occurred. Figure 3-6 shows the implications for Medicaid spending per recipient. Most strikingly, per-person Medicaid expenses for low-income children and related adults have been essentially flat—and are very low compared to per-person expenses for the elderly or disabled. All of the growth in Medicaid dollars for families and children is due to increases in the eligible population. In sharp contrast, per-person Medicaid spending for the elderly and disabled has increased steadily for over 2 decades. Medicaid spending on the elderly and disabled has been largely driven by increases in the per-person cost of services provided to this population, and not by population growth.

---

[5]In particular, Medicaid eligibility for children was de-linked from family AFDC eligibility. Currently, all children in families below 135 percent of the poverty line are eligible for Medicaid.

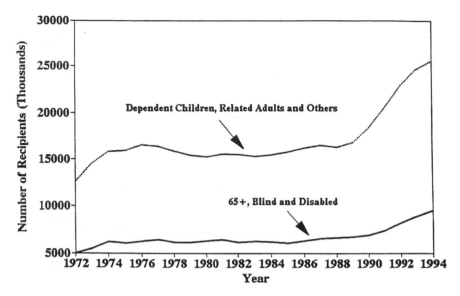

FIGURE 3-5 Number of Medicaid recipients by eligibility category. SOURCES: 1972 and 1994 from Social Security Administration (1995); 1973 from U.S. Department of Health, Education, and Welfare (1975); 1974 from U.S. Department of Health, Education, and Welfare (1976); 1975-1993 from U.S. Department of Health and Human Services (1995a).

PUBLIC ASSISTANCE PROGRAMS AND GOVERNMENT SPENDING

Ongoing federal budget deficits have resulted in increased pressure to cut all forms of federal spending. Many states operate under balanced budget requirements and are also constantly seeking areas where costs can be reduced in order to meet other public demands. Public assistance programs have often been a primary target in efforts to cut state and federal budgets. At least some of this is due to a misperception on the part of many Americans about the role played by public assistance in the budget. For instance, a 1995 CBS News/New York Times poll indicated that over 50 percent of the population thinks the federal government spends more than 20 percent of its budget on welfare programs (Roper Center for Public Opinion Research, 1995).

Figure 3-7 shows the composition of federal expenditures in 1995. Public assistance accounted for 14 percent of federal expenditures, of which 6 percent was due to Medicaid spending. While not an insignificant share, more was spent on Social Security, on defense, and on net interest on the debt.

Much of the growth in federal expenditures on public assistance is relatively recent, and it is heavily due to increases in Medicaid expenditures. Figure 3-8 shows the trends over time on government spending on social programs as a

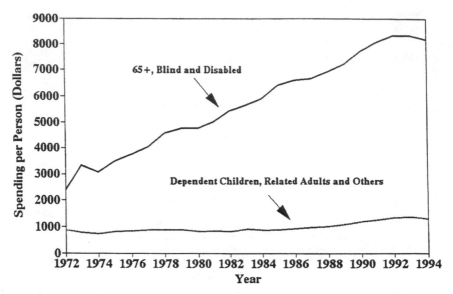

FIGURE 3-6   Medicaid spending per person by eligibility category (1995 dollars). SOURCES: 1972 and 1994 from Social Security Administration (1995); 1973 from U.S. Department of Health, Education, and Welfare (1975); 1974 from U.S. Department of Health, Education, and Welfare (1976); 1975-1993 from U.S. Department of Health and Human Services (1995a).

fraction of all outlays. Family support programs (primarily AFDC) have been flat at about 1-2 percent of the U.S. budget for decades.   If Food Stamps are added to family support, this accounts for a flat 2-3 percent of the U.S. budget. In these core public assistance programs—the programs that U.S. citizens are most likely to identify as "welfare"—there is no evidence of high or growing budget shares.

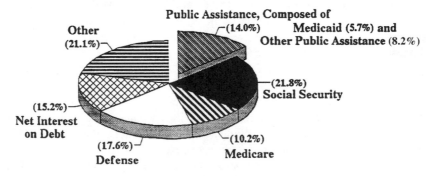

FIGURE 3-7   Federal expenditures for fiscal year 1995.   SOURCE: U.S. Office of Management and Budget (1995).

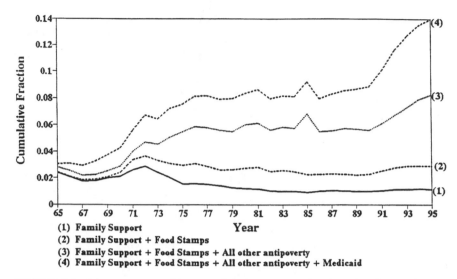

(1) Family Support
(2) Family Support + Food Stamps
(3) Family Support + Food Stamps + All other antipoverty
(4) Family Support + Food Stamps + All other antipoverty + Medicaid

FIGURE 3-8 Government spending on social programs as a fraction of outlays. NOTES: The category "Family Support" includes payments to states for AFDC benefits, administration, and child support enforcement. The category "All other antipoverty" includes child nutrition and special milk, supplemental feeding, commodity donation, legal services, day care assistance, Supplemental Security Income, and the Earned Income Tax Credit. SOURCE: U.S. Office of Management and Budget (1995).

The federal budget share for all antipoverty programs (except Medicaid) has risen from 6 to 8 percent over the past 5 years, primarily because of the growth in the EITC and SSI programs, discussed earlier. But the big budget-buster is Medicaid, which has increased from 5 to 8 percent of the federal budget in only a few years.

The effect of Medicaid on public budgets is even more visible at the state level. Figure 3-9 shows the breakdown of state expenditures for 1992, the most recent year for which these data are available. Medicaid accounts for 11 percent of the average state budget in that year; other public assistance accounts for only 3 percent. As at the federal level, the Medicaid share of state budgets has been growing dramatically over time. The result is that virtually all states are facing a crisis in their public assistance spending: All states are currently spending more for public assistance in total than they were 10 years ago, but almost all states are spending less on non-Medicaid assistance. In short, programs for low-income nonelderly and nondisabled families have been cut in order to accommodate the growth in spending on medical assistance. While many have decried the growing cost of public assistance faced by the states, few state governors have publicly discussed the primary cause of this problem—increasing costs in medical services (especially long-term care services) for elderly and disabled persons. In-

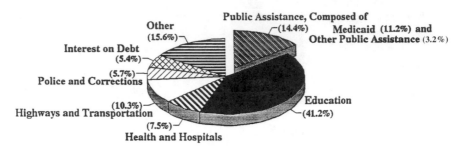

FIGURE 3-9   State expenditures for fiscal year 1992.   SOURCE: U.S. Bureau of the Census (1993).

stead, they have often mistakenly assumed that the problem is spending in other programs and have cut general assistance, lowered AFDC benefits, or taken other steps that limit public assistance spending in areas where costs have not been rising.

THE 1996 LEGISLATIVE CHANGES[6]

The 1996 welfare reform legislation has been described as a revolutionary change in the structure and emphasis of U.S. welfare programs. In reality, the changes are at once both less radical and more radical than is often claimed. They are less radical in the sense that the criticisms of existing antipoverty programs that they embody are not new and reflect concerns that have long been part of the U.S. debate over helping the poor. Encouraging work, strengthening families, and reducing government costs are not new ideas. On the other hand, this legislation has produced a more fundamental change in the federal government's role in antipoverty efforts than any legislation since the Social Security Act of 1935, giving the states much more control over programs and the federal government much less. This section summarizes some of the most important aspects of the new legislation.

The legislation creates a new block grant to the states, the Temporary Assistance for Needy Families (TANF) block grant. The AFDC program is abolished and states are given almost complete control over the design of their public assistance programs. States can use TANF money for any programs that accomplish the purposes of the block grant, which include providing assistance to needy families, ending the dependency of needy parents on government benefits, preventing and reducing out-of-wedlock pregnancies, and encouraging the formation of two-parent families.

---

[6]The description in this section closely follows that in Blank (1997b).

In giving states this expanded program authority, the legislation eliminates family entitlements to cash assistance. Under AFDC, any family that met the eligibility requirements had to be provided with assistance according to established rules and regulations. Under the new law, states have much more discretion in determining who should get funds and how much they should get. They can eliminate some groups from assistance, redirect money away from cash support toward services designed to prevent teen pregnancy and promote marriage, or impose behavioral requirements on the recipients of public assistance funds. If money runs short at the end of a budget year, families can be turned away.

State entitlements to open-ended federal payments are also at an end. AFDC was a matching grant program rather than a block grant program. If states spent more, federal dollars automatically increased. Under TANF, states will receive a fixed amount of money from the federal government in future years, equal to the federal payments they received in the early 1990s for AFDC and related welfare-to-work programs. This leaves states bearing the financial risk should there be an increase in poverty or unemployment; the federal government will not automatically increase payments if a state has to provide assistance to more people. The federal dollars are also fixed at the same nominal level, so they become less over time with inflation.

Although states have greater discretion to determine who is helped, the federal legislation imposes new mandates with regard to work requirements and payment limits for those who receive TANF funds. Any parent who has received 24 months of assistance in programs funded through TANF must be working or in a work program in order to receive further funding. By 1997, 25 percent of all families in the state receiving TANF support must be working at least 20 hours per week. By 2002, 50 percent of all families must be working at least 30 hours per week. (States have substantial discretion to define what counts as "work.") This vastly increases the share of the caseload who must be working, although these requirements are lowered if caseloads fall within the state. (Because of the recent decline in caseloads, in the short run a number of states will face much lower requirements.) The 1996 legislation provided no new federal funds to assist states in expanding their work programs, although some additional funds were added in the 1997 budget legislation.

TANF dollars are time-limited to any individual. No family can receive funding from TANF if an adult in that family has already received 60 months of assistance over his or her lifetime. (At their option, states can impose even shorter time limits.) States are allowed to exempt 20 percent of their caseload from this 5-year limit. States can also continue to support families with state-only funds, which will probably lead to some creative accounting with regard to which families are being supported on federal versus state dollars.

The enactment of time limits is the most dramatically new part of the legislation. At this point, however, it is unclear exactly what the impact of these time limits will be. If there is high unemployment or if many adults hit these time limits at a point when they are clearly unable to hold a full-time job, states may well try to negotiate for more extensive exemptions. In addition, enforcing this lifetime limit effectively will require state and national tracking systems that identify the cumulative months of support received by any individual in any state. But the legislation included no funds for establishing such systems, which may allow some recipients to avoid the time limits in the near term.

In terms of both dollars and numbers of people affected, the biggest impact of the 1996 legislation will be on those who were once AFDC participants and who now are subject to the state-designed programs funded by the TANF block grant. But a number of other provisions in this bill will affect other programs and other groups of people. The legislation sharply limited the availability of public assistance to immigrants (although some of these cuts were restored in later legislation in 1997); limited Food Stamp benefits to nonelderly, nondisabled adults without children; and narrowed eligibility categories for SSI.

LARGER PATTERNS IN PROGRAM CHANGES[7]

As noted above, the 1996 legislation pushed further and faster in some directions where changes in public assistance had already been occurring. This section discusses three of the major trends in the structure of public assistance programs over the past decade.

Increasing Emphasis on Behavioral Requirements as Part of Program Eligibility, with Particular Emphasis on Work Behavior

More than twenty-five years ago, President Nixon proposed to roll all cash and non-cash income assistance programs into one single cash assistance program, available to all families who met the income eligibility requirements. Commonly referred to as a negative income tax, such a system would provide cash support through the tax system. The pendulum has swung far in the other direction, so that Nixon's not-so-ancient proposal seems almost unbelievable in today's political climate.[8] The current emphasis is very much in the opposite direction: time-limited programs available for narrowly defined target groups, ensuring that large numbers of people are not eligible for substantial amounts of public assistance. Those who do receive assistance must establish their "deservingness" by enrolling in job training and placement programs or working and (in some states) limiting their future fertility, ensuring their children are appropriately cared for, or meeting other state requirements.

---

[7]This section closely follows parts of the discussion in Chapter 3 of Blank (1997a).

[8]Nixon's negative income tax proposal was the high-water mark of efforts to provide large-scale cash assistance to the poor, rather than behaviorally tied assistance. The earlier history of public aid shows an ongoing focus on behavioral regulations as a precondition for assistance.

These more targeted and behaviorally linked public assistance programs will face several major problems that have not yet been fully understood. First, such a proliferation of mandates and behavioral requirements is typically *more* expensive to run (per person) than are cash assistance programs, because the former require much more monitoring. The cheapest and most administratively efficient program is one that simply writes and mails a check each month. The more information that case workers have to regularly collect, process, and evaluate, the higher are administrative costs, and the greater is the potential for errors, misunderstandings, and management problems.

Second, this trend flies directly in the face of another desire that is often articulated at the same time: To reduce governmental interference in people's lives. By mandating behavioral conformance as well as income eligibility for public assistance programs, government's role in the lives of low-income people becomes much more intrusive.

The effectiveness of these behavioral mandates will depend upon exactly what they require and how easily they can be monitored and enforced. There is strong support for behavioral mandates that encourage parents who receive public assistance to enter job training and job search programs; that evict people from public housing who engage in criminal behavior; and that link job recommendations and placement with high school performance among youth. Other behavioral mandates are more controversial, such as cutting a family's public assistance benefits if the mother cannot keep a teenager in school or refusing public assistance to infants born to unmarried mothers.

Deciding which behavioral mandates make sense requires good judgment about what can be effectively implemented without vast increases in administrative complexity and cost, what mandates are likely to motivate changes in behavior (rather than being simply punitive), and what actions might produce unacceptable levels of need among mothers and children who could not meet the mandate. Programs with extensive but unmanageable requirements that end up having little effect may only make life harder for the poor and increase public cynicism about the ineffectiveness of government programs.

A Return to More Local and State Discretion in the Design of Programs

Public assistance in this country was entirely based at the county or township level 150 years ago. Over time, states took over more and more of the financing and operation of programs, and then, starting in the 1930s, the federal government entered the scene. The role of counties and states has always been important, however. The federal government has never directly administered public assistance programs. The people who actually run programs are all county, local, or state-level employees. The checks received by poor families or by those who run public services for the poor have always been drawn on state or municipal banks, and states have always provided substantial funding for many public assistance programs. Over time, however, the federal government has come to fund more programs and has imposed more regulations on how programs could be run. Over the 1980s, states were given the opportunity to apply for waivers to run programs that did not conform to federal rules, but these waivers tended to be limited in scope and often took a great deal of time and effort to negotiate. The enactment of TANF dramatically increases state discretion over public assistance programs.

The interest in returning more control to the state or local level grows out of four quite different perspectives. First, some argue that giving more discretion and control back to states will reduce the rigidities and bureaucratic nature of many current public assistance programs. Second, some who believe that we simply don't know enough to design effective nationally run antipoverty programs, advocate allowing states to experiment with a variety of programs like job training, education reform, or housing assistance. From this multiple experimentation will come better evidence on what works effectively and what does not. Third, those who are concerned about the growing scope of federal authority want to devolve centralized decision making away from the federal government and back to the states. Fourth, those who worry about the federal deficit and want to reduce federal spending see these changes as a way to cut federal spending on antipoverty programs and induce states to take greater fiscal responsibility for the maintenance of these programs.

Some of these arguments have much to recommend them. Certainly for programs like job training, where there are substantial differences across local areas in the nature of jobs available and the characteristics of the low-income population, running locally designed programs is necessary in order for programs to be effective. Indeed, the federal government has always largely left the specific design of job search and job training programs to state and local discretion. Similarly, in areas where existing programs have been largely ineffective, such as efforts to engage teenage high school dropouts in employment and training programs, allowing different states to experiment with different programs might result in useful new information.

On the other hand, there are also serious problems with limiting the federal role in public assistance programs to fixed levels of block grant funding. First, states have less ability to finance antipoverty programs than the federal government. The need for public assistance is at its largest when the economy is the rockiest. Thus, public assistance programs are necessarily countercyclical, expanding when the economy is in recession and contracting when the economy booms. Because most states operate under year-to-year balanced budget requirements, it is almost impossible for them to run major countercyclical programs. In economic recessions, tax revenue shrinks and this often means they must cut back on spending at exactly the time when need is increasing. These financial problems, faced by states in the Great Depression of the 1930s, were one of the main reasons the federal government became more involved in financing public assistance programs.

Second, while the federal government has been sometimes inept and sometimes foolish in the way that it has managed and run antipoverty programs, states hardly have a better track record. In fact, much of the impetus toward more centralized regulations and rules in the 1960s occurred because of concern over how these programs were being run by many states, where racist exclusions and arbitrary rule making were all too common. While there are always states that take the lead in implementing new management procedures, the federal government has been a key agent pushing states to reduce waste and fraud by decreasing errors in determining eligibility for assistance, by requiring regular program reports, and by encouraging states to upgrade computer systems.

Third, there continue to be concerns about the equity of state-run public assistance programs. For instance, if some states choose to dramatically cut all forms of cash assistance and other states maintain their current programs, benefit differences across states could become much larger than they already are. This may not only raise equity concerns, but could also cause substantial migration by low-income families, forcing those states that want to maintain more generous programs to cut them back because of growing low-income populations. This type of competition between states has been referred to as the "race to the bottom," meaning that when states are given complete control over public assistance benefits, there are incentives for all states to provide less than they might otherwise choose to, out of a fear of being a "magnet" for poor people.[9]

Cutbacks in Dollar Expenditures and Entitlements

The urge to cut the growth of government programs—all programs, not just public assistance—has been strong in recent years, driven by at least two forces. First, the rapid expansion of the federal deficit that occurred in the 1980s has led some observers to worry about long-term debt commitments. Cutting the deficit can be done by either increasing taxes or decreasing expenditures. While the second is not popular, the first has been political poison. Second, the long-term stagnation in wages among many workers (including actual declines for less skilled workers) has created economic fears about the cost of more extensive redistributive programs. Ongoing demands for lower taxes mean that there is unlikely to be any more revenue available for public assistance in the near future.

In this debate over government budgets, public assistance programs have often been targeted for disproportionately large cuts. In part, this is because low-income assistance programs often have few politically powerful supporters. Low-income adults typically vote at a lower rate and are less politically active. In part, these disproportionate cuts simply reflect the ongoing American discomfort with the whole idea of public assistance, especially for nonelderly adults.

---

[9]See Peterson (1995) for a discussion of this issue.

The urge to cut program dollars is in direct conflict with some other aspects of reform. Increases in behavioral mandates on program recipients may increase program expenses, as discussed above. Job training and placement programs for public assistance recipients can add to the cost of public assistance in the short run. A year into the enactment of welfare reform, many states have avoided these financial questions because of a very strong economy. Unemployment is low, labor markets are tight, and many state budgets are in surplus. Caseloads in many states fell dramatically after 1995, in part because of the strong economy and in part because of the enactment of "get-tough" welfare reforms by the states.[10] Given these circumstances, few states have had difficult funding more extensive job placement programs. At some point, however, the economy will slow down, unemployment will rise, and state revenues will become much tighter. Of course, it is exactly at this point that the demand for job placement assistance and for public assistance support will rise. It is not clear how states will deal with these multiple demands.

Looking at the decade ahead, we are almost certainly in a world where few government programs, especially public assistance programs, can expect increases in funding. The question is more likely to be, How big will the cuts be? rather than, What can we afford to do that is new and different (and perhaps more expensive)? This will be a major constraint on all efforts at welfare reform in the near future. It will almost surely continue to force hard choices on those who want to maintain public assistance programs at current levels of funding, and may particularly constrain states that want to use their expanded control over these policies to experiment with new and redesigned programs. States that want to cut their welfare budget *and* provide expanded job search and training programs for their public assistance recipients to move them into the labor market are going to face these contradictions most directly. Given the problems facing less skilled workers in the labor market, there will be no easy, quick, or cheap way for states to move public assistance recipients into economic self-sufficiency through employment.

For programs to maintain their funding and political support, it will be increasingly important to have evidence demonstrating their effectiveness. This means that reliable research, evaluating programs and their effects, may become increasingly important in the public discussion. It will also be important to build political coalitions that support and protect effective programs in the midst of budget-cutting fervor.

Overall, we are moving further away from a system that provides direct cash assistance payments to low-income families, toward a system that increasingly conditions its assistance much more closely on particular groups that meet behavioral as well as income qualifications. Dollars are shifting toward work-connected programs through increases in the Earned Income Tax Credit, more vigorous child support collection efforts, and subsidized job placement and training

---

[10]See Blank (1997c) for a discussion of the causes behind recent caseload changes.

efforts. It is not clear that these reconfigured public assistance programs will provide a cheaper or a more effective safety net than the one we have at present. It will be different, with a different set of management and incentive problems than are embedded in the current antipoverty system.

ACKNOWLEDGMENT

Leslie Moscow provided excellent research assistance.

REFERENCES

Blank, R.
    1997a   *It Takes a Nation: A New Agenda for Fighting Poverty.* Princeton, N.J.: Princeton University Press.
    1997b   Policy watch: The 1996 welfare reform. *Journal of Economic Perspectives* 11(1):169-177.
    1997c   *What Causes Public Assistance Caseloads to Grow?* National Bureau of Economic Research Working Paper 6343. Cambridge, MA: NBER.
Internal Revenue Service
  Various   *Statistics of Income—19xx Individual Income Tax Returns.* Washington, D.C.
  years (a)
  Various   *Statistics of Income Bulletin; Season 19xx.* Washington, D.C.
  years (b)
Peterson, P.
    1995   *The Price of Federalism.* Washington, D.C.: The Brookings Institute.
Roper Center for Public Opinion Research
    1995   CBS News/New York Times poll conducted April 1-4, 1995. Accessed via Dialogue, file 468, Public Opinion on Line.
Social Security Administration
    1995.   *Social Security Bulletin, Annual Statistical Supplement: 1995.* Washington, D.C.: U.S. Government Printing Office.
U.S. Bureau of the Census
    1993   *State Government Finance, 1992.* GF/92-3. Washington, D.C.: U.S. Government Printing Office.
U.S. Department of Health and Human Services
    1995a   *Health Care Financing Review: Statistical Supplement.* Baltimore, Md.: Health Care Financing Administration, Office of Research and Demonstrations.
    1995b   *Overview of the AFDC Program: Fiscal Year 1994.* Washington, D.C.: U.S. Government Printing Office.
U.S. Department of Health, Education, and Welfare
    1975   *Numbers of Recipients and Amounts of Payments Under Medicaid, Fiscal Year 1973.* Washington, D.C.
    1976   *Numbers of Recipients and Amounts of Payments Under Medicaid, Fiscal Year 1974.* Washington, D.C.
U.S. House of Representatives
    1994   *1994 Green Book: Overview of Entitlement Programs.* Washington, D.C.: U.S. Government Printing Office.
U.S. Office of Management and Budget
    1995   *Budget of the United States Government, Historical Tables, 1996.* Washington, D.C.: U.S. Government Printing Office.

4

The Effect of Welfare on Marriage and Fertility

Robert A. Moffitt

The research literature on the effects of welfare on marriage and fertility contains a large number of studies over the last 30 years. The studies use a variety of methodologies, employ several different datasets with different types of individuals, and cover different time periods. Several studies were conducted in the 1970s and early 1980s, but there has been a second wave of studies beginning in the mid-1980s and still under way. Based on the early studies, a consensus among researchers developed a decade or so ago that the welfare system had no effect on these demographic outcomes. However, a majority of the newer studies show that welfare has a significantly negative effect on marriage or a positive effect on fertility rather than none at all. Because of this shift in findings, the current consensus is that the welfare system probably has some effect on these demographic outcomes.

However, there is considerable uncertainty surrounding this consensus because a significant minority of the studies finds no effect at all, because the magnitudes of the estimated effects vary widely, and because there are puzzling and unexplained differences across the studies by race and methodological approach. For example, the findings show considerably stronger effects for white women than for black or nonwhite women, despite the greater participation rates of the latter group in the welfare system. Also, the findings often differ when demographic outcomes are correlated with welfare generosity in different ways—variation in welfare benefits across states in a particular year, for example, versus variation in welfare benefits over time. Whether the differences in study findings are the result of inherent differences in different datasets or differences in the way the data are analyzed—for example, in estimating techniques, definitions of variables, characteristics of the individuals examined, other influences controlled for, and so on—is difficult to determine because most authors do not systematically attempt to determine why their findings differ from those of other studies.

This chapter summarizes the literature and discusses these differences across studies. Because of the diversity of findings, methodological considerations necessarily must be a major focus of the discussion. The first section provides background on the U.S. welfare system and those aspects of its structure relevant to marriage and fertility, and discusses the context of social science theories of marriage and fertility in which the welfare system plays a role. The second section outlines the different questions of interest and discusses those questions that have been addressed in the research literature. The third section discusses the methodological approach taken in the research literature toward the question and contrasts the method of experimentation with the nonexperimental method of using natural program variation. Broad trends in the United States on demographic outcomes and the welfare system are presented in the following section; these trends establish a set of basic patterns in the data. The next section reviews the multivariate research studies on the question, compares and contrasts their approaches, and discusses possible reasons for the diversity of findings. Finally, suggestions for future research are outlined in the last section.

BACKGROUND

The U.S. welfare system is currently undergoing major change as the result of 1996 legislation, the Personal Responsibility and Work Opportunity Reconciliation Act. However, because the research whose review is the main focus of this chapter entirely concerns the welfare system prior to this legislation, only the old system is described here. The relevance of this research to the future welfare system is discussed in the last section.

Chapter 3 contains a discussion of the welfare system that provides a general background. In this chapter, only the features of the system specific to marriage and fertility are outlined.

The most well-known aspect of the welfare system bearing on marriage and fertility is the set of of eligibility rules in the Aid to Families with Dependent Children (AFDC) program that result in a high concentration of single mothers among recipients, a relatively tiny fraction of married couples on the rolls, and no families or individuals without children (single mothers are defined as women with children under 18 in the household but no spouse or cohabiting partner present). This feature is a result of the basic eligibility requirement, laid out in the 1935 Social Security Act, which created the AFDC program, that the program is intended to provide cash support only to children living without at least one of their biological parents. Thus children for whom one parent has died are eligible, but so are children whose parents never married but are living apart or whose parents are divorced or separated. The mother, or other caretaker relative, is also supported by the grant. Children who are living with both parents are eligible, along with their parents, only for the AFDC-UP (unemployed parent) program, but eligibility for those benefits has additional conditions requiring that at least one parent be unemployed, that this parent have a significant history of employment, and that the family meet the same stringent income and asset requirements as a single-parent family. As a result, AFDC-UP families constitute only a small fraction of the AFDC caseload.[1]

The Food Stamp program provides food coupons to low-income families regardless of family structure and hence does not have the same "bias" toward single-parent families as does AFDC. Eligibility and benefits for the program are based on the income and resources of a group of people who eat together, regardless of their relationship to each other. Thus two-parent as well as single-parent families are eligible, although the fixed upper income and asset limits knock more two-parent families than single-parent families out of eligibility.[2] Single individuals and childless families are also eligible.

The Medicaid program provides subsidized medical care assistance to poor families. Historically it has been made available primarily to AFDC recipients and therefore has the same bias toward single-parent families. However, in the last decade, eligibility for Medicaid benefits has been greatly broadened to include children in poor families even if both parents are present and the family is off AFDC. However, despite the growth of Medicaid recipients under these new eligibility rules, the program is still disproportionately composed of single-parent families.

Housing programs come in several different forms—public housing as well as subsidized private housing, for example—and provide housing at below-market rents to families with low income and assets. However, these programs are distinguished from the other programs so far discussed by their nonentitlement status. Expenditure allocations to local public housing authorities limit the amount of funds available and therefore limit the number of recipients that can be served. Eligible families who apply and are accepted but cannot be supported are put on waiting lists that can be quite long (e.g., several years). To choose from among the pool of eligibles, local housing authorities are required to give certain groups priority over others (called "preferences"). One of the preferred groups is AFDC recipients. This, along with the fact that family income (per family member) is lower among the single-parent population than the two-parent population, results in a high fraction of single-parent families receiving housing benefits. However, the preference is not absolute, and there have been been times in

---

[1] The eligibility rules have many other important facets which space does not permit discussing, especially rules governing eligibility of children living with cohabiting adults and whose caretaker parent has remarried. For details on these rules, see Moffitt et al. (1998).

[2] AFDC recipient families are automatically eligible for Food Stamp benefits, so this also results in a disproportionate number of single-parent families actually on the Food Stamp rolls.

the history of the program when middle-income families were preferred, so there are sizable representations of two-parent families in the housing program.

In summary, therefore, the conventional perception of the U.S. welfare system as largely favoring single-parent families over two-parent families and childless couples and individuals is essentially correct.[3] This favored treatment affects incentives to marry as well as incentives to have children. Fertility incentives are present in one additional way, however, which arises simply because benefits are based on the number of children present in the family unit. Hence the monetary cost of having an additional child is smaller in the presence of these welfare programs than it would be in their absence.

That these marriage and fertility incentives may have an effect on behavior can be understood both with common sense and from a variety of theoretical perspectives. The most natural modern conceptual framework is the economic theory of marriage and fertility as developed by Becker (1981) because that model emphasizes the economic gains to marriage and the economic benefits and costs of having children. However, one could easily understand incentives induced by the welfare system without the formalization of the Beckerian theory, for almost any framework in which economic factors play a role will predict that, if all else is held fixed, a welfare system biased against marriage and toward childbearing will change behavior in that direction (although the magnitude of the effect can, of course, be large or small).

Although more complex theories can give different predictions, the only simple economic theory that does so is that which conceptualizes single parenthood as an unlucky outcome of an attempt at marriage (or union formation in general) and in which benefits play the role of insurance against that outcome. Standard economic theories imply that government provision of such insurance— welfare benefits—would induce more individuals to attempt marriage in the same way that providing insurance to protect checking accounts against bank failure encourages individuals to put their money in banks. The difficulty with this way of viewing the problem is that it ignores what is called the "moral hazard" problem in insurance terminology—the simple fact that individuals who are given insurance have an incentive to put themselves more at risk or even to cause the insured-against event to happen; this means, in the case of welfare and family structure, simply that individuals have an incentive to take actions that lead, directly or indirectly, to single motherhood as an outcome.

---

[3]It is worth noting, however, that any program that provides benefits on the basis of the income of a family unit rather than the income of individuals will necessarily, and inherently, have at least a minimal amount of bias toward single-parent families. If bias is defined as occurring when the income gain to marrying, for example, is less in the presence of a government program than in its complete absence, then a welfare program will be nonbiasing only if benefits are completely unaffected if a single parent marries. But this violates the definition of a targeted transfer program, namely, one that concentrates its benefits on those with lower income. This is an example of the equity-efficiency economic principle.

Welfare effects on marital and fertility behavior occur necessarily through one of a fixed set of routes. An unmarried childless woman entering adulthood may have an child out of wedlock, for example, and welfare may affect the probability of this outcome. She may later marry and possibly have additional children within marriage, but then separate or divorce, returning to a state of single motherhood; welfare may also affect the likelihood of this outcome. Alternatively, she may have married and begun childbearing within marriage but then divorce or separate, which is a different path to the same eventual outcome. Once divorced or separated, she may have additional children out of wedlock; and she may or may not remarry. Both of these behaviors may be affected by the presence of welfare and the level of benefits.

Whether welfare is more likely to influence some of these behaviors than others is an empirical matter, but it is often argued on intuitive grounds that some "routes" to single motherhood are more likely to be affected than others. For example, it is often argued that an unmarried woman's second and subsequent out-of-wedlock births may be more influenced by welfare benefits, especially if the woman is already on welfare, than the first birth because the latter is more likely to be "unintended" and because awareness of welfare is less acute before a woman has been on welfare. It is also often argued that divorce and separation are likely to be less affected by welfare than remarriage probabilities, because divorce and separation are heavily influenced by other factors—most notably, whether the marital "match" is a good one—while remarriage is (so it is argued) more subject to rational calculation. These notions are useful as a starting point in thinking about differential motivations for women in different positions, but they should be regarded initially only as hypotheses to be tested.

When other determinants of marriage and fertility are considered, a rich set of conceptual models developed over decades of research is available. Some of the more important factors posited to affect marriage propensities and fertility rates are economic opportunities for women; economic opportunities for men (often hypothesized to have the opposite effects of those of women); sex and sex-employment ratios in the population; neighborhood effects; and the influence of education, family background, and other factors on social norms and values. Although enumerating these factors in detail would take us too far afield from the review exercise, it is important to emphasize that there are many influences on marriage and fertility other than welfare benefits, a point that is often deemphasized in studies whose sole focus is a single-minded search for welfare effects. Moreover, even if these other factors are not examined in detail when testing for the effects of the welfare system, it is always necessary either implicitly or explicitly to parcel out their influence relative to that of welfare, which means in most cases controlling for these other factors statistically, a point to be discussed further in the next section. Since a single mother does, after all, have alternatives to welfare, it is only the influence of the welfare benefit relative to the alternatives that should affect her choices.

Unfortunately, the large number and diversity of these alternative factors make it difficult empirically to control for them all and often leave the door open to doubts as to whether it is welfare that is affecting behavior or some other omitted factor, as discussed below in the review of the empirical research literature.

DIFFERENT QUESTIONS OF INTEREST

In turning from theories of welfare effects to the more specific issue of what empirical questions are of interest, an important distinction necessary to make at the outset is between what may properly be called a "time-series" question and a "cross-sectional" question. An important time-series question is why marriage rates have declined and nonmarital childbearing rates have increased in the United States. The corresponding welfare-related question is whether the welfare system has contributed to these trends. An important cross-sectional question, on the other hand, is whether welfare, if eliminated or reduced in generosity (for example), would raise marriage rates and lower nonmarital fertility rates, if all else is held fixed.

The answers to these questions need not be the same. One may simultaneously conclude, for example, that welfare is not a major contributor to the time-series trends in marriage and fertility but also that welfare, if reduced in generosity, would have the effects mentioned above, if all else is held fixed. Differing answers to these two questions are not necessarily inconsistent because all else is not held fixed in time series; many other factors are changing at the same time, most notably, changes in the economic and social environment and in social norms. These other factors could have been primarily responsible for the marriage and fertility trends, and could have outweighed any welfare effect. However, if it is concluded that welfare would have had an effect if nothing else had changed, one must also conclude that the time-series trend would have been different if welfare had not trended the way it did.

Both questions are of importance. Some analysts argue that the only important question is the time-series question. That question does receive much of the attention of the public. However, the cross-sectional question is also important because it bears on what would happen in the future if the welfare system were altered, regardless of what might have caused marriage and fertility trends in the past. If welfare has undesirable effects, for example, it could be used as a tool to increase marriage rates and reduce nonmarital fertility rates in the future. In any case, as the review below shows, virtually the entire research literature on the effect of welfare on demographic outcomes has focused on the cross-sectional question, not the time-series question. The majority of analyses have attempted to hold everything else fixed in a cross-sectional sense. Indeed, those studies that have utilized data over multiple time periods, which could conceivably examine time-series questions, have, by and large, deliberately eliminated the influence of time trends in the data and have based their welfare results on the cross-sectional variation in the data instead.[4]

METHODOLOGIES USED IN ESTIMATING WELFARE EFFECTS

Experimental Versus Nonexperimental Analysis

Although nonexperimental analysis is the norm in the social science research literature, experimental analysis is more familiar today to policy analysts involved in evaluations of welfare reforms. The most well-known experimental evaluations have examined the effects of various interventions on the employment, earnings, and welfare participation outcomes of welfare recipients (e.g., see the studies reviewed in Gueron and Pauly, 1991). However, experimental methods have not been widely applied to the study of welfare effects on fertility and marriage.[5] Because much of the discussion of reasons for differences in study findings turns on differences in nonexperimental methodologies—or, in the language of evaluation, the use of different nonexperimental comparison groups— a brief discussion of the reason that experimental methodologies have not been applied in this area is warranted.

The method of experimentation, wherein a randomly chosen experimental group of individuals is given a "treatment" and a randomly chosen control group is not, is a general methodology for inferring causal effects of a program or an alteration in a program. One can imagine experimenting with the level of welfare benefits, for example, giving the treatment group a higher level than the control group (or possibly giving the control group none, if it is the total effect of welfare that is of interest). Clearly the methodology cannot be applied in time series because the rest of society cannot be frozen in place and held fixed when the welfare system is altered. However, experimental methods are not always easily applied in cross section either, for a number of reasons. One is that the outcomes of interest under discussion here—marriage and fertility—do not respond quickly to changes in the welfare and socioeconomic environment, so any experiment to measure welfare effects might have to last several years for a credible estimate to be obtained. A second problem is that many welfare reforms are intended to have "community" effects—that is, effects that percolate through the community and affect general norms. Experiments cannot capture such outcomes unless the ex-

---

[4]In a regression framework, "eliminating the influence of time trends in the data" is meant to imply, for example, entering dummies for year or other time intervals into the equation.

[5]There are exceptions, and more experimental evaluations examining demographic outcomes are under way at this writing. See Chapter 6 for a discussion of state-level experiments on demographic outcomes. Also, the negative income tax (NIT) experiments of the 1980s were used to examine the effect of an NIT on marital stability (Hannan and Tuma, 1990; Cain and Wissoker, 1990) but, aside from being troubled by small sample sizes and design problems in the experiments, their results cannot be generalized to the AFDC program.

periments are "saturation site" in nature—that is, unless entire communities are made the unit of observation and all individuals within a community are either given the "treatment" or all are not. Saturation site experiments are rare and have never been very successful when tried. A third problem is that experiments can at best determine the effects of only one "bundle" of welfare reforms at a time, making it difficult to isolate the effects of any one piece of a welfare reform program from others that are part of the same reform package. This problem afflicts many of the welfare experiments undertaken in the last decade or so in the United States. Fourth, and relatedly, it is often difficult to extrapolate and generalize from experimental results, since experiments by and large test only one reform, or one bundle of welfare reforms, at a time. Fifth, for ethical reasons, experiments are limited in the types of reforms that can be tested (e.g., eliminating benefits entirely for the experimental group has, thus far, not been thought ethical).[6]

For these reasons, almost all of the research studies on the effects of welfare on marriage and fertility have utilized nonexperimental methods. Nonexperimental methods identify the effects of welfare by using natural variation in the welfare system, variation that generally arises through the political process, and by determining the existence and magnitude of correlations of such variation with variation in fertility and marital outcomes. Variations in benefits across states, across individuals within states, and over time across states have all been used for this purpose. Unfortunately, it is possible that different sources of welfare variation may have different empirical associations with marriage and fertility behavior—even though they should not "in theory"—and it is possible that this will lead to conflicting results across methods. Reconciling those differences requires determining why they yield different results and what confounding factors might be present in each.

Most of the research in this area has examined the effects and correlates of variation in the level of welfare benefits, rather than of variation in other features of welfare programs (e.g., earnings disregards, training programs, child support reform). While this may seem limiting from the point of view of a policy maker, for whom more specific programmatic reforms are generally of greater interest, much can be learned from the basic issue of whether welfare-eligible women alter their behavior in response to benefit levels. If they do so, it is not unreasonable to assume that they will respond as well to changes in other characteristics of the program that have, either directly or indirectly, monetary implications.

Types of Natural Variation Used in the Research Literature

Aside from time-series variation, three types of natural variation in the welfare system have been utilized in most studies. These are cross-state comparisons

---

[6]Even the 1996 welfare legislation does not eliminate welfare entirely for anyone, because some minimum number of years of receipt is guaranteed.

of levels, cross-state comparisons of changes over time, and within-state comparisons. The differences are important because welfare-effect estimates often differ depending on which is used.

A cross-state comparison of levels is the most common method in the literature and involves a determination of whether levels of welfare benefits are correlated with marriage and fertility behavior across states. Such comparisons need not literally be conducted at the state level, but rather can be conducted at the individual level so long as the data include individuals in multiple states. The widespread use of this technique is based upon the recognition that AFDC benefits are set at the state level and hence are generally the same within states, at least for families of the same size and with the same income and other characteristics. Consequently, when holding these family characteristics constant, benefits vary only across states. Using individual-level data, one can control for other confounding factors at the individual level (age, education, and the other factors referred to previously) and therefore get closer to determining the effect of welfare when all else is held fixed.

Cross-state comparisons of changes are less common but have recently gained popularity in the research literature, where they are often called "state fixed effects" models. In this case, changes over time in benefit levels across states are compared to changes over time in outcome variables such as marriage and fertility. A case can be made that such comparisons are superior to those using cross-state comparisons of levels, inasmuch as the levels of benefits and levels of marriage-fertility behavior may covary across states not only because of some true relationship but also for some other, spurious reason. For example, the low AFDC benefit levels and high marriage rates in most southern states may not be a reflection of a true welfare effect but may instead reflect the fact that the South is socially a relatively conservative region where social and cultural norms encourage marriage, as well as being a relatively conservative region politically where elected representatives do not legislate generous welfare benefits.[7] In this latter interpretation, a positive correlation between benefit levels and marriage (for example) would arise because there is a third variable—social, cultural, and political norms—that leads to them both, not because benefits affect marriage. In the method of cross-state comparisons of changes, changes in benefits over time are inspected instead of differences in levels. For example, as it turns out, benefit levels have been falling in the South more slowly than they have been falling in the Midwest over the last two decades; if there is a true effect of welfare on marriage, then marriage rates should fall less (or rise more) in the South than in the Midwest, even if the two regions started off at very different levels—that is, even if marriage levels were higher to begin with in the South for other reasons.

The method of cross-state comparisons of changes has its own difficulties, however. One important problem is the difficulty of measuring long-term re-

---

[7]This notion appears to have first been explicitly discussed and emphasized by Ellwood and Bane (1985).

sponses to changes in welfare benefits. If marriage and fertility behaviors do not respond quickly to benefit-level alterations, a fairly long time interval must be examined to measure changes in behavior.[8] If one attempts to examine long time intervals, an additional problem arises because significant state in- and out-migration may occur, which may change state-level average outcomes merely because the composition of the population has changed, not because a fixed set of individuals have changed their behavior. More generally, it has to be assumed that over long time intervals the "omitted" influences—for example, the social and cultural norms referred to previously—do not change and do not change differentially across states. In addition, a comparison of cross-state changes in welfare merely throws the bias problem back one stage because it then needs to be determined why some states increase their benefits faster, or lower them less rapidly, than other states, and whether omitted state-specific, time-varying influences might confound the welfare effect by being responsible both for benefit trends and for marriage-fertility trends.

Within-state comparisons are the most difficult and the least used because they rely on comparisons of outcomes for women within a state who are offered different benefit levels or comparisons between women who are eligible and women who are not eligible for welfare. The problem with this method is that, because the eligibility and benefit determination rules are generally the same statewide, benefit-level differences between women within a state are almost always associated with a demographic characteristic (e.g., having children) that by itself could have an impact on the outcomes of interest. A comparison of eligibles with ineligibles is an extreme version of this method.

Time-series analysis is a fourth method that is fraught with the difficulty already mentioned of controlling for alternative factors that are also changing over time.

BASIC TIME-SERIES PATTERNS IN WELFARE AND DEMOGRAPHIC OUTCOMES

Three of the methodologies—cross-state comparison of levels, cross-state comparison of changes, and time-series analysis—can be studied by examining trends over time in unadjusted state-level or national-level aggregates of demographic outcomes, on the one hand, and measures of welfare generosity, on the other. It is useful to present the basic patterns of these correlations with unadjusted aggregates before reviewing the multivariate analyses in the econometric literature. As it turns out, the patterns that appear in this analysis capture, in large

---

[8]A related possibility is that the comparison-of-changes method measures a short-term response, while the comparison-of-levels method measures a long-term response if it shows where marriage and fertility levels have ended up after several years of adjustment. Thus it may be that the two methods are simply not measuring the same thing.

degree, the patterns revealed by multivariate analyses. Consequently, much of the basic story is understandable in relatively simple terms and does not need recourse to controlling for additional variables or use of specialized statistical methods.

The pure time-series method involves a simple comparison of trends in welfare benefits and in demographic outcomes. Figure 4-1 shows the time trend in welfare benefits of different types in the United States over the period 1970-1993. It has been noted repeatedly that the time-series evidence for a welfare effect on marriage and fertility is weak because welfare benefits declined in real terms over the 1970s and 1980s while marriage rates declined and nonmarital childbearing increased; both trends have been noted in the overviews in Chapters 2 and 3. Figure 4-1 provides further confirmation, because it indicates that real AFDC benefits have fallen continuously since the early 1970s. Real Food Stamp benefits have remained roughly constant, primarily because they are indexed to inflation, while real Medicaid benefits were roughly fixed until the mid-1980s, when they began to rise. The sum of benefits therefore declined up to the late 1980s. It did begin to rise at that time, but this increase is too late to explain the secular trends in marriage and fertility. In addition, Medicaid benefits began to be available to many poor families off AFDC in the late 1980s, thereby weakening the link between welfare and the availability of medical care.

The inconsistency between benefit and demographic trends could mask the presence of long lags (Murray, 1993). The generosity of the transfer system

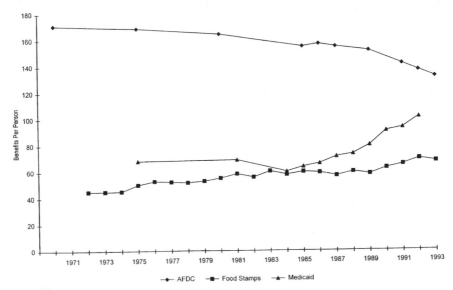

FIGURE 4-1   Trends in real monthly welfare benefits per person. SOURCE: U.S. House of Representatives (1994:378, 782, 806).

increased significantly in the late 1960s and early 1970s, as Food Stamps were mandated nationally and the Medicaid system was expanded. It is possible that this expansion of benefits resulted in increases in (say) nonmarital childbearing 10 years later, if the effect of the expansion took time to occur because social norms were slow to adjust. This is a difficult hypothesis to prove or disprove because the trends have been so universal. It is not possible to isolate specific communities where benefits increased much more than other communities, for example, and where the population was fixed for 10 years so that lagged effects could be measured. Consequently, the importance of this argument at the present time must rest to a great extent on whether one believes that low-income families react quickly or slowly to the monetary opportunities facing them.

As noted previously, the inconsistency between time trends in benefits and demographic outcomes may mean only that there have been other factors changing over time that masked the effect of welfare benefits; this is the major weakness of the method. There may have been changes in the other factors affecting marriage and divorce—economic opportunities for women and men, the availability of partners in the marriage market, and changes in social norms. More persuasive evidence on the effect of welfare per se might therefore be gained from cross-state comparisons of levels because these comparisons are made at a single point in time, across states, and hence are not complicated by such major time trends. Figure 4-2, drawn from Murray (1993), shows illegitimacy rates and welfare benefit levels among white women in different states in 1988.[9] A positive relationship between benefits and illegitimacy is clear from the figure. Much of the relationship comes from the concentration of southern states with low benefits and low rates of illegitimacy, although the relationship would still be positive (but weaker) if the South were omitted. Thus some evidence for a positive effect of welfare on out-of-wedlock childbearing is yielded by these data.

To ensure that this pattern is not special to the particular dataset, time period, and variables used by Murray, data from the Current Population Survey (CPS) for 1993 were obtained for this study, and tabulations of welfare benefits and rates of single motherhood by state were computed. Single motherhood rates rather than illegitimacy are examined because single motherhood is a broader and more inclusive measure of the demographic outcome of interest.[10] Figure 4-3 shows the cross-state result for white women.[11] Interestingly, very little relationship between headship and benefits appears in this figure, contrary to the results of

---

[9]The illegitimacy ratios are taken from vital statistics reports.

[10]This is because single motherhood is an overall category that can be reached by any of the routes discussed earlier—nonmarital childbearing, divorce or separation, and failure to remarry. Thus it is a summary measure of all these routes taken together.

[11]The March CPS is used. Single mothers are defined as women without a spouse in the household who have children under 18. Family and subfamily heads are included as separate observations. The rates are computed as a fraction of all women 18-64. The AFDC benefit variables are those for a family of four with no other income.

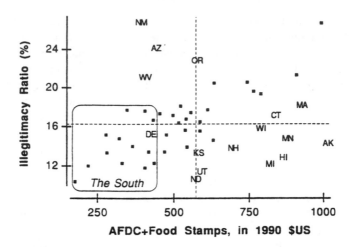

FIGURE 4-2   Illegitimacy rates and benefit levels for white women, 1988. SOURCE: Murray (1993).

Murray. A least-squares regression line, also shown in the figure, confirms this visual impression of only a slight positive relationship between the two variables. However, when women 20-44 and without a high school diploma are examined instead (Figure 4-4)—a subpopulation with relatively high welfare participation rates—the positive correlation reappears with a greater magnitude. Illegitimacy rates are no doubt more concentrated among the less educated, low-income population than are single mothers, who are fairly common in higher-income groups as well; this may explain why the positive correlation appears for illegitimacy rates even without restricting the sample to young, less educated women. This positive covariation extends to an examination of rates of never-married single mothers—that is, the fraction of women who have children but have never been married (thus omitting divorced, separated, and widowed single mothers)—where the relationship is, if anything stronger (figure not shown).

This simple analysis shows that the level of state welfare benefits is substantially correlated with single-motherhood rates. Many of the largest states such as New York, California, and Illinois have relatively generous welfare systems as well as high rates of single motherhood; another large state, Texas, has low benefits and low single-motherhood rates. Clearly, a major question is whether this simple correlation is the result of some other characteristic of the populations of these states or of their socioeconomic environments; however, as seen in the next section, this positive covariation persists even when other measurable influences are controlled for and therefore appears to be reasonably robust.

The positive relationship holds for other periods as well—all the way back to the 1960s, when CPS micro data are first available for these computations. It also

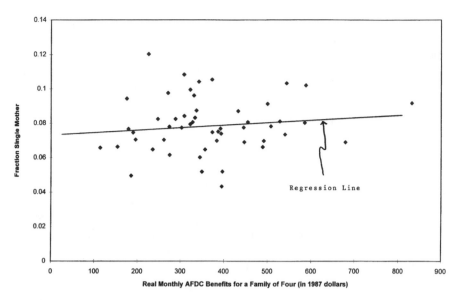

FIGURE 4-3   Single motherhood rates and real AFDC benefits by state: CPS, 1993, white women.

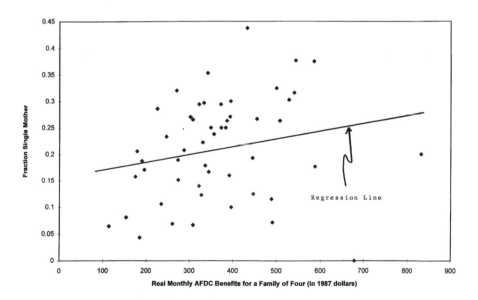

FIGURE 4-4   Single motherhood rates and real AFDC benefits by state: CPS, 1993, white women 20-44 without high school diploma.

holds when other measures of the welfare system—Medicaid, for example—are included. The relationship also appears in simple regional comparisons because the Northeast has high welfare benefits and high rates of single motherhood, while the South has the lowest benefits and lowest single motherhood rates. The Midwest and West have much higher benefits than the South and slightly higher rates of single motherhood.

To determine whether these comparisons of levels have the same implications as those from cross-state comparisons of changes, CPS data from a different year can be compared to the 1993 data. The tables discussed below use CPS information from 1977, a full 15 years prior to 1993, when benefit levels were quite a bit higher. Rates of single motherhood were lower in 1977 overall, but the issue here is whether those states that lowered their AFDC benefits the least— benefits fell in virtually all states—also had the largest increases in single motherhood; if so, this could be taken as evidence of an effect of welfare consistent with the pure cross-state comparison of levels.

As Figure 4-5 indicates, however, the relationship between benefit levels and single motherhood is extremely weak for young less educated white women when this type of comparison is made. Although different states lowered benefits over this period by different amounts, the increases in single motherhood across the states were fairly uniformly distributed. New Jersey, for example, which reduced its benefits by a very large amount over the period ($257 reduction per month) saw its single motherhood rate increase by about 5 percentage points,

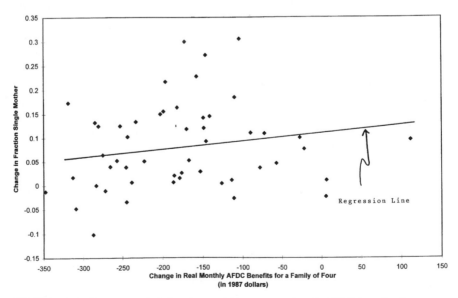

FIGURE 4-5 Never-married female headship rates and real AFDC benefits by state: CPS, 1993, white women 20-44 without high school diploma.

whereas Texas, which reduced its benefit by much less ($78 per month), saw about the same increase, 4 percentage points.

Mechanically, the difference in results between the different comparisons arises from two facts. First, over the 1970s and 1980s, states with high average welfare benefits had higher-than-average rates of single motherhood (as well as nonmarital fertility rates); this relationship held not just for 1993 but also for 1977 and other years. Second, over the course of the 1970s and 1980s, states that raised benefits more than others—or, more accurately, lowered them less than others—did not experience faster-than-average increases in single motherhood and fertility. Welfare benefits across U.S. regions converged slightly over the 1970s and 1980s, with the southern states lowering benefits the least and northeastern states lowering their benefits the most, for example, but this pattern does not correspond at all to rates of change of single motherhood among less educated white women (e.g., the Northeast experienced the greatest increase in single motherhood even though it, along with the industrial midwestern states, lowered benefits the most).

The difference between the results using these two sources of welfare variation may stem from the omission of factors in one or both of the two comparisons. One possibility is that the comparison of levels omits key state differences that affect both marriage and fertility behavior as well as benefits. For example, as mentioned earlier, southern states have strong promarriage social norms and also have low welfare benefits; the correlation between marriage and benefits may therefore arise coincidentally. The fact that the South did not lower its benefits very much over time, for example, and yet did not experience a high growth of single motherhood relative to regions like the Northeast, which lowered their benefits a great deal, suggests indeed that the cross-state levels relationship may have been spurious and due to other factors.[12] However, it may also be the case that the comparison of changes omits some factor that is causing benefits to change at different rates across states. Differences in rates of change in the economic performance of different states, in unemployment rates, and in related factors may have been responsible for both the change in benefits and the change in single motherhood. For example, the South experienced significant economic growth in the late 1970s and 1980s, and closed its economic gap with the rest of the country to some degree; this could have caused both its relative increase in welfare benefits and its relative decline in single motherhood. The place to begin in testing these hypotheses and attempting to reconcile the different forms of evidence (levels vs. changes) is to attempt to control for some of these omitted

---

[12]For example, Hoynes (1996) used data that followed individuals over time (i.e., panel data) to determine whether the correlation between changes in single motherhood at the individual level and changes in benefits is the same as that at the state level. She found this to be the case for white women. This supports the interpretation of the cross-state differences as traceable to differences in the types of women in those states.

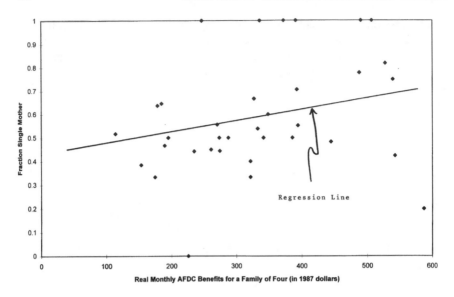

FIGURE 4-6   Female headship rates and real AFDC benefits by region: CPS, 1993, white women 20-44 without high school deploma.

variables in a multivariate analysis. This is one of the roles of the econometric research to be described momentarily.

The patterns for black women are roughly similar. As shown in Figure 4-6, the levels of single motherhood for young, less educated black women are positively related to welfare benefits. Also, a comparison of changes in single-motherhood rates and benefit levels also shows no relationship between the two, if not a negative relationship, as shown in Figure 4-7. Overall, single-motherhood rates grew quite a bit faster for black women than for white women over this period but, as for white women, the rate of growth across states was not closely related to the magnitude of changes in welfare benefits in the state. Single-motherhood rates for less educated black women grew at about the same rate in the South, the Northeast, and the Midwest, for example, despite very different changes in welfare benefits in those regions.

RESULTS FROM MULTIVARIATE ECONOMETRIC MODELS

The econometric studies in the literature are fairly large in number. A table listing many of the studies appears in the appendix to this chapter. A more detailed summary of each is available in Hudson and Moffitt (1997). These studies all use one of the four methods of obtaining welfare variation described in the discussion of methodologies, three of which have been discussed in graphical terms in the preceeding section (all except the use of within-state variation).

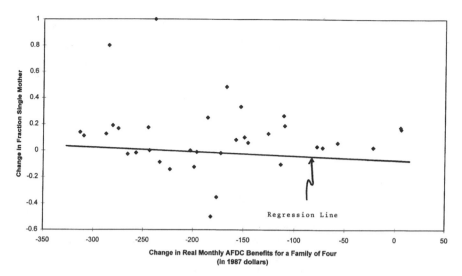

FIGURE 4-7   Change in female headship rates and real AFDC benefits by state from 1977 to 1993: CPS, white women 20-44 without high school diploma.

Relative to the graphical analysis, a simple question that can be answered here is whether the patterns of effects across states, over time and for different racial groups, is any different in a multivariate analysis where additional covariates are entered into the model and where more sophisticated methods of estimation are employed.

Table 4-1 summarizes the results of 68 different estimates from these studies, classified according to the method by which welfare variation was obtained and the nature of the result.[13] Over all types of studies, a slight majority find a significantly negative effect on marriage or positive effect on fertility rather than an insignificant effect (the mixed estimates, which could be classified in either way, are ignored). This may seem surprising in light of what was taken to be the

---

[13]The studies were located by searching the economics and sociology literature since 1970 and following references to other articles therein, as well as by a general search for articles on the subject since 1970 in a variety of other sources. All studies located were included that (1) had the estimation of the effect of AFDC on marriage, fertility, or a related demographic outcome as a significant, major focus of the study and (2) were either published or had been circulated in draft form by May 1996. No study was intentionally excluded that met these criteria. It should also be noted that there are 68 estimates but fewer individual studies than this because most studies provided estimates for both races. Estimates for outcomes other than marriage and fertility, (e.g., living arrangements) are excluded from the table but are indicated in the Appendix.

TABLE 4-1　Counts of Studies of Effect of Welfare on Marriage and Fertility, by Nature of Findings and Source of Welfare Variation

	All Races			White			Black or Nonwhite		
	Insig.	Sig.	Mixed	Insig.	Sig.	Mixed	Insig.	Sig.	Mixed
All types	8	5	1	8	13	5	10	12	6
By type									
Cross-state levels	6	3	1	2	9	4	7	6	3
Cross-state changes	1	2	—	4	4	—	1	5	2
Within state	1	—	—	1	—	—	1	—	—
Time series	—	—	—	1	—	1	1	1	1

NOTES: Entries denote number of studies of each type showing no statistically significant effect of welfare ("Insig."), a significantly negative effect of welfare on marriage or a positive effect on fertility or both ("Sig."), or a mixed pattern of results ("Mixed," implying some significant and some insignificant results). Studies listed under "All Races" did not report results separately by race. If a study presented more than one estimate or model, the author's preferred estimate is tabulated.

conventional wisdom approximately 10 years ago, when it was generally believed that the evidence did not support much of an effect of welfare on marriage and fertility at all. However, that consensus was based on studies from the 1970s, which indeed showed weaker results than the studies that have been conducted since then. Among analysts who work on the topic, there is now a rough consensus that the evidence does support some effect of welfare on marriage and fertility, although the magnitude of the effect remains in question. Whether this change in estimates has been a result of superior analysis methods in the later studies or an increase in the underlying effect of welfare on behavior is difficult to determine with certainty, but some evidence points to the latter (Moffitt, 1990).

However, the overall counts of estimates are misleading because they are disproportionately concentrated among studies using cross-state comparisons of levels—a much smaller number have used cross-state comparisons of changes and only a handful have used either time-series or within-state methods—and because the results differ notably by race. As Table 4-1 shows, a majority of the estimates from cross-state comparisons of levels show that welfare benefits have an effect on marriage or fertility—negative on the former, positive on the latter—but when the results are disaggregated by race, the studies show more of an effect for white women than for nonwhite or black women. For white women, nine studies show effects of welfare while only two show no effect. For black and nonwhite women, however, the split is almost exactly 50-50 between those that find an effect and those that find none. Thus these multivariate analyses are quite similar to those revealed by the simpler graphical analyses reported in the previous section, at least for white women. The implication, perhaps surprising, is that the additional covariates added in these studies—typically variables like age, educational level, and family background, as well as (sometimes) variables for the state unemployment rate, labor market wages, etc.—do not explain away the cross-state differences for white women in the simple unadjusted cross-state comparisons. For black women, however, these variables do appear to explain much of the raw difference; black women of similar characteristics in different states do not have significantly different demographic outcomes, at least in many of the studies in the literature, despite the differences in benefit levels across those states. It is not possible to determine the precise set of measured influences that account for the unadjusted difference across states noted earlier, but differences in urbanization may be one factor.[14]

The weaker effect for black women is unexpected in light of their greater rates of participation in the welfare system compared to those of white women. In general, it is possible that there is some omitted factor that differs between the races (including possibly cultural differences), but no such factor has yet been identified in the literature. Murray (1993) hypothesizes that the low-income black population is more geographically concentrated than the low-income white population and that neighborhood effects lead to changes in social norms that increase illegitimacy rates (for example) even in the face of low benefits. Thus the South, with its concentration of the black population, has high illegitimacy rates. However, if this argument is correct, it implies that the variation in illegitimacy between black women in different states is indeed a result of something other than the welfare system. The racial difference therefore must still be regarded as an unresolved puzzle.

As shown in Table 4-1, many fewer studies have conducted cross-state comparisons of changes instead of levels. Of those that have used this method, however, the estimated strength of the welfare system is quite different than the results of the levels method. For white women, the estimated welfare effect is quite weakened: the studies that compare changes are evenly spread over those that find an effect and those that find none. For black and nonwhite women, the estimated welfare effect is actually somewhat stronger in the comparison of changes than it was in the comparison of levels, in terms of the relative numbers of studies finding an effect. These results are, therefore, once again quite consistent with the simpler analysis reported in the last section for white women but only roughly so for black women, although even for black women there is about a 50-50 split between studies finding a significant effect and studies finding no effect. In addition, an implication of this pattern of results is that the differences between the comparisons of levels and changes,

---

[14]For example, see Moffitt (1994: Table 3). Adding age, education, urban residence, and a few other variables to an equation explaining black female headship rates changed a welfare-benefit coefficient from significance to insignificance. Urban residence, which is less common in the South than in other regions, for example, had a positive effect on headship rates.

and between the race differences within each, are not explained away by the typical covariates used in these analyses.

There has been considerable discussion in the research literature concerning the different results across methods but without any definitive resolution. Although it has been argued that the comparison of levels is subject to the biases noted earlier in the discussion of methodologies, the comparison of changes also has the defects noted there. In the absence of definitive evidence that either methodology is incorrect, an equal weighting of the two still leads to a conclusion that the welfare system has effects on marriage and fertility, even if not as strong as might be thought based on comparison-level methods alone.

There have been even fewer within-state and time-series studies, mainly for the reasons noted earlier: within-state comparisons must find some characteristic of women that affects their eligibility for benefits but does not independently affect their marriage and fertility outcomes, while time-series analyses inevitably have difficulty controlling for all alternative influences that are changing over time. For example, one study utilizing within-state variation did not examine benefits at all but found no effect of AFDC participation rates on demographic outcomes across races, a method that implicitly assumes there would be no racial difference in demographic outcomes in the absence of AFDC. Another study compared the divorce rates of women with and without children in states with high and low welfare benefits, thus implicitly assuming that divorce rates would be identical among women with and without children in the absence of AFDC. The implausibility of these assumptions shows the extreme weakness of the method. As for the time-series studies, most simply estimate a variety of bivariate relationships and find either no effect or mixed effects. The one study that found a negative effect regressed the illegitimacy ratio in a year on the lagged AFDC participation rate rather than on the AFDC benefit; yet the AFDC participation rate is an endogenous variable and is as much the product of time-series trends in illegitimacy as its cause. The within-state and time-series methods are sufficiently problematical that they should probably be dropped from any weighing of the evidence on the question.

While the discussion thus far has concentrated on what now appear to be unresolved differences between results using levels and changes comparisons, and between races, there is also a considerable variance of results within these types of studies and there are quite a few studies in each category that differ from the central tendency of the results for each type. Once again, without further analysis, it is difficult to resolve most of these differences. To be sure, there are a few studies that appear to suffer from a significant defect that could explain why their results differ from the central tendency. Many of these defects concern the use of endogenous variables either for the welfare benefit or in controlling for nonwelfare factors, where an endogenous variable is, roughly, a variable that is a result of women's marital and fertility choices themselves (rather than a cause of them). Among the studies of levels that find a significant cross-sectional welfare effect for black and nonwhite women, for example, one study replaced the welfare benefit ("instrumented" it, in econometric parlance) with such endogenous variables, while others included in the regression variables of questionable exogeneity such as the labor force participation rates and earnings levels of men and women. Other defects in the studies arise as well: one constrained the welfare benefit coefficient to be the same as the coefficient on other income, while another defined the dependent variable as AFDC receipt, which could by itself and separately be expected to respond to benefit levels. However, the number of studies that can be dropped from consideration for these reasons is relatively small, and even for these, it cannot be determined conclusively that a correction of the problem would have had a major quantitative effect on the results Thus most studies must be given some positive weight in a balancing of the evidence.[15]

One notable difference among the different studies behind Table 4-1 is their great diversity in the types of variables held fixed when estimating welfare effects. Duncan and Hoffman (1990), for example, control for differences in women's labor market opportunities and even for differences in the labor market opportunities of potential male marital partners. Schultz (1994) and Lundberg and Plotnick (1995) similarly attempt to control for labor market differences. Ellwood and Bane (1985) and Matthews et al. (1995) go the farthest in this direction, controlling for a large number of state characteristics, even including characteristics of state political systems. On the other hand, Murray (1993), in an intentional effort to keep his analysis simple and easy to understand, does not adjust for any other differences between women or across states besides welfare. Roughly speaking, the more variables that are controlled for in an analysis, the weaker is the estimated effect of welfare—although there is no logical reason why this need be so, which may also be responsible for some of the differences across studies. Determining whether this is the case would require reanalyzing some of the datasets under consideration and estimating similar specifications across datasets.[16]

In addition to these differences, however, the studies with different results vary in the dataset used, in the age range of the individuals examined, and in the

---

[15]These remarks are relevant to a common criticism of the "vote-counting" method used in Table 4-1—namely, that simply counting studies that have differing results without any adjustment for the quality of the study is misleading. The argument here is that only in rare instances can defects in the methodology in a study be determined to account for any nontrivial amount of the difference in estimates from another study, because too much else differs as well; hence the magnitude of the bias cannot be isolated.

[16]Although in general it is to be desired that as many alternative influences be controlled for as possible, this does not extend to endogenous variables, which were discussed previously and should not be included. However, as important as this distinction is, it is not necessary to discriminate between exogenous and endogenous variables when one is attempting merely to answer the simpler factual question of whether differences in regressor sets across studies account for their differences in estimated welfare impacts. Only after it has been determined which variable sets lead to what results can the question of which is "best" be addressed.

calendar years covered by the data. A simple way to summarize these differences is by ordinary least-squares regression, using as a dependent variable the strength of the estimated effect and as independent variables the characteristics of the study. By taking only the studies in the first two rows of Table 4-1 (levels and changes studies) and defining a dependent variable (Y) equal to 1 if an effect was found, 0 if not, and .5 if a mixed finding was obtained, the following regression-based summary of the importance of study characteristics results:

$$Y = -1.33 + .15*CHANGES - .07*BLACK + .016*YEAR + .022*AGE$$
$$(.16) (.13) (.015) (.010)$$
$$ + .12*VITAL + .08*NLSY - .12*PSID - .19*CPS$$
$$(.19) (.20) (.26) (.20)$$
$$ - .04*SM - .024*REMDIV$$
$$(.18) (.34)$$
$$n = 55, R^2 = .24$$

where CHANGES is a dummy variable equal to 1 if the study used the changes rather than levels method; BLACK is a dummy equal to 1 if the estimate in question is for the black or nonwhite population; YEAR is the median year of the data; AGE is the median age of the individuals in the data; VITAL, NLSY, PSID, and CPS are dummies equal to 1 if the study used vital statistics, National Longitudinal Survey of Youth (NLSY), Panel Study on Income Dynamics (PSID), or CPS data, respectively (omitted category is all other datasets); and SM and REMDIV are dummies equal to 1 if the study-dependent variable was single-motherhood or divorce-remarriage transitions (omitted category is a dependent variable pertaining to fertility, almost always nonmarital). Standard errors, in parentheses, are large because of the small sample size. Interestingly, the results imply that the changes studies yield stronger, rather than lesser, effects when the other variables are controlled; that estimated effects are larger in samples of older women (contrary to some of the hypotheses in the literature) and grow over time; and that the effects are stronger when vital statistics and NLSY data are used rather than CPS or PSID data.[17] The summary also indicates that welfare effects are weaker in studies that examine single motherhood as a single state, or remarriage or divorce, than studies that examine the effects on nonmarital fertility. When these results are taken at face value, they imply that the strongest effect of welfare occurs in nonmarital fertility but that these effects eventually disappear, perhaps because a woman eventually marries and her subsequent demographic behavior is unaffected by her having experienced an out-of-wedlock birth previ-

---

[17]Klerman (1996) argues that the sample sizes in all datasets save vital statistics are insufficient to detect effects of reasonable magnitudes. This is supported by the estimated coefficient on VITAL but not by the coefficient on CPS, which is the next largest dataset.

ously.[18] This finding bears further investigation because it means that the implications of early nonmarital childbearing for later family structure may not be as strong as imagined. Of course, there are many other differences in these studies that have not been controlled for. Once again, however, only a reanalysis of the various datasets and models can confirm these differences.

Studies that compare changes are thought by many analysts to be more reliable than studies that compare levels for the reasons noted previously—namely, that the level studies confound cross-sectional benefit variations and unobserved variations in economic, social, and political factors. If this view is taken, there are sufficiently small numbers of these studies to make more headway by making more detailed comparisons between specific individual studies. When the studies are examined at this more detailed level, many possible explanations for differences appear. For example, the stronger effects found by Jackson and Klerman (1995) hold only when effects on nonmarital fertility in isolation are estimated; when effects on marital fertility are examined as well, no effect of welfare on their relative magnitudes is found. This should properly move the study from one reporting a significant effect to one reporting an insignificant effect in Table 4-1. Clarke and Strauss (1995), who also find a significant effect of welfare, obtain strong effects with a two-stage least-squares procedure using state per capita income (among other variables) as an "instrument" for the benefit, but per capita income probably belongs in the main equation. Rosenzweig (1995) argues that his significant estimated effects of welfare result from separating out the low-income population for analysis, but a similar separation was conducted by Hoynes (1996), Moffitt (1994), and Robins and Fronstin (1996), who all found either no change in effects because of this separation or insignificant changes even for the disadvantaged population; this suggests that some other difference between the Rosenzweig study and the other three studies explains their different findings.[19] Finally, these studies differ dramatically in the extent to which other state-level influences are controlled in the regressions and the types of influences controlled for. Table 4-2 shows the different area-level controls used in the studies of changes. While some of the variables are potentially endogenous and therefore perhaps should be excluded, some of the studies

---

[18]This conclusion necessarily follows because a young woman who has a premarital birth necessarily becomes a single mother, thereby driving up the fraction of the population who are single mothers; but if the overall rate of single mothers is not significantly affected by welfare, it must be the case that these young mothers later marry so that, on average and over all ages, the single-motherhood rate ends up not much different than it would have been if the early premarital childbearing had not occurred. It should be noted that the vast majority of studies (about three-quarters) are of nonmarital fertility and that there is only one study of divorce, which is why it is lumped in with remarriage (for which there were only two studies).

[19]A notable difference, however, is that Rosenzweig stratified on the income of the family of origin, while the other three studies stratified on the education of the woman in question. Whether this could explain the differing results cannot be determined.

TABLE 4-2   State-Level Control Variables Used in Studies of Cross-State Changes

Study	Variables
Clarke and Strauss (1995)	Median wage of working women; median wage of working men; incarceration rate; unemployment rate; percent living in metropolitan area
Ellwood and Bane (1985)	Percentage nonwhite; percent high school graduates; mean wage; fraction of population under 18; unemployment rate; fraction of population living in metropolitan area
Hoynes (1996)	Average manufacturing wage; unemployment rate; per capita income; percent of population over 65; percent of population less than 18; percent black; Republican governor; Republican House; Republican Senate
Jackson and Klerman (1995)	Unemployment rate; mean wage; mean manufacturing wage; mean wage in retail trade
Lichter et al. (1996)	Sex ratio; male full-time median income; male education; male employment levels; female full-time median income; female education; percent population 65+; percent black; percent Hispanic; percent rural; population; percent Catholic; percent Latter Day Saints; percent anti-abortion Protestant
Moffitt (1994)	Unemployment rate; percent employed in manufacturing; percent employed in retail and wholesale trade; percent employed in services; percent employed in government
Robins and Fronstin (1996)	None
Rosenzweig (1995)	None

control for no area-level variables at all, which could easily explain some of the differences in findings.

A final important issue concerns the magnitudes of the estimated effects of welfare for those studies finding significant estimates. Not surprisingly, the estimated magnitudes have a wide dispersion as well. At the upper end are three studies (Fossett and Kiecolt, 1993; Hill and O'Neill, 1993; Rosenzweig, 1995) implying that a 25 percent reduction in welfare benefits would reduce the probability of a nonmarital birth by approximately .04 or .05.[20] If the mean probability is .16, this implies a reduction to a level of .11 or .12, or about a 30 percent

---

[20]The different studies define their dependent variables slightly differently; for two of them it is approximately the probability of ever having had a nonmarital birth up to a particular age (which is higher than the annual probability of the event). The 4 percentage point number is scaled from the numbers actually given in the articles.

reduction in the rate. In time series, the welfare benefit has indeed fallen by about 25 percent over the last 20 years (see Figure 4-1), while the nonmarital childbearing rate for this age group has doubled (U.S. Department of Health and Human Services, 1995: Figure II-1). One interpretation of these estimates is therefore that the historical increase in the nonmarital childbearing rate could have been cut by a significant amount if benefits had been reduced by twice the amount that they were. At the other end are studies obtaining estimates that are statistically significant but quite small in magnitude (Danziger et al., 1982; Duncan and Hoffman, 1990; Lichter et al., 1991, 1996). A typical and recent estimate is that of Lichter et al. (1996), who found that a 25 percent reduction in the welfare benefit would increase the percentage of women who are female heads by only .007, a small amount. Clearly, therefore, a resolution of the differences in these magnitudes is also a priority item for future research.

WHAT DO WE NEED TO KNOW?

This review of what we know about the effect of welfare on marriage and fertility has demonstrated that much has been learned from research regarding the basic patterns of relationship between welfare and the demographic outcomes, where a significant relationship appears and where it does not, and about the general robustness of the strength of the estimated relationship across different datasets and different methods. Based on this review, it is clear that a simple majority of the studies that have been conducted to date show a significant correlation between welfare benefits and marriage and fertility, suggesting the presence of such behavioral incentive effects. However, in addition to this finding not being able to explain the time-series increase in nonmarital fertility and decline in marriage, the majority finding itself is weakened by the sensitivity of the result to the methodology used and to numerous other differences in specifications across the studies. A neutral weighing of the evidence still leads to the conclusion that welfare has incentive effects on marriage and fertility, but the uncertainty introduced by the disparities in the research findings weakens the strength of that conclusion.

The resolution of the discrepancies between these studies is important for welfare policy at minimum because the issue of how demographic outcomes are affected by the overall level of welfare benefits is so basic to all discussions of welfare effects. It is also relevant to many of the reforms tested in the states in the past several years and to many of the changes enacted in the 1996 welfare legislation. Women who lose eligibility because of time limits or failure to comply with new rules, as well as women who do not choose to go onto welfare but would have otherwise, can be viewed as having suffered benefit reductions similar to those whose effects are studied by the research literature. More generally, the legislation is intended to reduce the welfare caseload and to lower the overall level of welfare benefits provided to low-income populations; it is explicitly intended to have effects on nonmarital fertility of the type with which the research literature is concerned.[21]

Although much of the analysis of the 1996 legislation will be conducted with program evaluation methodologies using experimental-control or treatment-comparison-group frameworks rather than the econometric approach underlying the studies in the research literature, the latter has a role to play in understanding the former. Ideally, the econometric research should be consistent with demonstration and evaluation evidence and any differences should be reconciled. If, for example, the New Jersey family cap experiment shows little effect of a family cap on fertility, it would increase the confidence in that finding considerably if it could be concluded from the research literature that incremental benefits in the range tested in New Jersey also appear to have no effect on fertility. Even more important—to continue to follow the New Jersey case—the research literature should be capable of providing estimates of the effects of benefit changes of greater magnitudes than that in New Jersey and for a greater number of states with differing economic and social environments. Regardless of the number of demonstration evaluations conducted, there will never be a sufficient number of them to provide the same range of alternative programs that occur naturally over time and across states. Econometric research using secondary data can make use of that larger range.

Unfortunately, the diversity in findings in the research necessarily reduces the power of that research to play this role. Moreover, studies that attempt to resolve the discrepancies have not been conducted. Three different types of studies are necessary. The first type involves *replication* studies, or studies that reanalyze the same dataset used by each study (or the major studies) to determine whether the results were correct as reported. The second type, *robustness* studies, conduct sensitivity testing to the model reported in each study to determine if the results are robust to variations in the specification. The third type—*reconciliation* studies—attempt to estimate common specifications across studies on common samples, in an attempt to reconcile why the studies achieved different findings. These types of studies—the three Rs of replication, robustness, and reconciliation—have not been applied to this literature. As in much other literature in which the main contributors are academic scholars, the lack of attention to the three Rs is primarily a result of the bias in academic publishing and research toward new findings, new techniques, and original analysis, and against mere replication of other researchers' results. This situation is unlikely to change without government or other funding to give researchers an incentive to conduct such studies.

---

[21]In addition, many of the states have adopted or will newly adopt family caps on payments to additional children, changes in the AFDC-UP program to encourage married-couple welfare participation, and other rules that directly affect fertility and marriage apart from simply reducing the caseload (see Chapter 6).

The most likely cause of the discrepancy across studies is the omission of different alternative influences on marriage and childbearing. Very few studies control for the same factors, and the studies using the different methodologies outlined here almost never attempt to control for the confounding influences appropriate to the method in question (e.g., alternative influences across states, across states over time, or in time series). Relatively little attention has been paid to nonwelfare influences, particularly those that might be correlated with welfare, in the analyses. This defect could also be addressed with additional research.

ACKNOWLEDGMENTS

The author would like to thank E. Michael Foster, John Haaga, Robert Haveman, Anne Hill, Hilary Hoynes, Daniel Lichter, Howard Rolston, and Barbara Wolfe for comments; Julie Hudson and Chris Ruebeck for research assistance; and grant R01-HD27248 from the National Institute of Child Health and Human Development (NICHD) for support. Assistance was also provided by NICHD grant P30-HD06268 to the Johns Hopkins University Population Center.

REFERENCES

Acs, G.
    1994   The impact of AFDC on young women's childbearing decisions. Washington, D.C.: Urban Institute.
    1996   The impact of welfare on young mother's subsequent childbearing decisions. *Journal of Human Resources* 31(4):898-915.
Allen, D.
    1993   Welfare and the family: The Canadian experience. *Journal of Labor Economics* 11(1, Part 2):S201-S223.
An, C., R. Haveman, and B. Wolfe
    1993   Teen out-of-wedlock births and welfare receipt: The role of childhood events and economic circumstance. *Review of Economics and Statistics* 75(2):195-208.
Becker, G.
    1981   *A Treatise on the Family*. Cambridge, Mass.: Harvard University Press.
Blank, R., C.C. George, and R.A. London
    1994   State Abortion Rates: The Impact of Policies, Providers, Politics, Demographics and Economic Environment. NBER Working Paper No. 1853. Cambridge, Mass.: National Bureau of Economic Research. September.
Cain, G., and D. Wissoker
    1990   A reanalysis of marital stability in the Seattle-Denver income-maintenance experiment. *American Journal of Sociology* 95:1235-1269.
Clarke, G., and R. Strauss
    1995   Children as Income Producing Assets: The Case of Teen Illegitimacy and Government Transfers. Mimeographed, Pittsburgh, Pa.: Carnegie-Mellon University. November.
Cutright, P.
    1970   AFDC, family allowances and illegitimacy. *Family Planning Perspectives* 2(4).
Danziger, S., G. Jakubson, S. Schwartz, and E. Smolensky
    1982   Work and welfare as determinants of female poverty and household headship. *Quarterly Journal of Economics* 97(August):519-534.

Darity, W., and S.L. Myers, Jr.
  1993   Changes in black family structure: Implications for welfare dependency. *American Economic Review* 83:59-64.
Duncan, G.J., and S.D. Hoffman
  1990   Welfare, economic opportunities and out-of-wedlock births among black teenager girls. *Demography* 27(4):519-535.
Ellwood, D., and M.J. Bane
  1985   The impact of AFDC on family structure and living arrangements. In R. Ehrenberg, ed., *Research in Labor Economics* Vol.7, Greenwich, Conn.: JAI Press.
Fossett M.A., and K.J. Kiecolt
  1993   Mate availability and family structure among African Americans in U.S. metropolitan areas. *Journal of Marriage and the Family* 55(May):288-302.
Freshnock, L. and P. Cutright
  1979   Models of illegitimacy: U.S. 1969. *Demography* 16(1):37-47.
Gueron, J., and E. Pauly
  1991   *From Welfare to Work.* New York: Russell Sage Foundation.
Hannan, M., and N. Tuma
  1990   A reassessment of the effect of income maintenance on marital dissolution in the Seattle-Denver experiment. *American Journal of Sociology* 95:1270-1298.
Hill, M.A., and J. O'Neill
  1993   Underclass behaviors in the United States: Measurement and analysis of determinants. New York: Center for the Study of Business and Government, Baruch College, The City University of New York. August.
Hoffman, S.D., and G.J. Duncan
  1988   A comparison of choice-based multinomial and nested logit models: The family structure and welfare use decisions of divorced or separated women. *Journal of Human Resources* 23(4):550-562.
Hoffman, S.D. and G.J. Duncan
  1995   The effect of incomes, wages and AFDC benefits on marital disruption. *Journal of Human Resources* 30(1):19-41.
Hoynes, H.W.
  1995   Does welfare play any role in female headship decisions? Berkeley, Calif.: University of California, Berkeley; and Cambridge, Mass.: National Bureau of Economic Research, April.
  1996   Does welfare play any role in female headship decisions? Berkeley, Calif: University of California, Berkeley; and Cambridge, Mass: National Bureau of Economic Research, June.
Hudson, J., and R. Moffitt
  1997   Welfare, nonmarital childbearing, and single motherhood: Literature results and summaries. Baltimore, Md.: Johns Hopkins University.
Hutchens, R.
  1979   Welfare, remarriage, and marital search. *American Economic Review* 69(3):369-379.
Hutchens, R., G. Jakubson, and S. Schwartz
  1989   AFDC and the formation of subfamilies. *Journal of Human Resources* 24(Fall):599-628.
Jackson, C., and J. Klerman
  1995   Welfare and American fertility. Mimeographed. Santa Monica, Calif.: Rand Corporation. January.
Janowitz, Barbara S.
  1976   The impact of AFDC on illegitimate birth rates. *Journal of Marriage and the Family* (August):485-494.
Klerman, J.
  1996   Power considerations in estimating policy effects on fertility. Mimeographed. Santa Monica, Calif: Rand Corporation.

Lichter, D.T., F.B. LeClere, and D.K. McLaughlin
  1991   Local marriage markets and the marital behavior of black and white women. *American Journal of Sociology* 96(4):843-867.
Lichter, D.T., D. McLaughlin, G. Kephart, and D.J. Landry
  1992   Race and the retreat from marriage: A shortage of marriageable men? *American Sociological Review* 57(December):781-799.
Lichter, D.T., D. McLaughlin, and D. Ribar
  1996   Welfare and the rise of female headed families. Mimeographed. University Park, Pa.: Pennsylvania State University. May.
Lundberg, S., and R. Plotnick
  1990   Effects of state welfare, abortion and family planning on premarital childbearing among white adolescents. *Family Planning Perspectives* 22(6):246-251,275.
  1995   Adolescent premarital childbearing: Do economic incentives matter? *Journal of Labor Economics* 13(2):177-200.
Matthews, S., D. Ribar, and M. Wilhelm
  1995   The effects of economic conditions and access to reproductive health services on state abortion and birth rates. University Park, Pa.: Pennsylvania State University. March.
Moffitt, R.
  1990   The effect of the U.S. welfare system on marital status. *Journal of Public Economics* 41:101-124.
  1992   Incentive effects of the U.S. welfare system: A review. *Journal of Economic Literature* 30(March):1-61.
  1994   Welfare effects on female headship with area effects. *Journal of Human Resources* 29(Spring):621-636.
Moffitt, R., R. Reveille, and A. Winkler
  1998   Beyond single mothers: Cohabitation and marriage in the AFDC program. *Demography* 35(3).
Moore, K.A., and S.B. Caldwell
  1977   The effect of government policies on out-of-wedlock sex and pregnancy. *Family Planning Perspectives* 9(4):164-169.
Moore, K.A., D.R. Morrison, and D.A. Glei
  1995   Welfare and adolescent sex: The effects of family history, benefit levels and community context. Washington, D.C.: Child Trends, Inc., March.
Murray, C.
  1993   Welfare and the family: The U.S. experience. *Journal of Labor Economics* 11(No. 1, Part. 2):S224-S262.
Ozawa, Martha
  1989   Welfare policies and illegitimate birth rates among adolescents: Analysis of state by state data. *Social Work Research and Abstracts* (March):5 11.
Plotnick, Robert D.
  1990   Welfare and out-of-wedlock childbearing: Evidence from the 1980s. *Journal of Marriage and the Family* 52(August):735-746.
Rank, Mark R.
  1989   Fertility among women on welfare: Incidence and determinants. *American Sociological Review* 54(April):296-304.
Robins, P., and P. Fronstin
  1996   Welfare benefits and birth decisions of never-married women. *Population Research and Policy Review* 15(February):21-43.
Rosenzweig, M.R.
  1995   Welfare, marital prospects and nonmarital childbearing. Mimeographed. University Park, Pa.: Pennsylvania State University. December.

Rosenzweig, M.R., and K.I. Wolpin
   1994   Inequality among young adult siblings, public assistance programs, and intergenerational
           living arrangements. *Journal of Human Resources* 29(Fall):1101-1125.
Schultz, T.P.
   1994   Marital status and fertility in the United States. *Journal of Human Resources*
           29(Spring):637-669.
   1995   Eroding the economic foundations of marriage and fertility in the United States. New
           Haven, Conn.: Yale University, March 17.
Southwick, L., Jr.
   1978   The effect of welfare programs on family stability. *Review of Social Economy*
           36(April):19-39.
U.S. Department of Health and Human Services
   1995   Report to Congress on out-of-wedlock childbearing. Washington, D.C.: U.S. Government
           Printing Office.
U.S. House of Representatives
   1994   Background material and data on programs within the jurisdiction of the Committee on
           Ways and Means. Washington, D.C.: U.S. Government Printing Office.
Winegarden, C.R.
   1988   AFDC and illegitimacy rates: A vector-autoregressive model. *Applied Econometrics.*
           20(December):1589-1601.
Winkler, A.E.
   1995   Does AFDC-UP encourage two parent families? *Journal of Policy Analysis and Manage-*
           ment 14(1):4-24.
Yelowitz, A.S.
   1993   Will extending Medicaid to two parent families encourage marriage? Cambridge, Mass.:
           Massachusetts Institute of Technology. November.

APPENDIX TABLE 4A Summary of Studies of the Effect of Welfare on the Family

Author, Date	Type of Study	Dataset	Main Sample	Dependent Variable	Welfare Result
Acs, 1993	Cross-state comparison of levels	National Longitudinal Survey of Youth 1979-1988	Women 14-23	Probability that woman has first birth	Not significant
			Unmarried women 14-23	Probability that unmarried woman has first birth	Not significant
			Women 14-23	Probability that woman has a birth and goes on AFDC	Positive
			Women 14-23 who have had a first birth	Probability that woman has second birth	Not significant
Acs, 1996	Cross-state comparison of levels	National Longitudinal Survey of Youth 1979-1988	Women 23-25 in 1988 who have had a child	Probability that woman has second birth	Not significant for blacks or for whites
			Women 23-25 in 1988 who have had a child and were on AFDC	Probability that woman has second birth	Not significant for blacks or for whites

TABLE 4A Continued

Author, Date	Type of Study	Dataset	Main Sample	Dependent Variable	Welfare Result
			Women 23-25 in 1988 who have had a child and were on AFDC and who grew up in a low-income single-parent home	Probability that woman has second birth	Not significant for blacks or for whites
Allen, 1993	Cross-province comparison of levels	Census of Canada 1986 micro data	Women less than 45 on or at poverty line	Probability that woman is a single parent	Positive
				Probability that woman has an out-of-wedlock birth	Positive
				Probability that woman is divorced	Positive
An et al., 1993	Cross-state comparison of levels	Panel Study on Income Dynamics 1968-1987	Women 19-25 in 1987	Probability of having an out-of-wedlock birth between ages 13 and 18	Not significant
Blank et al., 1994	Cross-state comparison of changes	Alan Guttmacher Institute data 1974-1988	All U.S. states	Abortion rate by state of occurrence	AFDC: Mixed but usually insignificant Medicaid: In-state restrictions—negative; border-state restrictions—positive

Study	Method	Data	Population	Dependent variable	Results
Blank et al., 1994	Cross-state comparison of changes	Alan Guttmacher Institute data 1974-1983	All U.S. states	Number of abortion providers in state	*AFDC:* Not significant *Medicaid:* In-state restrictions—not significant; border-state restrictions—negative
				Abortion rates for state residents (occurring inside or outside the state)	Not significant for both AFDC and Medicaid restriction variables
				Difference between abortion rates by state of occurrence and by state of residence	*AFDC:* Not significant *Medicaid:* In-state and border-state restrictions are significant with a larger gap associated with border-state Medicaid restrictions
Clarke and Strauss, 1995	Cross-state comparison of levels	Vital statistics 1980-1990	Unmarried women 15-19 (blacks: 36 states only)	Abortion rates by age and race. For groups: teens and nonteens, whites and nonwhites	
				Illegitimacy rate	*Whites and Blacks:* No effect in ordinary least squares but positive effect in two-stage least squares

TABLE 4A Continued

Author, Date	Type of Study	Dataset	Main Sample	Dependent Variable	Welfare Result
	Cross-state comparison of changes				*AFDC Guarantee:* White—positive in ordinary least squares and two-stage least squares; black—negative in ordinary least squares and positive in two-stage least squares. *Benefit differential:* Not significant for black or white women in any specification
Cutright, 1970	Time trend	Vital statistics 1940-1965	Annual aggregates 1940-1965	U.S. illegitimacy rates 1940-1965	Overall positive relationship holds but not for specific time periods, especially for blacks
	Cross-state comparison of levels		4 U.S. states	State illegitimacy ratio 1950-1964	States with higher benefit levels or recipiency rates do not have higher illegitimacy ratios
	Time trend		Several countries	International illegitimacy rates	Negative
Danziger et al., 1982	Cross-state comparison of levels	CPS 1975	Women 25-54 married or female heads	Female headship	Positive for white and nonwhite women
Darity and Myers, 1993	Time trend	Not reported 1955-1980	Annual aggregates	Ratio of black female-headed households to black non-female-headed households	Not significant

Study	Type of comparison	Data source	Sample	Outcome measure	Results
Duncan and Hoffman, 1990	Cross-state comparison of levels	Panel Study on Income Dynamics 1968-1985	Black women in 1985 who turned 19 between 1973 and 1985	Probability of an out-of-wedlock birth followed by AFDC receipt	Positive (weak) on AFDC-related births Not significant for non-AFDC-related births
Ellwood and Bane, 1985	Within-state comparison of women with different probabilities of being on AFDC	Survey of Income and Education 1976	All women 16-44	Probability that woman is an independent female head	Positive for whites and nonwhites ages 16-34 with higher significance levels for whites and higher magnitudes for nonwhites
				Probability that woman is a single mother	Not significant for nonwhites; positive for whites but age range is sensitive to specification
			Single mothers 16-44	Probability that single mother lives independently	Positive for whites and nonwhites ages 16-24
			Married mothers 16-44	Probability that woman is newly divorced	Not significant for whites or nonwhites
			Ever-married mothers 16-44	Probability that woman is currently divorced	Positive for whites and nonwhites ages 16-24 and for whites 25-30; not significant for older nonwhite women
			Unmarried women without children or with child < 1	Probability that woman has a nonmarital birth	Not significant for whites and nonwhites ages 16-24; positive for older white women ages 25-34

TABLE 4A Continued

Author, Date	Type of Study	Dataset	Main Sample	Dependent Variable	Welfare Result
			Never-married women 16-44	Probability that woman becomes a mother	Not significant for whites and nonwhites ages 16-24; positive for whites and nonwhites ages 25-34
	Within-state comparison of different eligibility types	Vital statistics, U.S. Census 1970	Selected states, women 14-44	Percent of ever-married mothers who are divorced or separated	Negative for whites and not significant for nonwhites
				Birth rate for unmarried women	Not significant for whites and nonwhites
				Ratio of percentage of ever-married mothers above age 14 who are divorced or separated to percentage of ever-married childless women above 14 who are divorced or separated	Not significant for whites and nonwhites
				Ratio of birth rate of unmarried women to birth rate of married women	Not significant for whites and nonwhites
	Cross-state comparison of changes	U.S. Census 1960, 1970	All U.S. states	Percent of women above 14 who are independent female heads	Not significant for whites or blacks

			Dependent variable	Finding
			Number of children living with a female head as a fraction of total children not living with both parents	Positive for 1960 and 1970 benefit levels of white and nonwhite women
			Percent of ever-married women above 14 who are divorced	Positive for whites in 1970; not significant for blacks in 1960 and 1970 or for whites in 1960
			Unmarried birth rate	Not significant for whites or blacks
Fossett and Kiecolt, 1993	Cross-city comparison of levels	U.S. Census 1980, vital statistics 1979-1981	270 Standard Metropolitan Statistical Areas	
			Percent of black men in metropolitan area who are married	Negative
			Percent of black women in metropolitan area who are married	Negative
			Percent of black women with children under 6 in metropolitan area	Negative
			Percent of black women with children under 18 in metropolitan area	Negative
			Percent of families with children under 6 in metropolitan area who are married	Negative

TABLE 4A Continued

Author, Date	Type of Study	Dataset	Main Sample	Dependent Variable	Welfare Result
				Percent of families with children under 18 in metropolitan area who are married	Negative
				Percent of children living in husband-wife families in metropolitan area	Negative
				Percent of births to black women in metropolitan area who are married	Negative for all four groups with a higher magnitude for black women 20-29 than for black teens
Freshnock and Cutright, 1979	Cross-county comparison of levels	Vital statistics 1970	Approximately 1,000 counties with usable data	Illegitimate birth rate for unmarried women	Not significant for teens; positive for never married whites ages 20-44; negative for blacks ages 20-44, with a larger magnitude in absolute value than that of whites
Hill and O'Neill, 1993	Cross-state comparison of levels	National Longitudinal Survey of Youth 1979-1987	Women 23-30 in 1987	Probability that woman has had a child but has never been married since 1979	Positive for white women; not significant for black women
				Probability that woman had an out-of-wedlock birth in the last year	Positive for white women; not significant for black women

89

Study	Method	Data	Sample	Dependent variable	Result
Hoffman and Duncan, 1988	Cross-state comparison of levels	Panel Study on Income Dynamics 1969-1982	Women who were divorced or separated 1969-1982 and were < 45 at time of event	Probability of remarriage	Not significant for blacks or whites
Hoffman and Duncan, 1995	Cross-state comparison of levels	Panel Study on Income Dynamics 1967-1985	Women with children and with a first marriage during 1967-1993	Probability of divorce	Positive for AFDC 5-year moving average; not significant for AFDC guarantee
Hoynes, 1995, 1996	Cross-state comparison of levels	Panel Study on Income Dynamics 1969-1989	Women 16-50 either married or household head in selected states	Probability that woman is a female head	Positive for blacks and whites, with larger magnitude for blacks
	Cross-state comparison of changes			Probability that woman is a female head	Zero and not significant for whites with fixed state and/or individual effects; positive for blacks with state fixed effects but zero and not significant with individual fixed effects
Hutchens, 1979	Cross-state comparison of levels	Panel Study on Income Dynamics 1968-1972	Female heads in 1970 in 20 states	Probability of 1970 female head remarrying or cohabiting by 1972	Negative
Hutchens et al., 1989	Cross-state comparison of levels	CPS 1984	Women less than 36, with at least one child, no husband present	Probability of being a household head	Positive for difference between household head and subfamily head benefit levels; not significant for benefit guarantee level alone

TABLE 4A Continued

Author, Date	Type of Study	Dataset	Main Sample	Dependent Variable	Welfare Result
				Probability that woman is on or off welfare and is household head or subfamily head	Difference between household head and subfamily head benefits significant positive only for household head versus subfamily head on welfare; all other effects insignificant
Jackson and Klerman, 1995	Cross-state comparison of levels	National Center for Health Statistics birth certificate tapes 1975-1990	All women 15-44	Birth rate for state in year (by age and race)	For both whites and blacks, negative for age < 21 and positive for age > 21
	Cross-state comparison of changes				Positive for whites through age 30 with largest magnitudes in early twenties; negative for blacks after age 33
				Birth rate for state in year for first births (by age and race)	Positive for whites 15-19 and for blacks 16-26
				Birth rate for state in year for higher-order births (by age and race)	Positive for whites above 17 and for blacks 18-21
			Selected states	Marital birth rate (marital births per total women)	Positive for blacks and whites
				Nonmarital birth rate (nonmarital births per total women)	Positive for blacks and whites

Author, year	Type of comparison	Data source	Sample	Dependent variable	Result
Janowitz, 1976	Cross-Standard Metropolitan Statistical Area comparison of levels	U.S. Census 1959, 1970, 1973; Department of Health, Education and Welfare data (1968, 1970)	58 Standard Metropolitan Statistical Areas > 250,000 with illegitimate data by race	Illegitimate birth rate among unmarried women	Positive for nonwhites 15-29; not significant for whites
Lichter et al., 1991	Cross-labor market area comparison of levels	U.S. Census 1980	328 labor market areas	Proportion of women currently married, ever married, recently married (5 years)	Negative for all three measures for blacks and whites
Lichter et al., 1992	Cross-labor market area comparison of levels	National Longitudinal Survey of Youth 1979-1986	Never-married women 18-28 from 1979 to 1986	Probability that woman will have a transition into marriage	Not significant
Lichter et al., 1996	Cross-county and state comparison of changes	U.S. Census 1980, 1990	All counties with sufficient sample size	Fraction of families with children under 18 headed by never-married or divorced women	Positive for whites and blacks; no effect for Latinos
Lundberg and Plotnick, 1990	Cross-state comparison of levels	National Longitudinal Survey of Youth 1979-1986	Unmarried white women 21-23 in 1986	Probability that teen will not marry conditional on having a birth	Positive
				Probability that teen carries pregnancy to term conditional on pregnancy	Negative

TABLE 4A Continued

Author, Date	Type of Study	Dataset	Main Sample	Dependent Variable	Welfare Result
Lundberg and Plotnick, 1995	Cross-state comparison of levels	National Longitudinal Survey of Youth 1979-1986	Unmarried women 21-23 in 1986	Probability that teen will become pregnant	Negative
				Probability teen will not marry conditional on having a birth	Positive for whites; not significant for blacks
				Probability that teen carries pregnancy to term conditional on having a pregnancy	Positive for whites; not significant for blacks
				Probability that teen becomes pregnant	Positive but small for whites; not significant for blacks
Matthews et al., 1995	Cross-state comparison of levels	U.S. state data 1978-1987	All U.S. states	Birth rate	Negative
				Abortion rate	Positive
	Cross-state comparison of changes			Birth rate	Positive
				Abortion rate	Insignificant
Moffitt, 1990	Cross-state comparison of levels	CPS 1969, 1977, 1985	Men and women 16-55	Probability of being married Probability of being female head	Insignificant for whites; negative for black men and mixed for black women

Study	Method	Data	Population	Outcome	Result
Moffitt, 1994	Cross-state comparison of levels	CPS 1968-1989	Women 20-44 with less than 12 years of education	Probability woman is a subfamily or household head	Effects for whites are positive and significant; effects for blacks are insignificant
	Cross-state comparison of changes				No effect for whites; negative effects for blacks
Moore and Caldwell, 1977	Cross-state comparison of levels	Kanter and Zelnik survey, 1971	Women 15-19	Probability teen is sexually active	Positive for whites ages 16-18 with AFDC benefit level but insignificant at other ages and for blacks
	Cross-state comparison of levels	Vital statistics 1974	Selected states	Probability teen becomes pregnant	Negative for blacks 12-15 but not significant at other ages or for whites
				Probability pregnant teen will obtain abortion	Negative
				Probability pregnant teen will marry before the birth	Not significant
				Probability pregnant teen will have out-of-wedlock birth	Not significant
				Out-of-wedlock birth rate of women ages 15-44	Insignificant for black or white women
Moore et al., 1995	Cross-state comparison of levels	National Survey of Children 1976, 1981, 1987	Individuals 11-17	Probability of first premarital sex	Insignificant for girls and boys

TABLE 4A Continued

Author, Date	Type of Study	Dataset	Main Sample	Dependent Variable	Welfare Result
Murray, 1993	Time trend	Vital statistics 1960-1988	Annual aggregates	Illegitimacy ratio	No simple correlation
	Cross-state comparison of levels		U.S. states	Illegitimacy ratio	Positive for white women starting in the mid-1960s; no relationship for black women
Ozawa, 1989	Cross-state comparison of levels	Vital statistics 1984	All U.S. states	Illegitimacy ratio for women under 19	Positive for white teens; not significant for black teens
Plotnick, 1990	Cross-state comparison of levels	National Longitudinal Survey of Youth 1979-1984	Women 19-20 in 1984	Probability teen has a nonmarital birth by age 19	Not significant for Hispanic or black women; sometimes positive and sometimes insignificant for white women
Rank, 1989	Within-state comparison of participants and nonparticipants	Wisconsin welfare records 1980-1983	2 percent sample of all cases on rolls in September 1980	Fertility rate	Negative effect
Robins and Fronstin, 1996	Cross-state or region comparison of changes	CPS 1980-1988	Never-married women 18-30 with zero or one child	Probability of giving birth to first child	Insignificant for whites and positive for blacks

The first row's welfare result reads: "Probability of contraceptive use conditional on premarital sex" under Dependent Variable, with "Not significant for girls or boys" under Welfare Result.

Study	Method	Data	Sample	Outcome	Results
	Cross-state comparison of changes in benefit increments	CPS 1980-1988	Never-married women 18-30 with zero or one child and with no high school diploma	Probability of giving birth to first child	Insignificant
			Never-married women 18-30 with at least one child	Probability that woman will give birth to another child	Negative for whites and positive for blacks for second birth only; higher-order births insignificant for both races
			Never-married women 18-30 with at least one child and with no high school diploma	Probability that woman will give birth to another child	Positive for second birth; not significant for higher-order births
Rosenzweig, 1995	Cross-state comparison of changes	National Longitudinal Survey of Youth 1979-1990	Women aged 22 from 1980 to 1987	Probability that woman has had premarital birth versus only marital births or no births	*Premarital birth versus no birth:* Positive with a higher magnitude for low-income women *Low income subsample:* Whites stronger than blacks *Marital births versus no births:* Not significant for blacks or whites in full- or low-income samples

TABLE 4A Continued

Author, Date	Type of Study	Dataset	Main Sample	Dependent Variable	Welfare Result
Rosenzweig and Wolpin, 1994	Cross-state comparison of levels	National Longitudinal Survey of Youth 1979-1987	Female siblings 22-29 in 1987	Probability that of coresiding with parents and not being on welfare vs. not coresiding with parents and not being on welfare	AFDC benefit has no effect but Food Stamp benefit has negative effect
Schultz, 1994	Cross-state comparison of levels	U.S. Census 1980	Women 15-65	Probability that woman is married	Negative at ages 15-24 for blacks and whites, not at other ages
				Number of children ever born	Positive for black women 25-34; negative for white women 15-24; insignificant at other ages
Schultz, 1995	Cross-state comparison of levels	U.S. Census 1990	Women 15-64	Probability that woman is married	Negative for blacks and whites
				Number of children ever born	Negative for blacks and whites
Southwick, 1978	Cross-state comparison of levels	1973 AFDC characteristics study	31 U.S. states	Percent of AFDC families with absent fathers	Positive
				Proportion of AFDC families where the father is not married to the mother	Positive for difference and ratio between income available to a two-parent family versus single-parent family

Study	Method	Dataset	Sample	Dependent variable	Result
Winegarden, 1988	Time trend	Aggregate U.S. data 1947–1983	Annual aggregates	Proportion of AFDC families with at least one illegitimate child	Negative
				Percent of AFDC families with divorce, legal separation, or separation without a court decree	Positive for divorce and legal separation; not significant for separation without a court decree
				Illegitimacy ratio	Positive for blacks but not for whites
Winkler, 1995	Cross-state comparison of levels	National Survey of Families and Households 1987	Mothers 19-35	Probability that mother lives in a AFDC-UP-defined two-parent family	Not significant
				Probability that mother is married	Negative for some specifications
Yelowitz, 1993	Cross-state comparison of changes	CPS 1989-1992	Women 18-55 with at least one child	Probability that mother is married	Having children in a family that is eligible for Medicaid has a positive effect

NOTES: All welfare results are reported by race if separate estimates by race were obtained. If no race is mentioned, the results apply to all women. "Dataset" refers only to the data source for the dependent variable. SOURCE: Hudson and Moffitt (1997).

5

Welfare Reform and Abortion

Jacob Alex Klerman

The impetus for the current round of welfare reform derives from two complementary arguments. First, there is simply a concern that too many resources are being transferred from taxpayers to a dependent class, welfare recipients.[1] Second, there is a concern that the welfare system itself induces undesirable behavior; in particular, the claim is that it induces women to have children when they cannot afford them and out of wedlock.[2]

Implicit in this second argument is that cutting welfare payments or radically restructuring the welfare system—in the words of President Clinton, "ending welfare as we know it"—will cut the number of children born to poor unmarried women. As we discuss in detail below, one way that this decline in the number of children could occur would be that women would not change their sexual behavior or their contraceptive behavior, but once they found themselves pregnant—and realizing that welfare would not support them and their child as it had previously—they would choose to abort the pregnancy. In net, fewer children would be born and fewer children would be on the welfare rolls.

This possibility that welfare reform might induce more women to have abortions has led many in the pro-life community to oppose some welfare reform

---

[1]See Senator Phil Gramm's announcement speech in his unsuccessful bid for the Republican presidential nomination, College Station Texas, February 24, 1995: "I want to ask the able-bodied men and women riding in the wagon on welfare to get out of the wagon and help the rest of us pull. We've got to stop giving people more and more money to have more and more children on welfare."

[2]On the evidence for this claim, see Chapter 4; see also Moffitt (1992); and Jackson and Klerman (1996).

proposals. For example, the Conference of Catholic Bishops issued a statement reading in part:

> Denying needed benefits for children born to mothers on welfare can hurt the children and pressure their mothers toward abortion and sterilization (Bishop John Richard, 1995:564).

The National Right to Life Committee argued the welfare reform-abortion link in more detail. The lead headline in its newsletter, *National Right to Life News,* for February 22, 1995 read "Welfare 'Reforms' Pose Threat to Unborn Babies." The article notes:

> National Right to Life has a long history of supporting alternatives to abortion since its formation in 1973. Consistent with this policy, National Right to Life is opposed to denying assistance to a newborn child who would otherwise qualify for assistance, based on the age or marital status of the mother or the fact that the mother is already receiving assistance for another child. NRLC is convinced that these proposals will result in the death of many additional children by abortion.

> NRLC President Wanda Franz, Ph.D., said *"What is at stake is a significant portion of the very limited aid that is available for classes of children who are among the most vulnerable to abortion, children of unmarried teens and of the poor. If we were to stand silently by and not have to* [sic, presumably it should be "the"] *courage to speak out against these proposals, then we could never look anyone in the eye again and say we support alternatives to abortion"* [emphasis in the original].

Proponents of the legislation seem to take two positions. Some grant that abortions will increase (if perhaps only in the short term) but argue that some increase in abortion is a worthwhile trade-off for a net decrease in children born onto welfare. For example, in congressional testimony, Charles Murray explained the effects of ending Aid to Families with Dependent Children (AFDC) as follows:

> (T)he need to find support forces a self-selection process. . . . It will lead others, watching what happens to their sisters, to take steps not to get pregnant. This is also good. Many others will get abortions. Whether this is good depends on what one thinks of abortion (testimony before the Subcommittee on Human Resources, House Committee on Ways and Means, July 29, 1994).

Or Marvin Olasky writing in the *Wall Street Journal* (Olasky, 1995).

> Most pro-lifers understand that the current welfare system is fundamentally wrong-headed. But they are frozen because we cannot say for sure that welfare reform might not lead to a very sad, short-term abortion increase. My own tendency in such situations is to visit the cliché hall of fame: Two wrongs don't make a right.

> Such an answer will not satisfy a single-issue opponent of abortion (and there is no better issue to be single-issue about) who might argue that welfare is

the lesser of two evils and thus justifiable. To such a person we need to explain that passing out welfare dollars to avoid abortion is like succumbing to extortion, and extortionists will want more and more.

Other proponents argue that the effect of the legislation will be to cut abortions because of changes in sexual behavior (Bauer and Gramm, 1995):

> To reduce abortions, we must reduce the out-of-wedlock pregnancy that creates a perceived "need" for abortion . . . . If it is true that preserving the current benefits package will save lives, presumably we could save even more lives by increasing the entitlements tenfold—or by expanding welfare without limit to create a pro-life socialism.
>
> If we are to reverse the trend in both illegitimacy and abortion, we must first acknowledge that illegitimacy and abortion are twin evils spawned by government policies that eliminate personal responsibility in favor of government responsibility.

The twin concerns that the welfare system was encouraging nonmarital fertility and that changes to the system would increase the number of abortions strongly shaped the Personal Responsibility and Work Opportunity Reconciliation Act of 1996 (hereafter, PRWORA). With respect to the first concern, illegitimacy, the official summary of the legislation (U.S. Congress, 1996: 6-8) explicitly names rising rates of "illegitimacy" and its negative consequences as a motivation for the reforms. To "reduce nonmarital births in general and teen births in particular," the legislation requires teen mothers to live at home and attend school, penalizes those who do not help to establish paternity, provides funding for abstinence education, requires reporting on state performance in reducing nonmarital birth ratios, and provides $1.4 billion in "performance bonuses" for states that reduce nonmarital births and illegitimacy ratios.

With respect to the second concern—abortion—several other steps were taken. First, $0.4 billion of the performance bonus funds were specifically allocated "for the five States that are the most successful in reducing the number of out-of-wedlock births *while decreasing abortion ratios*" [emphasis added] (U.S. Congress, 1996:18). In addition, the right-to-life community's strong lobbying forced the removal of a mandatory family cap from the final legislation.

This chapter attempts to draw together what we know today about the likely effects of welfare reform on abortion and to outline promising strategies for evaluating the actual effects of the limited reforms to date and the wider reforms that are likely to follow. The chapter opens with two sections that briefly review the legal status and demographic importance of abortion today.

The third section presents a simple rational choice model of a woman's choice of contraception, abortion, or fertility. The model focuses on the effect of welfare policy. The basic model implies that welfare reform will increase abortions. Several extensions to the model that might overturn the implication of the basic model are also considered. The section concludes with insights from the sociology and social psychology literature as to the likely magnitude of the effects.

The following section reviews possible data sources for analyses of effects on abortion. It begins with a review of the evidence that abortion is seriously underreported in survey data to the point where such data are nearly useless. It then discusses several more promising non-survey-based sources of data on abortion.

The fifth section provides a discussion of the methodological issues in evaluating the causal effects of welfare reform on the number of abortions. In the main, the issues raised here are likely to be common across most of the domains of possible demographic effects of welfare reform—concerns that simple cross-sectional or time-series results might reflect spurious correlation rather than the true causal effect of the policies and statistical approaches to this concern. These considerations suggest that even if household survey data were reliable, it seems unlikely that the survey data would have large enough samples to have power to detect effects of the size that seem plausible. There is some prospect of detecting effects using other data sources.

The next section combines the insights from our discussions of the theory, the data, and the methodological issues to try to draw some insights from the existing literature. The theoretical model suggests some analyses that might be insightful. The methods and data discussion suggests that many of the studies that might be insightful for the effects of welfare reform or abortions are unlikely to be empirically robust. Thus, this literature survey focuses on the papers that meet the data and method screens. Specifically, we explore the issues of whether welfare policy affects fertility and abortion and whether abortion policy affects contraceptive behavior, abortion, and fertility.

Using the perspectives gained from our discussion of data and methodological issues, the final section tries to put these pieces together to sketch potential research strategies to explore the actual effects of welfare reform on the level of abortions.

LEGAL STATUS OF ABORTION

We begin this section with a discussion of the legal status of abortion. Unless otherwise noted, this discussion is based on the Merz et al. (1996) summary of the regulation of abortion. Complete citations to the statutes and case law can be found in Merz et al. (1995).

Abortion in the United States has been legal, essentially without restriction, since the Supreme Court's *Roe v. Wade* decision in 1973. That decision capped a movement towards the liberalization of abortion laws at the state level that began in Colorado in 1966 and included 19 states by the time of *Roe v. Wade*.

Through the late-1980s, there were two major exceptions to the characterization of *Roe v. Wade* as guaranteeing abortion on demand: Medicaid funding and parental consent. Both exceptions figure prominently in the polemics of the right-to-life movement with respect to welfare reform.

Following *Roe v. Wade*, most state Medicaid programs nominally appear to have reimbursed abortion like any other medical procedure. As with other medical procedures, this reimbursement was funded through a combination of state allocations and federal matching funds. In practice, the rates of funding of abortions varied widely across states (Alan Guttmacher Institute, 1979; Klerman, 1996). Then in the late-1970s, even this de jure reimbursement policy changed. First in federal legislation known as the Hyde Amendment (first passed in 1976), the federal government stopped providing matching funds for state Medicaid expenditures for abortions. Then, after considerable controversy in the lower courts, a series of federal court decisions (*Beal v. Doe*, *Maher v. Roe*, and *Poelker v. Doe*, all in 1977, and *Harris v. McRae* in 1980) ruled that the states themselves did not have to fund abortions.

Given the resulting sharply higher cost to the states of funding abortions without federal matching funds, the opportunity to lower the cost of their Medicaid programs, and ideological/moral objection to abortion, most states promptly changed their policy from funding abortions under Medicaid to not funding abortions. Several states, however, have continued to fund abortions some by explicit legislation and some pursuant to the state supreme court's interpretation of either the federal or the state constitution. As of the mid-1990s, the following states were funding abortions under Medicaid: Alaska, District of Columbia, Hawaii, Maryland, New Mexico, New York, North Carolina, Washington, and West Virginia by statute or administrative action; and California, Connecticut, Illinois, Massachusetts, New Jersey, Oregon, Pennsylvania, and Vermont by order of their state supreme courts.

This state funding of abortions under Medicaid is a component of one of the pro-life community's antiwelfare reform arguments, which notes that "it is implausible that a change in welfare law will decrease teen sexuality while abortion on demand, often paid for by public funds, remains readily available for unintended pregnancies" (O'Steen, 1995).

The other major restriction on abortion allowed by the Supreme Court is a requirement for parental notification/consent. In a series of decisions in the early-1980s, the Supreme Court ruled that, as long as an appropriate bypass procedure to establish maturity is provided, states may require that parents be notified or even give their consent before an immature minor has an abortion. As of the mid-1990s, the following states had consent statutes in force: Alabama, Indiana, Kentucky, Louisiana, Maine, Massachusetts, Michigan, Mississippi, Missouri, North Dakota, Rhode Island, South Carolina, Wisconsin, and Wyoming. In addition, the following states had notification statutes in force: Arkansas, Georgia, Kansas, Minnesota, Nebraska, Ohio, Utah, and West Virginia.

The pro-life lobby claims that such parental notification laws are effective in lowering the number of births. Citing a drop in both abortions and teen births in

Minnesota following the passage of a parental consent law, the pro-life lobby proposes such laws as an alternative to welfare reform: "Apparently the knowledge that should pregnancy occur, the girl's parents will become aware of it either through continuation of pregnancy or notification of an abortion does have an effect on teen sexuality" (O'Steen, 1995).

This legal landscape of abortion limited only by parental consent/notification and lack of Medicaid funding is now shifting. The Supreme Court, which had struck down essentially all other limitations, changed its position with the *Casey* decision of 1990. In that decision, it upheld additional state efforts to circumscribe the right to abortion. Most noteworthy are "informed consent" requirements. These laws require that women seeking abortion receive prescribed information specifically intended to deter the woman from having an abortion.

DEMOGRAPHIC ROLE OF ABORTION

Abortion in the United States is far from demographically insignificant. In 1992, the most recent year for which final data are available, there were about 1.5 million abortions performed (Henshaw and Van Vort, 1994). This number should be compared against approximately 4 million births. Therefore, more than a quarter of all pregnancies (27.5 percent) are aborted (see Table 5-1).[3] Put differently, about 2.6 percent of women of childbearing age (15-44) have an abortion each year.

The demographic importance of abortion varies widely across subgroups (see Table 5-1). Abortion rates (abortions per woman) are highest among women in their early 20s, but the abortion ratios (abortions per pregnancy[4]) are high for both young and older women (unless otherwise noted all of the figures in this section are from Ventura et al., 1995, and refer to 1991). More than a third of pregnancies to women over 40 and under 20 are aborted. For women under 15, the figure is half. Both the abortion rate and the abortion ratio are nearly twice as high for nonwhites as for whites.

These rates represent a decline of about 10 percent from their highs in the early 1980s (all the figures in this paragraph are from Henshaw and Van Vort, 1994). The overall abortion rate (abortions per 1,000 women age

---

[3]Several other definitions of the abortion ratio are used in the literature. In some publications of the Centers for Disease Control and Prevention, the abortion ratio is defined as abortions divided by births (i.e., abortions are not included in the denominator; see for example Koonin et al., 1995). In some publications of the National Center for Health Statistics, the denominator includes abortions and an estimate of the number of pregnancies ending in miscarriages (see, for example Ventura et al., 1995).

[4]In this abortion ratio, pregnancies are defined as induced abortions plus births. Miscarriages and spontaneous abortions are excluded from the denominator. Some sources use an abortion ratio that includes an estimate of miscarriages (e.g., Ventura et al., 1995).

TABLE 5-1 Abortion Rates and Ratios by Subgroups

	Rate[a]			Ratio (%)[b]		
	1976	1980	1991	1976	1980	1991
Age						
<15	1.6	1.7	1.4	57	61	50
15-17	24.2	30.1	24.3	42	48	39
18-19	49.3	60.6	55.9	38	42	37
20-24	39.6	51.6	56.6	26	31	33
25-29	24.1	31.0	33.7	18	22	22
30-34	15.0	17.2	19.1	22	22	19
35-39	9.3	9.4	10.4	33	32	25
40+	3.7	3.5	3.0	45	46	34
Married		10.5	8.4		10	9
Unmarried		54.4	47.8		65	51
White	18.8	24.4	20.3	23	27	23
Married		8.6	6.6		8	7
Unmarried		47.4	39.1		72	53
Other Races	56.3	57.0	53.8	41	41	40
Married		24.7	20.6		21	19
Unmarried		82.7	75.8		52	49
Overall	29.4	26.3	25.9	30	27	27

[a]Rate: abortions per 1,000 women.
[b]Ratio: abortions/(abortions + live births); note that this is not the definition used in the source.
SOURCE: Computed from Ventura et al. (1995: Tables 1, 3, and 4).

15 to 44) increased nearly fivefold from first legalization in 1970 through 1980.[5] Even from the first full year following national legalization, 1974, there was an increase of about a half; from 19.3 to 29.3. Then the abortion rate declined to 25.9 in 1992. The abortion ratio also declined from its peak of 30.1 in 1981 to 27.5 in 1992. Preliminary data from the Centers for Disease Control (CDC) suggest a further 7 percent drop in the number of abortions from 1992 to 1994.

Furthermore, abortion ratios are much higher among unmarried women—those who might be eligible for AFDC if they did not abort. While in 1991 only 10 percent of pregnancies to married women ended in abortions, over half (51 percent) of pregnancies to unmarried women ended in abortion.[6] Especially for

---

[5]It seems likely that not all of this increase in abortions in the early 1970s was real. Some of it is probably the reporting of what previously would have been illegal and unreported abortions.

[6]Marital status is defined at the time of the pregnancy outcome—abortion or live birth. In the absence of abortion, some of these aborted pregnancies would probably result in postconception marriage and marital births. With the abortion option, such pregnancies instead result in nonmarital abortions. On the interaction between abortion availability and marriage, see Akerloff et al. (1996), Kane and Staiger (1996), and the theoretical discussion in the next section.

whites, the abortion ratio for nonmarried women appears to have fallen over the last decade (from 72 percent in 1980 to 53 percent in 1991). This decline in abortion among nonmarried women has been used to explain some of the increase over the 1980s in nonmarital birth rates (U.S. Department of Health and Human Services, 1995).[7]

A THEORETICAL PERSPECTIVE

In this section, we outline a simple rational choice model of fertility.[8] The model is developed to emphasize that because welfare reform will make having a child less attractive, some women will chose to avoid a birth through abortion. Given that goal, the model deliberately excludes many of the other features of the standard proximate determinants approach to fertility.[9] This basic model suggests that abortions will increase with welfare reform, but that the magnitude of the increase is crucially dependent on whether fertility effects are achieved through improved contraception or through abortion. The sociology literature on adolescent pregnancy is then surveyed for insights into this question. The section concludes with a consideration of alternative model features that overturn the strong result of the basic model.

Model Structure

Given the nature of the abortion decision as temporally subsequent to decisions about sexual activity and contraceptive practice, but temporally prior to receipt of welfare, it is useful to consider the abortion decision among the sequence of decisions leading from sexual activity to welfare receipt. Figure 5-1 represents the sequence of decisions graphically. Time unfolds in four periods. At period 1 (labeled "Sex"), the woman chooses a level of sexual activity and contraceptive practice. Those decisions imply a probability of pregnancy. At period 2 (labeled "Conception"), nature "moves" and the woman does or does not become pregnant according to the probability implicit in her decisions about sexual activity and contraceptive practice. At period 3 (labeled "Abortion"), those women who conceive choose whether or not to abort. At period 4 (labeled "Marriage/Welfare"), those women who conceive, but choose not to abort, then

---

[7]While striking, this stratification based on marital status is problematic. The model presented in the next section treats marital status as a choice. In particular, it was once true that many nonmarital conceptions resulted in marital births. The likelihood of such marriages might itself vary with welfare reform.

[8]Similar models can be found in Plotnick (1993), Lundberg and Plotnick (1995), and Jackson and Klerman (1996).

[9]Among the features ignored are the wantedness of pregnancies and the availability of contraception and abortion. For a more conventional proximate determinants approach, see U.S. Department of Health and Human Services (1995:39 ff. and Chapter 1, in this volume).

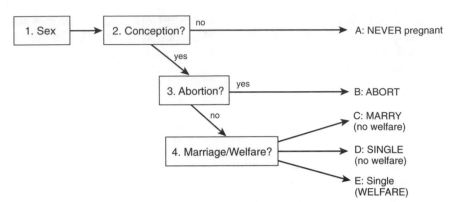

FIGURE 5-1: Model Schematic. NOTE: labels in capital letters are used in the text to refer to the final outcomes.

choose among marriage (and no welfare), no marriage and no welfare, or no marriage and welfare. To simplify the following theoretical discussion, we refer to these final outcomes as NEVER, ABORT, MARRY, SINGLE (no welfare), and WELFARE (single, welfare). In addition, we often refer to the pre-PRWORA welfare system as "before" and to the post-PRWORA welfare system as "after."

Implications for the Effects of Welfare Reform

In this simple model, what would be the effect of a welfare reform that made WELFARE less attractive for every woman? We begin the analysis by considering the standard rational choice assumptions—when a woman makes decisions about sexual activity and contraception, she knows what she would do (ABORT, MARRY, SINGLE, WELFARE) if she became pregnant. Furthermore, she makes her decisions about sexual activity and contraception based on what she would do if she conceived. We refer to these assumptions as the "basic model." We consider the effect of relaxing these assumptions below.

The insight of this sequential approach follows from dividing women into one of four groups based on the choice they would make if they found themselves pregnant before welfare reform: ABORT, MARRY, SINGLE, or WELFARE. Any woman who before welfare reform would have chosen MARRY, SINGLE, or ABORT, will still make that choice. Finding herself pregnant, she would not have chosen WELFARE before welfare reform. After welfare reform, WELFARE is less attractive; she certainly would not choose it. Furthermore, since the choice of such a woman if she became pregnant is unchanged, her contraceptive choices (at period 1, "Sex") are also unchanged.

In particular, the group of women who finding themselves pregnant would have chosen ABORT (before welfare reform) will not change their contraceptive practices. Their probability of conceiving is thus unchanged. If they conceive, they will still abort. It follows therefore that the number of abortions will not decrease with welfare reform. The only way that the number of abortions could decrease would be if some women who had chosen to abort before reform, will choose not to abort after reform. We have, however, argued that any woman who would have aborted before will change neither her contraceptive practices nor her abortion decision if she becomes pregnant.

Welfare reform will thus affect only women who finding themselves pregnant would—before welfare reform—have chosen WELFARE. Finding that choice less attractive after welfare reform, some of them will change their behavior in one of three ways. First, some of them may "contracept" more effectively (or become less sexually active). Second, conditional on finding themselves pregnant, some of them may choose ABORT. Third, more of those who find themselves pregnant and choose not to abort will not choose SINGLE or MARRY rather than WELFARE.

These changes are likely to lead to a larger number of abortions. Some women will choose to contracept more aggressively. Nevertheless, those methods will not be perfectly effective. Having tried to contracept and failed, some of them will abort. Furthermore, knowing that abortion is available, some women will continue to choose not to contracept.

Thus, the implication of the basic model is that welfare reform will not lower abortions. Any women who would have aborted before welfare reform will still abort. Some women who would have gone on welfare before welfare reform will now abort. This later result is true despite the fact that, given that welfare is less attractive after welfare reform, women who before would have gone on welfare if they became pregnant may now (after) contracept more aggressively, and such more aggressive contraception would lower the number of pregnancies.

On Contraceptive Behavior

The rational choice perspective of the previous section is strikingly at variance with the tenor of much of the writing about adolescent fertility (e.g., Ellwood, 1987; Musick, 1993; Luker, 1996). Ellwood (1987:16), for example, writes "There seems to be ample evidence to support almost any model of teenage behavior except a model of pure rational choice." There is much to be said against applying a model of rational choice to teenage fertility choices.

Adolescence is the time when humans develop a sense of the long-term consequences of their actions (Petersen, 1988; Keating, 1990). Adolescents often view themselves as invincible, leading to risk-taking behavior. Adolescents who currently have children are disproportionately drawn from the bottom quartile of the reading and math skill distribution (Pittman and Govan, 1986). Each of these considerations points to the possibility that adolescents might not consciously choose to have a child. Furthermore, even given such a choice, they might have trouble implementing it.

The right-to-life community sometimes takes this position. O'Steen (1995), discussing the effects of parental involvement laws, quotes a Dr. Franz:

> Adolescent thinking and reasoning tends to be concrete rather than abstract and focused on the immediate rather than the long-term consequence of an action. Hence, adolescents have difficulties with rational analysis that requires them to determine cause and effect, choose delayed over immediate gratification, and realistically assess the likely consequences of their choices. This makes them very vulnerable to the incessant stimulation of our sex-drenched culture, which stresses immediate gratification. It also makes it very unlikely that they will forego sexual activity just because sometime in the future there won't be any welfare payments.

That is, at least among adolescents, adjustments to PRWORA would be primarily through abortion. The right-to-life community appears to be of two minds about this question. Elsewhere in the same article, however, O'Steen argues that the Minnesota law had resulted in a drop in pregnancies, i.e., that changing abortion policy changed teenage sexual activity.

The basic model suggests that welfare reform will cause nonmarital fertility to decline. The strong form of this literature on adolescent decision making would imply that, in neither the prereform period nor the postreform period, have/will adolescents adjusted/adjust their fertility to the generosity of the welfare system. Chapter 4 reviews the empirical evidence on that question and its implications for the effects of welfare reform. Note, in particular, that a woman's decisions need not be "totally rational" in order for her to adjust her behavior with the changes in the generosity of the welfare system with welfare reform.

In particular, a woman need not adjust her sexual practices and contraceptive strategies. For there to be a fertility effect, it is sufficient that, finding herself pregnant, she choose to abort the pregnancy. The logic of the literature on adolescent decision making suggests that behavioral changes are more likely after conception. At that point, the issue is no longer one of risk taking. Failure to act will result in the birth of a child. Thus, this line of argument suggests both that the magnitude of the changes in fertility is likely to be small and that any changes in fertility will be accomplished mostly through abortion.

It is important to note, however, that there is an alternative theme in the literature. This theme emphasizes that for many poor adolescent girls, all options are unattractive. Motherhood may not be sufficiently worse than the other choices to make worthwhile the aggressive contraceptive strategies and high financial and emotional cost of abortion. For many girls, motherhood may actually look more attractive. Having a child gives her a clear role and certifies that she is an adult. The child is someone on whom the new mother can shower affection and from whom the new mother can expect unconditional love. The child is a chance to "start over," to make up for the errors of the previous generation (Luker, 1996; Musick, 1993:Chapter 5).

Furthermore, the child brings an entitlement to welfare. Welfare will provide a way for the new mother to establish a household of her own, away from her parents. It will provide her with an independent source of income. Finally, the new child will free the woman from the pressures and expectations of the world of school and work.

The preceding paragraph, of course, describes the prereform choice of motherhood and welfare. PRWORA was deliberately designed to make having a child out of wedlock less attractive. Under PRWORA, a minor mother must live with one of her parents. She will be expected to finish school. The payments will often be smaller. They will be of strictly limited duration. The payments are deliberately only "temporary assistance." Perhaps this worsening of the welfare option will be enough to cause women to change their preconception behaviors.

If for women currently on welfare, having a child was a choice (or at least, they did not choose to take sufficiently aggressive efforts to avoid the birth of a child), then there is some hope that women might achieve changes in fertility through changes in coital frequency and contraceptive strategies. Certainly, social disapproval of abortion would push some women in that direction.

Even if women who would have gone onto welfare want to avoid births, it is not clear that they can succeed in avoiding pregnancy. Effective use of contraception is eased by a settled, regular life-style; regular sexual activity; and a supportive partner. Adolescent sexuality, however, tends to be irregular, partners change frequently, and men are not always supportive (Luker, 1996; Zabin and Clark, 1981; Zelnik and Shah, 1983; Alan Guttmacher Institute, 1994; Kost and Forrest, 1989). Some of the sex is involuntary or close to involuntary (Moore et al., 1989). Social norms about women looking too "ready" discourage women from contracepting outside of an ongoing relationship (Luker, 1996).

In sum, the sociology and social psychology literatures suggest that many women will have trouble contracepting effectively. Inasmuch as they react to welfare reform by desiring fewer children, these theoretical literatures suggest that much of the adjustment will be through abortion, rather than changed contraceptive usage. Nevertheless, some women do contracept successfully now. Some women who formerly would have gone on welfare will after reform also decrease their coital frequency and contracept more effectively, leading to fewer pregnancies.

Below we consider evidence on this question from reactions to other policy changes. By combining information on the response of abortions and fertility to policy changes, in principle we can infer something about the relative size of the changes in fertility due to changes in abortion and those due to changes in sexual behavior. For example, if a state raises the cost of an abortion (by stopping Medicaid funding, requiring parental notification/consent, etc.), the change in abortions Δa, can be decomposed into Δc, the change in conceptions due to better contracepting, and Δb, the change in births (where $\Delta a = \Delta c + \Delta b$). Since Δa and Δb are observable (more precisely, can in principle be estimated from the data), we can compute Δc by subtraction. Similarly, if a state lowers its welfare payments (or in some other way makes welfare less attractive), any change in fertility, Δb, can be decomposed into a change in abortions, Δa, and by subtraction a change due to contraceptive practice ($\Delta c = \Delta b - \Delta a$).

Generalizations of the Basic Model

Logically, welfare reform could cause abortions to decline only if it induced some of the women, who before welfare reform would choose to abort, to choose some other outcome—either to contracept more effectively or, conditional on pregnancy, to choose some option other than abortion. The analysis of our basic model showed that the standard rational choice assumptions rule out that possibility. Here we consider several modifications to the model that might overturn this strong theoretical result.

The strong theoretical result—that abortions must increase—follows directly from the assumption that, when they choose a contraceptive strategy, women know exactly what they would do if they became pregnant. If new information will arrive after conception, then it is not appropriate to assume that a woman who currently chooses ABORT, knew with certainty that this would be her choice if she became pregnant. Such a woman would need to consider all of the possible types of information that would arrive. If some arriving information would make WELFARE the best option, then even a woman who currently chooses ABORT would need to consider the value of the welfare package in making her contraceptive choices.[10] In particular, she might choose to contracept better. Such better contraception would lower the number of abortions.

Over the appropriate time span of under 3 months, a woman is unlikely to learn a lot about life in general—her ability, her earnings prospects, etc. Pregnancy, however, might directly cause the arrival of new information. The obvious information is how the woman feels about being pregnant.

Another learning has occupied a central place in the literature on abortion. In the model of Kane and Staiger (1996), women become pregnant partially to determine if the potential father will "support" the child.[11] If, however, unlike in Kane and Staiger's paper, the woman chooses WELFARE (not MARRY) when the father indicates that he will support the child, and ABORT when he does not,

---

[10] In the standard expected utility formulation, she would compute the probability that, given her knowledge at conception, she would choose each of the options—ABORT, MARRY, SINGLE, and WELFARE. Then she would make her choice of contraceptive strategy considering the probability of each final decision conditional on pregnancy. In this formulation, even women who before reform did choose ABORT, need to consider the welfare payment when choosing a contraceptive strategy.

[11] In Kane and Staiger (1996), the choice is between MARRY and ABORT. Since these women would have married, welfare reform has no effect on their choices. Our discussion generalizes their model to the choice between WELFARE and ABORT. This model makes sense only if fathers provide support to their children even when the mother collects WELFARE.

then abortions could increase with welfare reform. If welfare reform makes WELFARE less attractive, then fewer women would become pregnant to determine if the father would support the child. By eliminating some of the pregnancies in which the man would have not "committed," this could lower the number of abortions. Presumably, finding themselves pregnant, some women who before would have chosen WELFARE, now find WELFARE less attractive and will choose ABORT. Again, the net effect is ambiguous. This analysis rests on the plausibility of the assumption that when the man commits, the woman chooses WELFARE and when he does not, she chooses ABORT. The alternative choices of MARRY/ABORT (for commit/don't commit) or MARRY/WELFARE seem more likely than WELFARE/ABORT.[12]

All of the preceding arguments assume that women know correctly what they would do if they became pregnant. Some women who had planned WELFARE if they became pregnant would—when faced with the reality of pregnancy and the real possibility of parenthood—choose to abort. We refer to any such discrepancy between the planned action and actual behavior as "time inconsistency." Welfare reform lowers the utility of having a child. This would induce some of these women to change their sexual behavior to make conceptions less likely. Fewer women would find themselves pregnant and choose to abort. Thus, this time-inconsistency scenario implies that welfare reform could *decrease* the number of abortions. Other cases imply that, as in the base case, the possibility of time inconsistency will cause welfare reform to increase the number of abortions.

Table 5-2 enumerates the possible cases. The first row is the case just discussed. Before reform, women would have planned WELFARE and then actually chosen ABORT. After welfare reform, these women contracept better and never become pregnant. To understand the next four rows of the table, note that after welfare reform, some of the women who expected to choose WELFARE will now expect to choose the other choices (NEVER, ABORT, MARRY, and SINGLE). Finding themselves pregnant, they previously would have chosen ABORT. The other choices have not gotten any better, so they would still choose ABORT. The net effect in this first panel is to decrease abortions.

Consider, however, the second panel (Plan = E , Action = E). It is composed of people who before welfare reform planned WELFARE and when pregnant actually chose WELFARE. After welfare reform, welfare looks less attractive, so they will be less likely to plan to choose WELFARE if they became pregnant. Recall that these are women who are likely to find ABORT more attractive when pregnant than they expected when making contraceptive decisions. Thus, some of those who planned MARRY, SINGLE, or WELFARE will choose ABORT.

---

[12]See Akerlof et al., 1996, who argue that a marriage MARRY/WELFARE pairing along with changes in contraceptive technology might explain the increase in black nonmarital fertility.

TABLE 5-2   Effects of Time Inconsistency

Before[a]		After[b]		Change in Abortions[b]
Plan	Action	Plan	Action	
E	B	A	A	–
		B	B	=
		C	B	+
		D	B	+
		E	B	+
E	E	A	A	=
		B	B	=
		C	C	=
		C	B	+
		D	D	=
		D	B	+
		E	E	=
		E	B	+
B	E	B	B	+
		B	C	=
		B	D	=
		B	E	=

NOTE: Letters refer to final states in Figure 5-1: A = NEVER pregnant; B = ABORT; C = MARRY; D = SINGLE (no welfare); E = single (WELFARE). + = increase; – = decrease; = is no change.
[a] "Before" = before welfare reform.
[b] "After" = after welfare reform.
[c] "Change in Abortions" gives the change in abortions with welfare reform.

All of these time inconsistencies increase the number of abortions. This increase is in addition to the time-consistent increase in abortions from the basic model.

Similarly (the third panel of the table: Plan = B, Action = E), some women who plan to choose ABORT if they become pregnant, would in fact not be able to "go through with it" when they have to make the decision. Encouraging this outcome appears to be the intent of the "informed consent" statutes noted earlier. For those who would have chosen WELFARE before reform, there is an increase in abortions. If welfare reform lowers the utility of having the child, then more of these women would have the abortion. This reinforces the earlier results based on the basic model. Welfare reform should increase the number of abortions.

An alternative pathway through which welfare reform could induce some of the women to change from ABORT to not ABORT would be for welfare reform to change the utility of the other options.[13] For example, if states respond to the

_____

[13]Note that some relaxations of this form strengthen the basic result. For example, Jackson and Klerman (1996) note that welfare reform will also affect the utility of the other states. Some women

performance bonuses by increasing funding for family-planning services (and such services are effective; see Meier and McFarlane, 1993), contraception would become cheaper, women would contracept more effectively, and fewer women would find themselves pregnant such that they needed to choose ABORT. Similarly, if the abstinence education programs funded by the legislation are successful in changing the behavior of women who would have aborted, then abortions would again decline.

The earlier quotes from the right-to-life movement suggest another mechanism. Welfare receipt makes women categorically eligible for Medicaid. In many states, Medicaid funds abortions. If PRWORA makes few women eligible for Medicaid, abortions will become more expensive. After such a change in Medicaid eligibility, some women who, finding themselves pregnant, would have chosen abortion will instead choose one of the other three options and all women who would have chosen abortion will take more aggressive steps to avoid pregnancy. The details of PRWORA make this outcome unlikely. PRWORA specifically continues Medicaid eligibility for women who would have been eligible for AFDC under the prereform rules. Thus, PRWORA will only lower Medicaid eligibility if it induces a large number of women to marry at their first pregnancy or to go to work and have earned incomes so high that they would not have been eligible for AFDC.

Finally, some proponents of welfare reform suggest that it will induce a broad change in social attitudes towards nonmarital sexual relations, abortion, and nonmarital childbearing. In this view, the current generous welfare system encourages a general climate of promiscuity and high levels of unprotected sexual activity. With welfare reform, women who would have chosen welfare will individually be more "careful." This will result in a lowering of the peer pressure for sexual relations (Musick, 1993; Luker, 1996), the pressures against contraceptive use, and the social acceptance of nonmarital fertility. Such a result would probably emerge from models of the marriage market such as that of Willis (1995) or Akerlof et al. (1996). With lower coital frequency, more effective contraception, and more marriage, the number of abortions might fall. On the other hand, an increase in the stigma attached to nonmarital fertility might increase abortion. The net effect is ambiguous among those who become pregnant.

Implications for Abortion Regulation

The model also has predictions about the effects of abortion regulation. Most forms of abortion regulation—in particular, making it illegal, requiring

---

who have the child, but do not immediately go on welfare, may nevertheless treat welfare payments as "insurance," potential income if the marriage breaks up. If welfare reform makes welfare not as effective as insurance, then some women who would have chosen MARRY or SINGLE, will choose ABORT after welfare reform.

parental notification or consent, not funding it through Medicaid—have the effect of making abortion more expensive (with "cost" viewed not merely in terms of out-of-pocket costs). This makes the choice of abortion more expensive.

The analysis then proceeds as in the analysis of the effects of welfare reform. The only women who would be affected by welfare reform are those who would have chosen abortion had they found themselves pregnant. In general, the model predicts that these women will be less likely to choose abortion and more likely to choose each of the other options. In particular, they will contracept more aggressively (or lower coital frequency). Finding themselves pregnant, they will be more likely to choose the other three options: MARRY, WELFARE, and SINGLE. Thus, in net the total number of abortions performed will go down and the number of births—overall, marital, nonmarital—will go up. The abortion ratio—the ratio of abortions to live births—will also decrease.

The generalizations continue to apply. In particular, under the Kane and Staiger (1996) model in which fathers reveal whether or not they will support the child, births could go down. It is now more expensive to learn whether the father will support the child (because if he does not, the necessary abortion is more expensive). Thus, women will contracept more effectively. Fewer women will become pregnant to determine if the father would support the child. In net, there will be both fewer births and fewer abortions.

Time inconsistency could also overturn these results. Consider the case of women who thought ex ante that they would abort, but ex post would not. Knowing that abortion was more expensive (and thinking that they would abort), they would contracept more aggressively. Since they would not abort, the smaller number of pregnancies yields a smaller number of births. The net effect is of course a function of the relative size of the two groups (the time-consistent group and the time-inconsistent group) and the relative magnitude of the effects.

Note also that time inconsistency could plausibly have the opposite effect. Women who thought they would not abort if they became pregnant, in fact do abort. Their preconception behavior is unaffected, but finding the cost of the abortion higher, they are less likely to abort. This possibility would reinforce the conclusion that with regulation of abortion, abortions would decrease and births would increase.

ABORTION DATA

More than most other subfields of demography, empirical research on abortion—its levels, its determinants, and its effects—is limited by the available data. Abortion is close to the archetypical "sensitive topic" for survey research. Public opinion polling finds that a large fraction of the population is strongly opposed to abortion, so issues of interviewer/public approval are likely to lead to underreporting. Similarly, many Americans are themselves conflicted in their attitudes towards abortion and the decision is likely to have come at a difficult time, so suppressing unpleasant memories is also likely to result in underreporting.

AGI Provider Surveys

The best reports of the number of abortions in the United States appear to be collected by the Alan Guttmacher Institute (AGI).[14] AGI does an approximately annual survey of abortion providers. Provider surveys were conducted annually from 1973 to the present, except for 1983, 1986, 1989, 1990, and 1992. Henshaw and Van Vort (1994) provide a description of their methods.

Given the origin of that organization as a semiautonomous division of Planned Parenthood Federation of America, more than anyone else, they are able to gain the confidence of abortion providers. Nevertheless, their survey undoubtedly misses some small providers (e.g., gynecologists providing individual abortions to mature, long-term private patients). Also, AGI estimates abortions because some of the larger commercial abortion providers do not report (at all or partially) for business reasons.

The AGI survey of providers is subject to two important drawbacks. First, it collects no covariate information. AGI simply collects the number of abortions performed. An occasional AGI survey (the most recent one in 1994-1995; see Henshaw and Kost, 1996) of women having abortions collects some information, but this patient survey is far from annual. In addition, refusals are a problem in the patient survey. Many providers refuse to allow the patient survey; many patients refuse to participate.

The other major problem with the AGI data is that, being a provider-based survey, it records *state of occurrence*. For most population-based analyses—and in particular the effects of welfare reform—we would like to know the number of abortions by the woman's *state of residence*. CDC (1997) reports that for 8.3 percent of abortions, the woman's state of residence is not the state in which the abortion occurs. These CDC estimates are likely to be a lower bound. See the discussion of this issue in Blank et al. (1996). They note, for example, that interstate travel is the most plausible explanation for why the District of Columbia's abortion rate is four times that of any other state.

AGI also provides an estimate of abortions by state of residence. The algo-

---

[14]See for example the statement of Jones and Forrest (1992a): "The AGI statistics nevertheless are widely accepted as the best available estimates of the incidence of abortion in the United States." This quotation is followed by a citation to the *Statistical Abstract*, which, in fact, reports the AGI numbers. It should be noted that both Jones and Forrest are senior staff members at AGI.

rithm for transforming AGI's state-of-occurrence data into state-of-residence estimates is given in Henshaw and Van Vort (1992). Particularly relevant for the methodological discussion below, the algorithm would not capture policy-induced changes in the demographic characteristics of women going out of state for an abortion. A consistent series is available for 1978-1988 (except for 1983 and 1986 when the underlying survey was not conducted). Earlier estimates using a different algorithm are available for 1974-1977. Blank et al. (1996) note that the series do not appear to splice well, and they do not use the earlier series.

CDC Surveillance Data

The Centers for Disease Control has an ongoing Abortion Surveillance Program. That program publishes annual data (1974-present, some data for earlier years) on abortions by state of occurrence, state of residence, race, and age. The data are compiled from reports of state central health agencies (for 47 reporting areas: 44 states, the District of Columbia, New York City, and the balance of New York State), supplemented with other sources including direct contacts with abortion providers (from five reporting areas; unless otherwise noted the information in this section is drawn from Koonin et al., 1995).

The data are clearly incomplete. Not all states provide reports to CDC. Among those states that do provide reports, the reported number of abortions is often well below the AGI numbers (overall, 12 percent lower). Also not all reporting states provided information on the characteristics of the woman (only 43 reporting areas provide information on the age of the woman; only 36 reporting areas provide information on the race of the woman) or distinguish between state of occurrence and state of residence (10 reporting areas do not attempt to record out-of-state abortions). Most states report marital status of the woman and her ethnicity (Hispanic/non-Hispanic), but those data often have high missing data rates. Nevertheless, these are the only data that provide any demographic covariates. Standard practice at both AGI and CDC has been to use the AGI estimates for the total number of abortions and the CDC data to estimate the national distribution of abortions by age and race.

Micro Data from Vital Statistics

All states require individual-level data on births from their vital registration systems for births (i.e., doctors/hospitals are required to report all births on a "birth certificate"). In contrast, not all states require individual-level reports of abortions. Only 14 states make similar individual-level data for abortions available: Colorado, Indiana, Kansas, Maine, Missouri, Montana, New York, Oregon, Rhode Island, South Carolina, Tennessee, Utah, Vermont, and Virginia (Kochanek, 1989).

These vital statistics systems have two potential problems. First, despite a reporting requirement, compliance is not always complete. Joyce and Kaestner (1995) note severe underreporting (more than 15 percent below the comparable AGI figures) for Colorado, Kansas, New York, and Oregon. Second, many states do not collect data on out-of-state abortions to their own residents (Joyce and Kaestner, 1995, note that this is an issue for Maine, but not for Illinois). Even among those states that do collect data on out-of-state abortions to their own residents, the quality of the data is often suspect (Joyce and Kaestner, 1995, note severe problems with the data from Virginia and suspect that the problem is abortions performed in the District of Columbia).

Survey Data

Several major surveys of individuals (as opposed to the AGI survey of providers, or the CDC survey of state health departments)—among them the National Survey of Family Growth (NSFG) and the National Longitudinal Survey-Youth (NLS-Y)—include questions on abortions. The effectiveness of these questions has been explored by Jones and Forest (1992a). They compare the survey reports with the age-race-time period appropriate national rates (estimated from AGI-CDC data). They conclude that in all of the surveys they examined, abortions are severely underreported. For most of the surveys and subsamples they consider, fewer than half of the abortions are recorded. The underreporting appears to be most severe among unmarried and nonwhite women. No clear pattern by age of the respondent is evident. Attempts by the NLS-Y to use a self-administered questionnaire to increase response rates appear to have been largely unsuccessful.

This problem has been noted in most studies of fertility-related behaviors using survey data (Lundberg and Plotnick, 1990, 1995; Currie et al., 1996). The magnitude of the underreporting and its differential nature with different sub-populations suggest that in evaluating the literature the published studies using survey data should be heavily downweighted.[15] Thus, survey data-based analy-

---

[15]It should be noted that this problem of underreported abortions calls into question several other sets of results from survey data. In particular, the NSFG has been used to compute contraceptive termination, switching, and failure rates (e.g., Grady et al., 1983, 1989). Given the high abortion ratio, these findings should also be considered suspect. In particular, if there was a pregnancy that was terminated by an unreported abortion, then there must be some problem with the NSFG calendar. Among the possibilities are the following: (1) a contraceptive failure is reported as a period of continual usage, when in fact abortion terminated an unwanted pregnancy; (2) a period of contraceptive use was reported as a period of nonuse to suppress the true failure (and the subsequent abortion); (3) the conception occurred during a period of nonuse (and the abortion was not reported). See Jones and Forrest (1989, 1992b) and Grady et al. (1986) for an attempt to address this problem. See also Currie et al. (1996), who propose and implement a strategy for estimating the effects of restrictions on abortions on pregnancy outcomes that is robust to this data problem.

ses do not seem promising for evaluations of the effects of welfare reform on abortion rates.

METHODS

In this section, we review two methodological issues in estimating the effects of welfare policy on abortion rates. First, we consider under what conditions comparing abortion rates in states with different policies recovers the true effect of the policy (i.e., the effect of changing the policy in a given state in a given year). Second, we consider the required sample sizes to detect substantively important effects.

Estimating the Effects of Government Policies

If good data are available, the obvious testing/estimation strategy is to regress a measure of abortions (or fertility) on policy variables and controls. As discussed in Chapter 4, the appropriateness of this approach depends crucially on how states choose policies. If policies are randomly assigned, such regressions would recover the causal effect of the policy. However, if states with otherwise high or low abortion rates choose a given policy, then such a regression would ascribe to the policy both its direct effect and the variation in the baseline level of abortion in the states that choose the policy. Similarly, if we estimate the effect of a policy change by the change in abortion rates for a state through time, we would ascribe to the policy both its true effect and the effect of other social changes occurring simultaneously. A crucial methodological issue is thus how to estimate the true effect of the law while controlling for persistent differences in the states adopting policies and other social changes.

One approach to these issues is to exploit the available data on abortion and fertility rates for states through time. With such time series of cross-sectional data, we can include in the regression dummy regressors for each year and for each state. Such models can be interpreted as follows. The year dummies control for otherwise unmeasured national social changes. The state dummies control for persistent, otherwise unmeasured, differences across states. Some analyses (e.g., Matthews et al., 1995; Jackson and Klerman, 1996) also include state-specific linear time trends and find them to be significant. Most analyses also include detailed controls for state economic conditions. Considerable evidence is now emerging that empirical results are quite sensitive to the inclusion of such dummy variables (see, for example, Moffitt, 1994, on female headship).

Nevertheless, these dummy variable estimators are essentially conventional linear regression in which we are using the dummy variables to control for the unobservables. Implicitly, the method assumes that the remaining variation in the crucial policy variable (i.e., after regressing it on the dummy variables and the other regression controls) is random. There is no reason to believe this, except that we have controlled, as well as we can, for the obvious observable variation.

As Ellwood and Bane (1985) noted in their seminal paper on these issues, state policies themselves do not arrive deus ex machina. They are determined by a political process. We could alternatively argue that the state policies and the outcomes of interest (abortion or fertility) are jointly caused by some unobserved effect. If so, then the estimated effects are spurious.

There are at least three possible constructive approaches to this critique. First as Meyer (1995, among others) notes, we often have strong ex ante expectations about the relative size of the effect across subgroups. If so, we can stratify the analysis and check if our expectations are confirmed. In the context of abortion policy, such an approach would involve differentially exploring policy effects by age and education groups. We presume that welfare policy and Medicaid funding should primarily effect younger and less educated women. Their earnings prospects are worse, and therefore welfare is likely to be relatively more attractive. This will lead their decisions to be marginal with respect to Medicaid reimbursement for abortion or the details of welfare policy (see Klerman, 1996, for an empirical application of this idea). Application of this idea to abortion policy, however, is limited by the data. We noted that, due to the collection of abortion statistics from providers, abortion data stratified by covariates are even less available than high quality abortion data in general.[16] The limited amount of covariate information makes it difficult to apply these stratification ideas to abortion rates.

Second, for some cases, we can assert that a policy should have zero effect on a subgroup. When this is a good assumption, we can estimate the effect of the policy by comparing rates for the affected group to those for the unaffected group. The regression analogue is to include dummy variables for every state-year combination. In the context of abortion policy, the obvious example would be parental consent laws. They potentially have effects on minors (women who are 17 or below during the first trimester of their pregnancy) and no effect on women 18 and above at that time. Thus, while including age-year and age-state dummy variables (and perhaps age-state linear time trends), we can also differentiate younger women from older women. This would control for state-year effects, which are common across minor and adult women.

Doing so is more subtle than it seems. The levels of fertility rates, abortion rates, and abortion ratios are quite different for minors and adults. Thus, it seems implausible that there is a common dummy variable in the level of abortions (Meyer, 1995, makes a similar point). A common dummy variable in the logs (i.e., multiplicative) seems more attractive.

---

[16]See Blank et al. (1996) and Haas-Wilson (1996). Both papers stratify by age.

Third, the nature of the legal battles on abortion policy suggests another approach. Presumably the sentiment effects operate most strongly at the level of the state legislatures, and much less so in the courts. The contentiousness of the abortion issue and the constitutional rights under *Roe v. Wade* have led to almost every piece of abortion legislation being litigated in the courts (see Merz et al., 1995, 1996 for details). The length of time from passage to implementation varies enormously. The correlation between the timing of passage of a restriction on abortion and the actual implementation is very weak. Thus, we can use periods in which a restriction is unenforced as a test for the importance of joint causation (rather than direct causation from policy to demographic rates). Blank et al. (1996), Currie et al. (1996), and Haas-Wilson (1996) implement this approach for abortion.

Sample Size Considerations

Beyond these issues in estimating the true causal effect of the policy, there is a concern about the required sample sizes for the analysis. Several things conspire to make the required sample sizes for analyses of the effects of public policies on abortion and fertility much larger than they are for other types of analyses. First, fertility and abortion are discrete events. Compared to continuous outcomes, discrete outcomes will in general require larger samples to identify regression effects.

Second, the event in question is relatively rare. Overall, about 2.6 women in 100 (aged 15-44) have an abortion in a year. Thus, if the expected effect size is a 40 percentage point change in the age-specific birth/abortion rate, we are looking for a 1 percentage point change in the number of women having the event. Given a binary regressor (state abortion regulations, implementation of a particular discrete element of welfare reform), simple normal approximations to the variance of a binomial outcome imply sample sizes of several thousand. Consider the example of a simple before-after comparison. Assume that a third of the population experiences a change in welfare/abortion policy and the abortion rate is 2.6 percent (the national average). Then, if the sample size is 50,000 both before and after the change in regime, one standard error of the estimate is 6.5 percent of the mean abortion rate (0.17 abortion per 100 women).[17] Even if the

---

[17]The implied calculation is as follows. The variance of a binomial variable is simply pq/n. So the standard error of the difference-of-differences (before/after, experimental states/control states) is the variance of the sum of four binomial variables (two with population zN and two with population $(1 - z)N$ where z is the fraction of the population experiencing the change in regime; we assume that the mean is p in each term):

$$SD = \sqrt{2 * \left\{ \frac{pq}{zN} + \frac{pq}{(1-z)N} \right\}}$$

comparison yielded an estimate equal to a true effect of 12 percent, an analyst using 2 years of a survey including 50,000 women of childbearing age would be unable to reject the hypothesis that the deviation was due to chance! This is approximately the size of the largest ongoing survey in the United States—the Current Population Survey. It does not record abortions.

In many ways, these estimates are too optimistic. The change in the abortion rate corresponding to the above calculations is over all women of childbearing age. If we expect welfare reform to only affect abortion for a minority of the population, the equivalent effect size in that subpopulation would need to be even larger.[18] Most reforms are likely to be implemented in fewer than a third of the states or more than two-thirds of the states. As the fraction of states with the policy becomes more extreme, the required sample sizes increase. Stratifying on covariates (race, age, marital status) will further increase the required sample size.

Third, this binomial formula applies only in the absence of covariates. The inclusion of dummy variables washes out much of the variation in the policies. When dummy variables for state are included in the regression model, the only sample that contributes towards the power computation of the previous paragraph are states that change policy during the period under study. States that do not change policy contribute nothing. When dummy variables for state and year are included, states in which no change in policy occurs help to estimate more precisely the year effects but the general point remains.

Fourth, the simple binomial formula calculations apply only in the case where—up to sampling variability—the regression model exactly describes the rates. Jackson and Klerman (1996) present a simple superpopulation formulation in which this statement is meaningful even for vital statistics. If, as seems likely, there are unmodeled components that affect everyone in the state, these simple sample size computations are too conservative. Even larger samples—in particular more states and years—will be needed.

Jackson and Klerman (1996) formulate the equivalent model for the log of the proportion (e.g., Madalla, 1983). They compute that this state-year specific error is about 3 percent of fertility. Thus, despite the apparently large sample sizes in vital statistics calculations, small changes in fertility rates cannot be

---

[18]Some of the implied increase in required sample size is counteracted by the higher abortion rates among the current AFDC population. The estimates in Henshaw and Kost (1992) imply that women with family income below $15,000 have an abortion rate 1.86 times as high as the U.S. average. For those covered by Medicaid, the corresponding figure is 2.04. The pessimistic evaluation in the body of this chapter assumes the use of a general survey of both the affected population and the unaffected population. In that case, the smaller affected population will outweigh any increase in the rate in the affected population. However, if the sample is drawn only from the affected population, then the higher abortion rates for the affected subsample would lower the required sample size for the population of interest by about 30 percent.

detected in year-to-year changes. Instead, several years of pre- and postchange data will be needed to detect all but the largest effects. In practice, this means that several years of postreform data will be needed; thus, rapid evaluation will not be possible.

These sample size considerations are not crucial for studies using AGI or CDC data on aggregate abortion rates. There are now about 60 million women of childbearing age in the United States. Most analyses analyze the full time series of cross sections. In doing so, they implicitly pool several years for "before" data and several years for "after" data. This pooling makes up for the fact that (at least until recently) few states had implemented parental consent laws and few states changed their Medicaid funding policies.

These power considerations are, however, relevant for two other cases. First, even if individual-level survey data were of high quality (e.g., the NLS-Y or the NSFG), the sample sizes would not be large enough. We have argued that such dummy variable models are a minimal requirement for estimating causal effects of state policies. Similar arguments would apply to any ad hoc survey to monitor the effects of welfare reform. In addition for such an ad hoc survey, we would need to worry about both the size of the baseline sample (for "before" data) and the size of the postreform sample (for "after" data).

Second, these sample size considerations imply that it will be difficult to do reliable "instant policy analysis." Consider a policy put into place in January of 1996, the year of the workshop for which this paper was written. Experience with the 1992 and 1994 data suggests that preliminary CDC data will be released in late 1998 or early 1999. Detailed CDC data, including the crucial disaggregation by age, will not be released until mid-2000. Furthermore, these power considerations suggest that reliable estimates will require several years of postreform data.

Clearly these results hold to a lesser degree the larger the expected effect of a given reform. However, the effects of most reforms on the overall abortion rate will be moderate to small. Among the current welfare population, neither fertility nor abortions will fall to zero. Since only about a tenth of newborns are on welfare shortly after birth (Jackson and Klerman, 1996), the effect on overall abortion and birth rates will be much smaller. Thus, the largest plausible percentage changes in overall fertility and abortion rates are well under 5 percent.

EXISTING LITERATURE

In this section, we review the existing empirical literature for insights into the likely effects of welfare reform on abortion rates. We begin with a review of the limited literature on the effects of AFDC payment levels on abortion rates.

We then survey the literature on the effects of Medicaid funding on abortion. As is noted in the right-to-life literature, one possible pathway for the effect of welfare reform on abortions is through a change in the eligibility requirements for

Medicaid. If welfare reform has the effect of making fewer women eligible for Medicaid and Medicaid funding of abortions increases abortion rates, then welfare reform would lower abortion rates.

Finally, we discuss the relative magnitude of the birth and abortion effects of changes in abortion policy and economic conditions. We have noted in the previous section that this comparison of relative magnitudes might provide some insight into the extent to which any effect of welfare on births would come through changes in contraceptive behavior/coital frequency or through abortion.

Welfare and Abortion

The theoretical model outlined earlier suggests that higher AFDC payments should decrease abortions. Six studies have explored the effect of welfare payments on abortion levels. Two early cross-sectional studies of teenagers (Moore and Caldwell, 1977; Singh, 1986) find little support for this hypothesis. Moore and Caldwell, using small survey samples, find no effect. Singh, using AGI data for 1 year, finds a negative effect.

Lundberg and Plotnick (1995) estimate a nested logit model of adolescent childbearing using NLS-Y data (1,089 whites, 462 blacks). The model does not include dummy variables for state or year. They estimate that a 20 percent decrease in welfare payments lowers the probability of pregnancy for a white adolescent by 0.2 percentage point (a fifth of a percentage point based on a coefficient with a t-statistic of over 5). It, however, lowers the conditional probability of a live birth by 2.9 percentage points. The abortion rate therefore declines by 1.6 percentage points. There is no statistically significant effect on black adolescents. Thus, these results imply that most of the adjustment to variation in welfare payments is through abortion. Note, however, that these results are subject to the earlier caveats about sample sizes, lack of dummy variables, and the sizable underreporting of abortion in survey data.

Blank et al. (1996) use both AGI and CDC data on abortions for 1974-1988 and state and year dummy variables to explore the determinants of state abortion rates including AFDC payment levels. Their AFDC results are not robust to different specifications reported in their paper. Their basic model with state and year dummy variables shows no effect of AFDC payment levels. This result is robust to whether they use the more reliable data on state of occurrence (of the abortion) or the conceptually more appropriate data on state of residence. They suggest that this is due to lack of variation in the welfare variable, but this suggestion is not consistent with equivalent models estimated on births (which do find a welfare effect). It would, however, be consistent with problems in the abortion data, particularly in the state-of-residence data. Consistent with Singh's (1986) results, models without state dummy variables show the "wrong" sign (higher AFDC payments raise abortion rates) and are significant at the 1 percent level.

Alternative results using the CDC data also find this "wrong" sign result. The result appears to be due to the subset of states. Regressions on the AGI sample (used in their basic model) for the CDC subset of states also show this positive effect. The advantage of the CDC data is that they make possible disaggregated analyses. Such disaggregated analyses do not appear to provide important additional insights. Using the CDC data, the effects of AFDC on teens versus nonteens and nonwhites versus whites are statistically indistinguishable.

Matthews et al. (1997) explore the effects of AFDC (as well as other policies, economic conditions, and health care availability) on both abortions and births. Like Blank et al. (1996), they use state and year dummy variables on aggregate rates (not disaggregated by age or race). Their results for abortions are similar to those of Blank et al. (1996). AFDC payments significantly increase abortions in a specification without dummy variables, but with dummy variables (with or without state-specific linear time trends), there is no effect of AFDC on abortions. On births, they do find a significant positive effect of AFDC. Taken at face value, this result implies that the adjustment of births to AFDC does not occur through abortions.

McKinnish and Sanders (1996) also use state and year dummy variables on aggregate data on births and abortions by state of occurrence. Unlike Blank et al. (1996) and Matthews et al. (1997), they use a nested logit model for aggregate data. Nevertheless, they also find no effect of AFDC on abortion and a highly significant effect on births.

Finally, Joyce and Kaestner (1996) explore the effects of another component of the prereform welfare package—health benefits through Medicaid—on fertility. They consider the effects of the Medicaid expansions of the late 1980s on abortion ratios using individual-level data from vital statistics reports on abortions in South Carolina, Tennessee, and Virginia. In addition to using cross-state differences in the timing of the expansion, they compare abortion ratios among women who were more or less likely to be eligible for Medicaid if they carried the child to term. Implicitly, they assume that any change in the relative abortion ratios of the more and less likely groups across the expansions (within a state) is due to the expansions.

Joyce and Kaestner find large results. For white women 23 to 27 years old, they note that their estimates imply that the Medicaid expansions cut the abortion ratio by 2 to 5 percentage points (depending on which specification's estimates are used). This is equivalent to a 27 to 68 percent drop in the abortion ratio for Medicaid-eligible women. Even given the Long et al. (1994) estimate (cited by Joyce and Kaestner) that the value of the Medicaid expansion for prenatal care, delivery, and infant care is $6,850, these are large effects. This estimate of the cost to Medicaid of the expansions is likely to be an overestimate of the savings to mothers. Some of this care—in particular, the large component due to the costs of childbirth—would have been provided anyway, either in pubic hospitals or as charity care.

Medicaid Funding of Abortions

There is a moderate-sized literature exploring the effects of Medicaid funding of abortions on abortion rates and birth rates. As discussed earlier, the extensive litigation and changing state policies provide a rich environment in which to explore policy effects.

The classic study in the literature is Trussell et al. (1980). They explored the time-series data on births and abortions around the end of Medicaid funding in Ohio and Georgia (using Michigan, which continued funding, as a control). They found that the number of abortions in Ohio and Georgia fell by more than a quarter (while abortions were approximately constant in Michigan), but that births were approximately constant in all three states. These results are consistent with the hypothesis that Medicaid funding does increase abortion rates. They are also consistent with the conclusion that women adjust contraceptive practice in response to changes in the price of abortion.

A more recent study of the end of Medicaid funding in Michigan in 1988 comes to the opposite conclusion with respect to fertility (Evans et al., 1993). Compared to the controls (Ohio and Indiana), births in Michigan rose, though by less than abortions fell. Again, funding affects abortion rates. This result suggests that changes in welfare policy would have effects on both contraceptive practice and abortion rates.

Blank et al. (1996) also consider the effect of Medicaid funding. They find that Medicaid funding raises abortion rates in analyses of the state of occurrence data. This result washes out in analyses of state-of-residence. Medicaid funding should be a function of state of residence. Funding should not be available to women who have abortions in states with a funding policy if their state of residence does not fund. Similarly, Medicaid should fund even if the abortion is performed out of state. Their strong negative effects of Medicaid funding in bordering states is, therefore, also anomalous. They conclude that the Medicaid funding results are spurious.

Matthews et al. (1997) also find a positive Medicaid funding effect on abortions. Their effect, however, becomes statistically insignificant when state-specific time trends are included.

Levine et al. (1996) perform similar computations on several of the Medicaid funding changes. With respect to the 1981 Supreme Court ruling allowing states not to fund abortions through Medicaid, they find a drop in abortions, but also an increase in births. More careful consideration of which states to include as controls leads them to conclude that the change in births is spurious (see their discussion of Ohio versus Pennsylvania, pp. 12-13; and Texas versus Colorado and Michigan discussed in footnote 20, p. 14).

These results are robust in their multivariate analyses. Medicaid funding raises abortions by 1-1.5 per 1,000 women. The larger effect is in models without state-specific time trends; the smaller effect, in models with them. In models without state-specific time trends, Medicaid funding raises births (against the theory), but this effect washes out with the inclusion of state-specific time trends.[19]

Haas-Wilson (1996) applies both ordinary least squares and state dummy variables (without year dummy variables) to explore the effect of abortion restrictions on the abortion rate of minors using the CDC data. In both specifications, she finds a strong positive effect of Medicaid funding on abortions.

Korenbrot et al. (1990) examine both births and abortions in three states that changed their funding policies between 1984 and 1985 (Colorado, South Carolina, and Pennsylvania). They conclude that ending funding lowers abortions and raises fertility, with the absolute value of the effect usually being larger on abortions. Disaggregated analyses for Colorado suggest that the birth effects are largest for blacks, but the North Carolina results do not support that suggestion.

Changes in Abortion Versus Changes in Contraception

We have noted earlier that welfare reform is likely to induce women who formerly would have had children and received AFDC to instead attempt to avoid births. For the concerns of this chapter, the crucial question is the extent to which they do so through lower coital frequency and more effective contraception or through abortion once they become pregnant. Papers that explore both births and abortions provide an opportunity to explore the relative importance of changes in abortion and changes in contraception for other policies that change birth rates. As noted in our theoretical discussion, there are two experiments. The first involves changes in the perceived value of children. The second involves changes in the perceived total cost of an abortion.

The results for changes in the perceived value of children are striking. American fertility has a pronounced (highly statistically significant) procyclical pattern (e.g., Silver, 1965; Jackson and Klerman, 1996; Black et al., 1996). Matthews et al. (1997) also find this pattern in their regression coefficients for male and female wages (measured using CPS data on workers, with and without standard selection corrections). Nevertheless, their point estimates for the effect on abortion is positive, but statistically insignificant. In some of their alternative specifications, this positive effect of business cycle conditions is statistically signifi-

---

[19]They also report results using the NLS-Y. Those results are consistent with their aggregate data results. Those data allow them to identify women who are more likely to be Medicaid eligible. We are inclined to downweight those results due to the small sample sizes, the misreporting of abortions, and the absence of any dummy variables.

cant (i.e., per capita total personal income). This positive point estimate is consistent with the results in Blank et al. (1996) both for state of occurrence and for state of residence.[20] Such a positive point estimate is not consistent with changes in births with the business cycle being achieved through abortions.

The results with respect to abortion policy and access are also consistent with this conclusion. Matthews et al. (1997) find a negative effect of Medicaid abortion funding decisions in their models with dummy variables (it is only significant in their models without state-specific time trends). The effect on births is, however, also negative (again significant in models without state-specific time trends, insignificant in models with state-specific time trends). If there was no effect on contraception, we would expect abortions to rise.

Similar results appear for parental notification/consent statutes. Consistent with the theory, abortions fall, but not consistent with the theory, births also fall. Again the results are only significant in the models without state-specific time trends.

Their results for access to abortion providers also have a similar pattern. Access to abortion providers (by several measures) is strongly associated with more abortions (significantly both in models without and in models with state-specific time trends). The effect on births has the theoretically expected sign (negative) in the no-state-specific time-trends model, but it is much smaller in absolute value (in the log scale and also when transformed to rates). In the state-specific time-trends models the effect is positive, but insignificant.

Finally, in empirical tests of their theory, Kane and Staiger (1996) also find evidence that adjustments are through contraception. Kane and Staiger's theory suggested that if women use the availability of abortion to determine whether a father would support a child, then both abortions and fertility would rise as abortion became more available. More women would become pregnant, some of them would abort, some would deliver. In net, easier access to abortion could increase both births and abortions. They test this hypothesis using time series of cross-sectional data on fertility at the county level. Their fixed-effects results for

---

[20]This is not Blank et al.'s interpretation of their results. They discuss their economic results as follows: "Once state and year fixed effects are included, changes in economic or demographic variables over time within a state appear to have relatively small effects on state abortion rates. The strongest remaining effect is the positive relationship between unemployment and abortion rates. As the economy moves into recession, a 1-point rise in the unemployment rate leads to about a 3 percent increase in abortion rates. Estimates with slightly less precision but still significant at the 5 percent level, decreases in marriage rates and increases in per capita income lead to an increase in abortion rates." Note, however, that the unemployment rate result is not robust to the switch to state-of-residence data, but the positive per capita income result is robust and grows in statistical significance. Lundberg and Plotnick (1995) also explore Medicaid funding. They find that funding lowers abortion rates and raises birth rates. For the reasons discussed in the previous paragraph, we are inclined to downweight these results.

all three of their abortion access measures—Medicaid funding, parental consent laws, and distance to an abortion clinic—are all consistent with the hypothesis that births *increase* as abortions access improves. This could only happen if women are adjusting their contraceptive practices in response to abortion access. A simple adjustment of abortion conditional on fertility would imply that fertility would fall with improved abortion access. Consideration of the timing of the effects suggests that the Medicaid funding and parental consent results may be spurious, but the results based on distance to an abortion clinic are consistent with their theory.

In all three cases, against the conventional wisdom (e.g., Hofferth, 1987), the implication is that rather than adjust abortions, women adjust contraceptive patterns. Note, however, that the effect on abortions itself is sensitive to specification. Blank et al. (1996) do not find any effect of parental notification/consent laws, and their effect of Medicaid funding washes out in the models using the preferred state-of-residence concept (which is what Matthews et al., 1996, use). Similarly, the preponderance of evidence in the Medicaid funding literature is that abortions change in the expected direction, but if there is any effect on births (at least in the theoretically expected direction), it is much smaller. Thus, these results should be interpreted with caution. More faith should be put in results based on the economic conditions. They appear to be robust (but see footnote 20).

CONCLUSIONS

Congress has identified the effect of PRWORA on abortions as an important indicator of its success. Reducing nonmarital fertility is an explicit goal of the legislation. If there is a reduction in nonmarital fertility but it comes as a result of increases in the number of abortions, many of the legislation's proponents will judge the legislation to have been a mistake. Thus, evaluation of the net effect of the legislation and developing additional rounds of welfare reform will require information on the causal effect of the legislation on the number of nonmarital births and abortions. For some, the concern will be relative: in achieving any decline in nonmarital fertility, what was the relative importance of changes in abortion versus changes in coital frequency and contraceptive practice?

This chapter has considered the likely effects of PRWORA on abortion and the research considerations in exploring that issue. While it is possible to construct theories with alternative implications, it seems reasonable to assume that, inasmuch as PRWORA decreases fertility, it will do so partially by increasing the number of abortions. Finding themselves pregnant and facing a less generous welfare option, more women will choose to abort rather than give birth. This is true despite the fact that the theory also suggests that a less attractive welfare option is likely to make women more aggressive contraceptors.

We then also note that the data on abortion are poor. Survey data on abortion are unreliable and the sample sizes are too small to allow the estimation of policy effects. The AGI data, the best aggregate data available, lack covariate information. The AGI provider survey data are the most important data resource for the study of effects on abortion. The CDC abortion surveillance data allow partial corrections to those data for abortions to nonresidents and estimates of effects disaggregated by covariates. Continuation of both of these data collection efforts will be crucial for any attempt to evaluate the effects of welfare reform on abortion. An additional analysis strategy worthy of further consideration is analysis of those states that release individual-level records on abortions. For at least four states, those data appear to be nearly complete and to include out-of-state abortions (see Joyce and Kaestner, 1995, 1996).

The chapter has also reviewed the existing empirical literature and noted its sensitivity to the exact specification used. State dummy variables effects are crucial. The inclusion of state-specific time trends (which on a priori grounds are appropriate) makes estimated effects smaller. Also, there is some evidence for heterogeneity of effects by demographic group (which is difficult to explore using abortion data).

Given these caveats, the existing literature finds no effect of AFDC payments on abortion. This is true even when using the state and year dummy variables approaches that do find effects on births. This discrepancy between the fertility and abortion results might be real (welfare affects contraception, not abortion), or it could also be explained by the poorer quality of the abortion data (larger measurement error in the dependent variable leading to less precise estimates of regression coefficients).

The literature does find significant effects of Medicaid funding on abortions (in the expected direction). There is some controversy about whether those effects are causal. At this point, a causal interpretation seems appropriate. Whether there is an effect on births remains an open question. Some studies find, against the theory, that births increase with Medicaid funding of abortion.

Finally, the evidence is mixed on the extent to which adjustments to fertility occur through contraception or through abortions. The Medicaid funding literature seems to suggest an effect on abortions. The welfare literature and the economic conditions literature seem to suggest an effect through contraception. The difference may partially be due to differential effects by subpopulation.

ACKNOWLEDGMENTS

This work was partially supported RAND and the National Institute of Child Health and Human Development (NICHD) (under Grants R01 HD31203 and P50 HD12639). This chapter reflects on every page the input of my co-principal investigator on one of the NICHD-sponsored projects, Catherine A. Jackson. Most of the ideas discussed here were developed as part of our joint research. The comments of the discussant, Jacqueline Darroch, significantly improved this chapter. As usual, the responsibility for any opinions or errors remains solely with the author.

REFERENCES

Akerlof, G.A., J.L. Yellen, and M.L. Katz
    1996   An analysis of out-of-wedlock childbearing in the United States. *Quarterly Journal of Economics* 11(2):277-317.
Alan Guttmacher Institute (AGI)
    1979   *Abortions and the Poor: Private Morality, Public Responsibility.* New York: Alan Guttmacher Institute.
    1994   *Sex and America's Teenagers.* New York: Alan Guttmacher Institute
Bauer, G. and P. Gramm
    1995   Why pro-lifers should support welfare reform. *The Wall Street Journal* (August 30):10.
Black, D., D. Kermit, and S. Sanders
    1996   How much does economic growth help the poor: Evidence from the Appalachian Coal Boom and Bust. Heinz School Working Paper. Pittsburgh, Pa.: Carnegie Mellon University.
Blank, R., C. George, and R. London
    1996   State abortion rates: The impact of policy, provider availability, political climate, demography and economics. *Journal of Health Economics* 15(5):513-553.
Centers for Disease Control (CDC)
    1997   Abortion surveillance: Preliminary Analysis—United States, 1995. *Morbidity and Mortality Weekly Report* 46(48).
Currie, J., L. Nixon, and N. Cole
    1996   Restrictions on Medicaid funding of abortion: effects on birth weight and pregnancy resolutions. *Journal of Human Resources* 31(1):159-188.
Dash, L.
    1989   *When Children Want Children: The Urban Crisis of Teenage Childbearing.* New York: William Morrow.
Ellwood, D.
    1987   Understanding Dependency: Choices, Confidence, or Culture. Report prepared for U.S. Department of Health and Human Services (Executive Summary), Center for Human Resources, Heller Graduate School, Brandeis University.
Ellwood, D., and M. Bane
    1985   The impact of AFDC on family structure and living arrangements. *Research in Labor Economics* 7:165-195.
Evans, M., E. Geicher, E. Feingold, M. Johnson, and R. Sokol
    1993   The fiscal impact of the Medicaid funding ban in Michigan. *Obstetrics and Gynecology* (October):555-560.
Geronimus, A.T., and S. Korenman
    1992   The socioeconomic consequences of teen childbearing reconsidered. *Quarterly Journal of Economics* 107(4):1187-1214.
Grady, W.R., M. Hayward, and J. Yagi
    1986   Contraceptive failure in the United States: estimates from the 1982 National Survey of Family Growth. *Family Planning Perspectives* 18:200-209.
Grady, W.R., M.B. Hirsch, N. Keen, and B. Vaughan
    1983   Contraceptive failure and continuation among married women in the United States, 1970-75. *Family Planning Perspectives* 14(1):9-19.
Grady, W.R., M. Hayward, J. Billy, and F. Florey
    1989   Contraceptive switching among currently married women in the United States. *Journal of Biosocial Science* 20:143-156.

Gruber, J.
1994   The incidence of mandated maternity benefits. *American Economic Review* 84:622-641.
Haas-Wilson, D.
1996   The impact of state abortion restrictions on minor's demand for abortions. *Journal of Human Resources* 31(1):140-158.
Henshaw, S., and K. Kost
1992   Parental involvement in minors' abortion decisions. *Family Planning Perspectives.* 24:196-207, 213.
1996   Abortion patients in 1994-1995: Characteristics and contraceptive use. *Family Planning Perspectives* 28(4):140-147,158.
Henshaw, S., and J. Silverman
1988   The characteristics and prior contraceptive use of U.S. abortion patients. *Family Planning Perspectives* 27:120-122.
Henshaw, S., and J. Van Vort, eds.
1992   *Abortion Factbook, 1992 Edition.* New York: Alan Guttmacher Institute.
Henshaw, S., and J. Van Vort
1994   Abortion services in the United States, 1991 and 1992. *Family Planning Perspectives* 26:100-106.
Henshaw, S., L.M. Koonin, and J.C. Smith
1991   Characteristics of women having abortions, 1987. *Family Planning Perspectives* 23:75-81.
Hofferth, S.
1987   Contraceptive decision-making among adolescents. In S. Hofferth and C. Hayes, eds., *Risking the Future: Adolescent Sexuality, Pregnancy, and Childbearing*, (Volume II), Washington, D.C.: National Academy Press.
Jackson, C.A., and J.A. Klerman
1996   Welfare and American fertility. National Bureau of Economic Research, Summer Institute, Cambridge, Mass., July, 1995. Revised October 1996.
Jones, E.F., and J.D. Forrest
1989   Contraceptive failure in the United States: Revised estimates from the 1982 national survey of family growth. *Family Planning Perspectives* 21(3):103-109.
1992a   Underreporting of abortion in surveys of U.S. women: 1976 to 1988. *Demography* 29:113-126.
1992b   Contraceptive Failure Rates Based on the 1988 NSFG. *Family Planning Perspectives* 24(1):12-19.
Joyce, T., and R. Kaestner
1995   The Effect of Parental Involvement Laws on Pregnancy Resolution. Presented at the 1995 Population Association of America Annual Meetings, San Francisco, April 6.
1996   The effect of Medicaid income eligibility expansions on abortion. *Demography* 33(2):181-192.
Kane, T., and D. Staiger
1996   Teen motherhood and abortion access. *Quarterly Journal of Economics* 111(2):467-506.
Keating, D.
1990   Adolescent thinking. Pp. 54-92 in S. Feldman and G. Elliott, eds., *At the Threshold: The Developing Adolescent.* Cambridge, Mass.: Harvard University Press.
Klerman, J.A.
1996   Fertility effects of Medicaid funding of abortions: A disaggregated analysis. Mimeo, RAND, Santa Monica, Calif.
Kochanek, K.D.
1989   Induced terminations of pregnancy: Reporting states, 1987. *Monthly Vital Statistics Report* 38(9, suppl.), Hyattsville, Md.: U.S. Public Health Service.

Koonin, L.M., J.C. Smith, and M. Ramick
    1995   Abortion surveillance—United States, 1991. *CDC Surveillance Summaries, Morbidity and Mortality Weekly Report* 44:SS-2.

Korenbrot, C.C., C. Brinis, and F. Priddy
    1990   Trends in live births and abortions following state restrictions on public funding of abortions. *Public Health Reports* 105:6, 555-562.

Kost, K., and J.D. Forrest
    1989   American women's sexual behavior and exposure to risk of sexually transmitted disease. *Family Planning Perspectives* 6 (November-December):244-254.

Levine, P., A. Trainor, and D. Zimmerman
    1996   The effects of Medicaid abortion funding restrictions on abortions, pregnancies, and births. *Journal of Health Economics* 15:555-578.

Long, S.H., M.S. Marquis, and E.R. Harrison
    1994   The costs of financing of perinatal care in the United States. *American Journal of Public Health* 84:1473-1478.

Luker, K.
    1979   *Taking Chances: Abortion and the Decision Not to Contracept.* Berkeley, Calif.: University of California Press.
    1996   *Dubious Conceptions: The Politics of Teenage Pregnancy.* Berkeley, Calif.: University of California Press.

Lundberg, S., and R. Plotnick
    1990   Effects of state welfare, abortion, and family planning policies on premarital childbearing among white adolescents. *Family Planning Perspectives* 22:246-251.
    1995   Adolescent premarital childbearing: Do economic incentives matter? *Journal of Labor Economics* 13:177-201.

Maddala, G.S.
    1983   *Limited-dependent and Qualitative Dependent Variables in Econometrics.* Cambridge, England: Cambridge University Press.

Matthews, S., D. Ribar, and M. Wilhelm
    1997   The effects of economic conditions and access to reproductive health services on state abortion and birth rates. *Family Planning Perspectives* 29(2):52-61.

McKinnish, T., and S. Sanders
    1996   Who is right: The Pope or Newt Gingrich? Mimeo, Carnegie Mellon University, Pittsburgh, Pa.

Meier, M.H., and D.R. McFarlane
    1993   State Family Planning and Abortion Expenditures: Their Effects on Public Health. *American Journal of Public Health* 84:1468-1472.

Merz, J.F., J.A. Klerman, and C.A. Jackson
    1995   A review of abortion legality, Medicaid funding, and parental involvement laws, 1967-1994. *Rutger's Women's Law Reporter.*
    1996   *A chronicle of abortion legality, Medicaid funding, and parental involvement laws, 1967-1994.* Labor and Population Program Working Paper 96-08. RAND, Santa Monica, Calif.

Meyer, B.
    1995   Natural and quasi-natural experiments. *Journal of Business and Economic Statistics* 13(2):151-162.

Moffitt, R.
    1992   Incentive effects of the U.S. welfare system. *Journal of Economic Literature* 30(1):1-61.
    1994   Welfare effects on female headship with area effects. *Journal of Human Resources* 29(2):621-636.

Moore, K., and S. Caldwell
    1977   The effect of government policies in out-of-wedlock sex and pregnancy. *Family Planning Perspectives* 9:164-169.

Moore, K., C. Winquist, and J.L. Peterson
    1989   Nonvoluntary sexual activity among adolescents. *Family Planning Perspectives* 21(3):
            110-114.
Musick, J.S.
    1993   *Young, Poor, and Pregnant: The Psychology of Teenage Motherhood.* New Haven,
            Conn.: Yale University Press.
Olasky, M.
    1995   Dismantle the poverty panopticon: Pro-life, anti-welfare. *The Wall Street Journal* (March)
            22:16.
O'Steen, D.N.
    1995   Welfare 'reforms' pose threat to unborn babies. *National Right to Life News* (February
            22):1 ff.
Petersen, A.
    1988   Adolescent development. *Annual Review of Psychology* 39:583-607.
Pittman, K., and C. Govan
    1986   *Model Programs: Preventing Adolescent Pregnancy and Building Youth Self-Sufficiency.*
            Washington, D.C.: Children's Defense Fund.
Plotnick, R.
    1993   Welfare and Out-of-Wedlock Childbearing: Evidence from the 1980s. *Journal of Mar-
            riage and the Family* 52:735-746.
Richard, Bishop John
    1997   The factors of genuine welfare reform. *Origins* 24(34):564-566.
Silver, N.
    1965   Births, marriages, and business cycles in the United States. *Journal of Political Economy*
            73:237-255.
Singh, S.
    1986   Adolescent pregnancy in the United States: An interstate analysis. *Family Planning
            Perspectives* 18(5):210-220.
Trussell, J., J. Menken, B.L. Lindheim, and B. Vaughan
    1980   The impact of restricting medicaid financing for abortion. *Family Planning Perspectives*
            12(3):120-130.
U.S. Congress, Committee on Ways and Means
    1996   Summary of the Welfare Reforms Made by Public Law 104-193: The Personal Responsi-
            bility and Work Opportunity Act and Associated Legislation. WMCP 104-15, Washing-
            ton, D.C., November 6.
U.S. Department of Health and Human Services
    1995   Report to Congress on Out-of-Wedlock Childbearing. DHHS Pub. No. (PHS) 95-1257.
            Hyattsville, Md.
Ventura, S., J. Taffel, W. Mosher, J. Wilson, and S. Henshaw
    1995   Trends in pregnancies and pregnancy rates: Estimates for the United States, 1980-92.
            Monthly Vital Statistics Report 43(11, Suppl.) Hyattsville, Md.: National Center for Health
            Statistics.
Willis, R.J.
    1995   A Theory of Out-of-Wedlock Childbearing. Presented at The Symposium on the Eco-
            nomic Analysis of Social Behavior Convened by the Fraser Institute on the Occasion of
            Gary Becker's 65th Birthday, Chicago.
Zabin, L. Schwab, and S. Clark, Jr.
    1981   Why they delay: A study of teenage family planning clinic patients. *Family Planning
            Perspectives* 13(5):205-207, 211-217.
Zelnik, M., and F. Shah
    1983   First intercourse among young Americans. *Family Planning Perspectives* 15(2):64-70.
Zelnik, M., and K. Ford
    1981   *Sex and Pregnancy in Adolescence.* Beverly Hills, Calif.: Sage Publications.

6

Changing Family Formation Behavior Through Welfare Reform

Rebecca Maynard, Elisabeth Boehnen, Tom Corbett, and Gary Sandefur, with Jane Mosley

Aid to Families with Dependent Children (AFDC), the signature program of federal welfare policy and the traditional focal point of welfare reform discussions, was replaced by Temporary Assistance for Needy Families (TANF) when Congress passed and President Clinton signed the Personal Responsibility and Work Opportunity Reconciliation Act (hereafter PRWORA) on August 22, 1996. Among other things, this legislation ends entitlement to program benefits and devolves program authority to the states in the form of block grants or fixed federal fiscal contributions. PRWORA sets forth four principal goals: (1) to provide assistance to needy families so that children may be cared for in their own homes; (2) to end the dependency of needy parents on government support by promoting job preparation, employment, and marriage; (3) to prevent and reduce the incidence of out-of-wedlock and teen pregnancies and births and to establish annual numerical goals for preventing and reducing the incidence of these pregnancies; and (4) to encourage the formation and maintenance of two-parent families (U.S. House of Representatives, 1996b).

The goals of PRWORA mirror those of many state welfare reform demonstrations that were initiated under what were termed Section 1115 waivers of federal welfare policies.[1] By the mid-1990s, states were proposing sweeping and dramatic changes in their AFDC programs, with strong encouragement from the

---

[1]Section 1115 of the Social Security Act, added in 1962, authorized research and experimentation with federal welfare policies. In the 1980s and 1990s, Section 1115 became the means by which states endeavored to initiate welfare reforms involving departures from requirements or principles of federal law.

Clinton administration. PRWORA was seen as another logical step toward the devolution of welfare policy authority from Washington. Indeed, many states that have submitted new welfare reform plans under PRWORA propose to continue the programs and policies they initiated with these waivers.

Whether PRWORA actually results in greater autonomy and flexibility at the state and local levels remains to be seen. It may actually diminish local flexibility in at least two ways. First, it imposes a whole set of expectations and mandates on states, including time limits on federal benefits, restrictions on federal benefits for teen parents, and penalties if states do not achieve enhanced work objectives for recipients. Second, PRWORA increases the fiscal risk of innovation on the part of states by making states responsible for all expenditures above a *fixed* federal contribution. In effect, this increases the marginal price to states of investing in disadvantaged families with children, thereby discouraging states from investing in areas with uncertain returns.

There are important concerns about how states will respond to these policy changes. With the increase in fiscal risks associated with state and local policy, do states have sufficient research evidence from the reforms begun under Section 1115 waiver demonstrations to assume additional responsibility for the design and operation of welfare policy? As described in more detail below, despite the extent of policy innovation and related evaluations over the past decade, we have but modest hard evidence to guide states in many of the important decisions they face as they assume the lead role in providing a social safety net for their poor.

The nature of the waiver demonstration programs changed over the years. As the number of demonstrations expanded, the focus of reform initiatives also shifted. The early waiver reforms were directed primarily at enhancing the labor supply of AFDC adult caretakers through work-related policies and programs. More recently, other recipient behaviors have emerged as the focus of attention, including personal decisions about marriage and cohabitation, decisions affecting family stability (for example, divorce and other family composition changes), fertility decisions, and the quality of parenting. Reform activity increasingly was directed toward what were termed "strategies to promote responsible behavior"—in effect, a new strain of social engineering using welfare policies and rules to encourage socially desirable behaviors.

In theory, then, the explosion of waiver-based demonstrations, accompanied by federally mandated rigorous evaluations, promised a wealth of information by which states might make decisions in a postfederal world. This chapter examines those state waiver demonstrations that were designed specifically to influence fertility, family formation, and family maintenance behaviors. It seeks to identify what useful lessons were generated to guide states in their design of welfare programs under TANF. We then reflect on how one might better capitalize on the opportunities for knowledge development presented to us by the massive natural experiment that encompasses both the state welfare reform demonstrations of recent years and those reforms now being implemented under PRWORA.

MOTIVATION FOR REFORM

The recent welfare reform debate that led to the shift from AFDC to TANF was framed by several premises. First, it was widely accepted that AFDC was seriously flawed and required radical repair. Both welfare dependency and child poverty had reached record levels and AFDC was regarded by many state and federal officials as worsening these problems. AFDC caseloads exceeded the 5 million mark in 1994 for the first time, an increase of almost one-third in 5 years. Meanwhile, child poverty rates also increased from 19.6 percent in 1989 to 21.8 percent in 1994.[2]

Second, it was assumed that the era of "solutions from the center" was over and that the future of welfare innovation should and would derive largely from state and local initiatives. Public officials at all levels, as well as the public itself, argued for devolution of authority over welfare policy from the federal government to state and local governments, which presumably could craft solutions sensitive to the particular needs of the client population and in accord with local conditions and labor markets.

Third, there was growing acceptance that reforms should redirect the goals of welfare policy from fairly straightforward objectives, such as reducing income poverty or increasing the labor market participation of adults in welfare families, toward more complex objectives involving fundamental changes in individual and community behaviors. This change in attitude was affected, in part, by the observations that 89 percent of children on AFDC lived in households with no father present; that the out-of-wedlock birth rate more than tripled after 1960; and that half of children in never-married households and over three-fourths of children born to teenage mothers ended up on welfare. Finally, it has been assumed that states are the ideal laboratories of reform and, through experimentation, will promote both more effective welfare policies and improved knowledge about effective design, implementation, and management of these policies.

Arguably, however, the dominant motivation for reform was the growing perception that welfare, especially AFDC, promoted irresponsible and/or self-destructive behaviors. Historically, welfare has embodied work disincentives, issuing the largest benefits to those who do not work and reducing benefits as earnings rise, sometimes drastically, among those recipients who do work. The result has been marginal tax rates, "notch" effects, and penalties for savings that are greater than those imposed on other income classes. A second argument was that welfare discourages marriage by making it easier for single-parent families than for two-parent families to receive benefits and by treating earnings among single-parent families more generously in calculating welfare benefits. A third

---

[2]Since 1994 there has been a decline in both national AFDC caseloads and child poverty. At the time the welfare reform debate was fully engaged, however, it appeared we had the worst of possible worlds—worsening welfare dependency and rising rates of child poverty (U.S. House of Representatives, 1996b).

notion is that welfare lowers the cost of childbearing among poor women and thus may encourage more childbearing among welfare recipients and teenagers than otherwise would be the case.[3] Finally it is argued that welfare creates incentives for noncustodial parents not to report their child support payments or to avoid their child support responsibilities, since all but a modest amount of child support payments were used to offset AFDC benefits rather than to increase support of the children.

Policy makers and analysts began focusing on incentive issues in the 1960s, when they set up the various negative income tax experiments. However, it was not until the waiver authority vested in the Secretary of the federal Department of Health and Human Services (DHHS) was liberalized in the 1980s that states began to explore, on a large scale and systematically, alternatives for responding to these issues. Table 6-1 classifies waivers into several major types. As the last column of Table 6-1 shows, by August 1996, 42 states had applied for one or more waivers of federal welfare regulations and the federal government had approved 452 separate state waivers of welfare policies. Column 1 of Table 6-1 shows that 33 states had received waivers of 46 provisions related to the eligibility criteria for unemployed parents. As we move across the top of the table, we see that 40 states had waivers that changed more than 150 provisions related to ongoing program participation requirements. Thirty-seven states had waivers changing 142 provisions related to benefits and services. And 37 states had waivers changing 107 provisions related to the treatment of earnings and assets in the calculation of benefits.

As the pace of waiver requests increased in the 1990s, so too did the complexity of the proposed policy changes. Many of the more recent waiver requests reflected substantial "borrowing" of ideas from other states and jurisdictions and "bundling" of policy changes to form complex and sometimes radically different welfare policies. Over time, state reforms became increasingly ambitious and were more likely to encompass multiple goals: promoting labor supply, encouraging family formation and stability, encouraging school attendance, mandating immunization of children, altering fertility decisions, and promoting improved parenting. So too, more reforms focused on target populations other than the adult caretaker—children in the assistance group, minor teenage parents receiving assistance, immigrant beneficiaries, and nonresident fathers of recipient children. Many reforms included multiple strategies for achieving these various goals: testing a variety of behavioral incentives for various household members and, in some cases, nonresident parents; testing incentives for employers to hire recipients; and testing incentives designed to alter welfare agency cultures. There

---

[3]Some have even argued that many teens may have babies just to get welfare and be able to set up independent homes. So too, some have argued that many welfare mothers have additional children in order to increase their grants. The research base fails to support these claims (see further discussion below).

TABLE 6-1   Number of Waivers of Federal Welfare Policies as of August 1996, by Type and State

	Number of Different Waiver Provisions Related To				
	Eligibility for Benefits	Ongoing Welfare Participation Requirements	Benefits and Services	Income and Asset Disregards	Total
States with Provision	33	40	37	37	42
Total Provisions	46	157	142	107	452
Arizona	1	1	3	1	6
Arkansas	0	1	1	0	2
California	1	2	8	5	16
Colorado	0	1	1	2	4
Connecticut	2	1	6	3	12
Delaware	1	5	5	3	14
Florida	2	3	4	5	14
Georgia	1	3	4	2	10
Hawaii	2	0	1	0	3
Illinois	0	6	2	2	10
Indiana	2	5	4	3	14
Iowa	0	5	7	3	15
Kansas	3	4	3	4	14
Louisiana	0	3	1	0	4
Maine	0	5	3	1	9
Maryland	1	7	5	4	17
Massachusetts	1	6	5	3	15
Michigan	1	5	0	3	9
Minnesota	2	1	2	3	8
Mississippi	1	3	5	1	10
Missouri	1	4	2	4	11
Montana	2	3	3	3	11
Nebraska	1	3	4	4	14
New Hampshire	2	5	3	4	14
New York	0	3	2	0	5
North Carolina	1	6	4	2	13
North Dakota	1	1	0	0	2
Ohio	1	5	5	3	14
Oklahoma	1	2	4	1	8
Oregon	2	3	4	3	12
Pennsylvania	2	9	6	6	23
South Carolina	1	9	5	7	22
South Dakota	1	1	1	1	4
Tennessee	1	7	4	5	17
Texas	1	7	3	2	13
Utah	2	2	2	2	8
Vermont	1	1	2	1	5
Virginia	1	7	5	2	15
Washington	0	2	1	3	6
West Virginia	1		4	2	7
Wisconsin	2	7	6	3	18
Wyoming	0	3	2	1	6

SOURCES: U.S. Department of Health and Human Services, Administration for Children and Families (various years). See also U.S. Department of Health and Human Services (1997).

also was substantial variation in the focus of the various state welfare demonstrations and in the particulars of the individual initiatives.[4]

Some common themes do, however, appear in the waivers. As Table 6-2 shows, the most common waiver provisions of the majority of approved demonstrations fall within four categories of change: (1) eligibility of two-parent families, 34 states; (2) welfare participation requirements, 40 states; (3) benefits and services, 37 states; and (4) income and assets disregards, 37 states.

With regard to the eligibility of two-parent families for benefits, 34 states eliminated the 100-hour work rule (discussed below) and 25 states expanded eligibility for unemployed parents; 40 states required ongoing work participation of some form, including mandatory participation in work-related activities (36 states) and financial incentives and sanctions imposed depending on work participation (30 states). Many states (37) made changes in their benefit structure and services: 25 states obtained waivers designed explicitly to impose time limits on benefits, while 22 states chose to expand transitional child care and Medicaid programs to ease the financial burden of moving from welfare to work. Waivers were obtained by 21 states to impose family caps on benefits to discourage (or at least not reward) childbearing among welfare recipients. Many states obtained waivers to liberalize their policies regarding the use of income and assets in the calculation of welfare benefits. Some increased the value of an automobile (26) or other assets (23) individuals could own and still receive public assistance, and some increased the amount of earned income that is disregarded in computing benefit amounts (25).

FAMILY STRUCTURE AS THE FOCUS OF REFORM

State waiver demonstrations systematically explored remedies for the perceived adverse behavioral consequences associated with AFDC. Other than improving labor market attachment, nowhere has this search been more vigorous than in the area of family structure. Moreover, while PRWORA changes myriad aspects of the economic and social safety net, the provisions related to family structure have been especially important in the political debate over the reforms. Two specific areas have attracted the greatest public attention in the welfare reform discussions, in large part because of their anticipated links to behavioral consequences that could change the future of poverty and welfare policy—*family caps* (also termed child exclusion provisions) and the *unemployed parent* (UP, or two-parent family) provisions.

Family caps, the policy of not adjusting cash assistance benefits when AFDC recipients have additional children, reflect a relatively new and, to many, radical

---

[4]Considerable variability prevailed in the number and mix of provisions implemented in states (and sometimes within local areas). For instance, although many states requested waivers to make changes in the benefit eligibility rules for two-parent (or unemployed-parent) families, only two of those provisions were present in waivers granted to large numbers of states (see Table 6-2).

TABLE 6-2 Common Provisions of State Welfare Waiver Demonstrations: 1986-August 1996

Provision	Number of States
Eligibility of Two-Parent Families for Benefits	*34*
Elimination of 100-hour work rule	34
Expanded eligibility for unemployed parents	25
Ongoing Welfare Participation Requirements	*40*
Mandatory participation in work-related activities	36
Financial incentives and sanctions	30
Financial sanctions	28
Financial incentives	5
School attendance and/or performance for children and/or teenage parents	25
Children must receive appropriate immunizations and health services	19
Teenage parents must live at home or in supervised settings	17
Recipients must cooperate with child support enforcement	13
Participants must have self-sufficiency plans	13
Changes in Benefits and Services	*37*
Time limits on benefits	25
Expansions in transitional child care and Medicaid	22
Caps on benefits based on initial family size (family caps)	21
Cash-out of food stamp benefits	13
JOBS' services for noncustodial parents	12
Increases in the child support pass-through	10
Changes in Income and Asset Disregards	*37*
Increases in limit on value of an automobile	26
Increases in resource limits	23
Increases in earnings disregard	25
Expansions in disregards for college assistance, work study, or student earnings	13

NOTE: This table includes only provisions found in 10 or more state waivers.
SOURCE: U.S. Department of Health and Human Services, Administration for Children and Families (various years). See also U.S. Department of Health and Human Services (1997).

change in welfare policy. New Jersey was the first state to implement family caps, doing so on an experimental basis in 1992. In contrast, virtually all states had AFDC-UP programs as of July 1990, although UP recipients remained only a small portion of the AFDC caseload. Between 1961, when federal legislation allowed states to offer AFDC to two-parent families, and 1988, when the Family Support Act mandated that all states offer AFDC coverage to poor, two-parent families in which one worker had a recent work history, only about half of the states voluntarily enacted AFDC-UP programs. Less than 10 percent of the total AFDC caseload represented UP families. Recent reforms related to family caps and the unemployed parent policies share programmatic goals with PRWORA and are of special interest to states as they design and implement their TANF reforms.[5]

Family Cap Rules

Generally the family cap provisions under the waivers in effect at the time PRWORA was passed contained the stipulation that an AFDC family would not receive additional cash assistance for those children born while the family was receiving AFDC benefits. Under PRWORA, states have the option of imposing family caps, but are not required to do so.

By the time PRWORA passed, 21 states had obtained federally approved waivers containing family cap provisions (Table 6-3). States were given the flexibility to modify existing waiver terms and conditions under PRWORA, though many chose not to do so, at least in the short run.

The New Jersey family cap, implemented in 1992 as a provision of the state's Family Development Program, has been the most widely publicized such provision and became somewhat of a model for other states. Under it, AFDC families received no assistance for a child born more than 10 months after AFDC application (there also was a 10-month grace period for current recipients), with three exceptions: (1) the first child of a minor already included in an AFDC grant; (2) families who left AFDC due to earnings, remained employed for 90 days, then terminated employment for good cause; and (3) families who left AFDC for any reason and remained off welfare for 12 consecutive months. New Jersey also offered an additional earned income disregard for employed mothers with infants who are subject to the cap, allowing them to keep more of their earnings.

Family cap initiatives were characterized by two features during the pre-PRWORA period. First, as in New Jersey, the "typical" family cap provision was not initiated as a stand-alone provision, but was embedded within larger, more complex welfare reform initiatives.[6] Seventeen of the twenty-one states with family caps overlap with states that obtained waivers altering their two-parent family provisions (see further below). Second, there existed considerable varia-

---

[5]There are additional waiver provisions and goals in PRWORA that may also have an affect on family formation (such as requiring minor parents to live with an adult). However, this chapter limits its focus to the family cap and the two-parent family provisions.

[6]For example, the New Jersey Family Development Program includes expanded employment, education, and training services; provisions reducing the marriage penalties; and modifications to earnings disregards. The Virginia Independence Program (VIP) contains a family cap provision as well as provisions for time limits, earnings subsidies, modifications to income disregards, changes in JOBS sanctions and exemptions, and links between benefits and school attendance. North Carolina's Work First demonstration includes a family cap as well as benefit time limits, modifications to income disregards, elimination of the 100-hour rule, and changes in JOBS sanctions and exemptions (U.S. Department of Health and Human Services, various dates, and U.S. Department of Health and Human Services, 1997).

TABLE 6-3 Key Features of Family Cap Provisions of State Waiver Demonstrations: 1986–August 1996

State and Program Name	Date Approved	Date Implemented	Statewide	Time Limit Exclusion (months)
Number of states with provision	21	—	19	20
AZ—(EMPOWER) Employing and Moving People Off Welfare and Encouraging Responsibility	5/95	11/95	X	10
AR—AFDC-M	4/94	7/94		10
CA—(WPDP) Work Pays Demonstration Project	3/94	4/94	X	10
(CWPDP-M) Work Pays Demonstraton Project Modified	8/96	8/96	X	24
CT—Reach Jobs 1st	12/95	12/95	X	10
DE—BETTER CHANCE	5/95	10/95	X	10
FL—Family Responsibility Act	6/96	6/96[d]	X	10
GA—Personal Accountability and Responsibility Act	11/93	1/94	X	24
IL—Work and Responsibility	9/95	9/95[d]	X	10
IN—IMPACT	12/94	5/95	X	10
IMPACT—M	8/96	8/96[d]	X	
KS—Actively Creating Tomorrow	8/96	8/96	X	10
MD—Family Investment Program	8/95	10/95	X	10
MA—Transitional AFDC Program (Welfare Reform '95)	8/95	11/95	X	10
MS—New Direction —Modifications	8/95	11/95	X	10

Liberalized Treatment of Earnings and Child Support	Benefits Vary by Number of Children[a]	Exemptions			
		Incest/Rape	Birth to Minor[b]	Residence Requirement[c]	Conceived During Period of No Benefits
8	3	14	8	5	6
X		X			X
		X	X		
X		X			
	X	X	X	X	X
X		X	X	X	X
X	X				
		X			
		X	X	X	X
		X			
X					
		X			

TABLE 6-3 Continued

State and Program Name	Date Approved	Date Implemented	Statewide	Time Limit Exclusion (months)
NE—Welfare Reform Demonstration Project	2/95	10/95	X	10
NJ—Family Development Program	7/92	10/92	X	10
NC—WORK First	2/96	2/96[d]	X	10
OK—Mutual Agreement	3/95	3/95[d]		
SC—Family Independence Program (FIP)	3/96	3/96[d]	X	10
TN—Families First	7/96	7/96[d]	X	10
VA—Virginia Independence Program (VIP)	7/95	7/95	X	10
WI—Parental And Family Act (PFR)[e]	4/92	7/94		10
Work Not Welfare	11/93	1/95		10
AFDC Benefit Cap Demonstration Project (ABC)[f]	6/94	11/96	X	10

NOTE: Twenty-one states have implemented a total of 25 demonstrations that include a family cap provision. In addition, three states, New Hampshire, Texas, and Wyoming require parents to participate in JOBS activities sooner after giving birth to a child conceived while on cash assistance, but continue to increase the cash grant (U.S. Department of Health and Human Services, 1997: Table III).

[a]Percentage of benefits changes as number of children increases.

[b]These provisions exempt first-born minors already receiving benefits.

Liberalized Treatment of Earnings and Child Support	Benefits Vary by Number of Children[a]	Exemptions			Conceived During Period of No Benefits
		Incest/Rape	Birth to Minor[b]	Residence Requirement[c]	
X		X	X	X	
X			X		X
		X			
		X			
		X	X		
X					
	X				
		X			X
		X	X	X	

[c]These provisions exempt children not living with the parent.
[d]Actual implementation date may be different or program might not have been implemented. Kansas and Oklahoma appear not to have implemented their family cap policies at all (U. S. Department of Health and Human Services, 1997: Table III).
[e]This provision applies only to specific population groups, designated by age.
[f]Family cap is a single waiver and not part of the larger waiver request.
SOURCE: U.S. Department of Health and Human Services, Administration for Children and Families (various years).

tion in the design and execution of the provisions. Although most states excluded from the cap children born within 10 months of application, two states (California and Illinois) had 24-month exclusions. Most exempted children who were conceived through incest or rape. Eight states (Arkansas, Connecticut, Delaware, Indiana, Nebraska, New Jersey, Tennessee, and Wisconsin) exempted the first-born children of minors who were already receiving benefits as a child of a welfare recipient. Six states (Arizona, Connecticut, Delaware, Indiana, New Jersey, and Wisconsin) exempted children conceived while the parent was not receiving benefits.

There were also variations by the recipient's age and the birth order of the children. The Kansas waiver permitted a second child to receive benefits; the third child received 50 percent of the benefits normally allotted for an additional dependent; and subsequent children received no benefits. Wisconsin's Parental and Family Responsibility Initiative (which included only recipients under the age of 20 at the beginning of the program) provided 50 percent of the otherwise available benefits for a second child, and no benefits for a third or subsequent child (Center for Law and Social Policy, 1995).

Some states accompanied the family cap provisions with exemptions that changed the treatment of family earnings for women with infants and/or women who received child support. For example, Arizona, Massachusetts, and New Jersey liberalized their treatment of earnings for women with infants. California, Virginia, and Florida exempted child support from countable income, while Nebraska and Delaware discounted child support in computing countable income.

Unemployed Parent Rules

Thirty-three states and the District of Columbia obtained waivers to eliminate some or all of the eligibility restrictions on two-parent families (Table 6-4). Under the AFDC-UP program, three primary provisions restricted the benefit eligibility of two-parent families. Under *the 100-hour rule*, an AFDC-UP family lost eligibility if the principal wage earner was employed for 100 hours or more a month, even if the family's wages from employment were so low that the family would still be eligible for AFDC. Under *the work history requirement*, an AFDC-UP family had to demonstrate a "connection to the work force" in one of two ways—the principal wage earner must have received or been eligible for unemployment compensation benefits or must have had $50 or more of earnings in at least 6 of 13 quarters ending within a year before applying for AFDC. Under *the 30-day waiting period requirement*, an AFDC-UP family could not receive aid for 30 days after the principal wage earner became unemployed (Center for Law and Social Policy, 1995).

All of the states (including the District of Columbia) with waivers related to the unemployed parent provisions eliminated the 100-hour rule, and 25 states requested, and most received, waivers eliminating both the 100-hour rule and the

TABLE 6-4 Key Two-Parent Provisions of State Waiver Demonstrations: 1986-August 1996

State and Program Name	Date Approved	Date Implemented	Statewide	Rules Eliminated		
				100-Hour Work Limit	Work History	30-Day Waiting Period
Number of states with provision			25	34	25	18
AL Avenues to Self Sufficiency Through Employment and Training (ASSETS)	10/89	5/90		X	X	
AZ Employing and Moving People Off Welfare and Encouraging Responsibility Program (EMPOWER)	5/95	11/95	X	X		
CA Assistance Payment Demonstration Project (APDP)	10/92	10/92	X	X		
Work Pays Demonstration Project (WPDP)	3/94	4/94	X	X		
CT Reach for Jobs First	12/95	1/96	X	X	X	X
DE Better Chance	5/95	10/95	X	X	X	X
DC Project on Work Employment and Responsibility (POWER)	8/96	8/96[a]	X	X		
FL Family Transition Program (FTP)	1/94	2/94		X	X	X
Family Transition Program—Expansion (FTP-M)	9/95	9/95	X	X	X	X
HI Pursuit of New Opportunities	8/96	10/96	X	X	X	X
IL Fresh Start	8/93	11/93	X	X	X	X

TABLE 6-4 Continued

State and Program Name	Date Approved	Date Implemented	Statewide	Rules Eliminated		
				100-Hour Work Limit	Work History	30-Day Waiting Period
IN Impacting Families Welfare Reform Demonstration Project (IMPACT)	12/94	5/95	X	X		
IA Family Investment Program (FIP)	8/93	10/93	X	X	X	
KS Actively Creating Tomorrow	8/96	9/96	X	X	X	X
MD Family Investment Program	8/95	10/95	X	X	X	X
Family Investment Program—Amendments	8/96	8/96	X	X	X	X
MA Welfare Reform	8/95	11/95	X	X		
MI To Strengthen Michigan's Families (TSMF)	8/92	11/92	X	X	X	
To Strengthen Michigan's Families—M (TSMF-M)	8/94	10/94	X	X	X	
MN Family Investment Program (FIP)	3/94	4/94	X	X	X	X
Barrier Removal	8/96	10/96	X	X	X	X
MS New Direction Program	12/94	11/95	X	X	X	X
MO Twenty-First Century	1/93	1/93[a]		X		
Missouri Families Mutual Responsibility Plan-I (MFMRP-1)	4/95	6/95	X	X	X	
MT Families Achieving Independence in Montana (FAIM)	4/95	2/96	X	X	X	X
NE Welfare Reform Demonstration Project	2/95	10/95	X	X	X	X

State	Program	Date	Date[a]				
NY	Jobs First	10/94	10/94[a]		X	X	X
NC	Work First	3/96	3/96[a]		X	X	X
ND	Training, Education, Employment and Management Program (TEEM)	9/95	7/96		X		
OH	Communities of Opportunity	3/95	1/96		X		
	Ohio First	3/96	6/96	X	X	X	X
OK	Mutual Agreement: A Plan for Success (MAAPS)	3/95	3/95[a]		X		
OR	Oregon Option	3/96	3/96[a]	X	X	X	
PA	Pathways	11/94	11/94[a]		X	X	X
SC	Family Independence Act	5/96	6/96	X	X	X	X
TN	Families First	7/96	9/96	X	X	X	X
TX	Achieving Change for Texans	3/96	7/96	X	X	X	
UT	Single Parent Employment Demonstration Project-Modified (SPEDP-M)	8/95	8/95		X		
VT	Welfare Restructuring Project	7/94	9/94	X	X	X	X
WA	Success Through Employment Program	10/95	7/96	X	X	X	
WI	Parental and Family Responsibility Act (PFR)	4/92	7/94	X	X	X	X
	Work Not Welfare (WNW)	11/93	1/95	X	X		
	Pay for Performance (PFP)	8/95	3/96	X	X		

NOTES: Thirty-three states plus the District of Columbia have implemented a total of 43 two-parent family demonstrations.

[a]Actual implementation date may be different or program might not have been implemented.

SOURCES: U.S. Department of Health and Human Services, Administration for Children and Families (various years). See also U.S. Department of Health and Human Services (1997).

work history requirements. Eighteen states eliminated all three rules. Eliminating these rules allowed working fathers to remain with their families and report their actual hours of work without loss of benefits to the families.

As with the family cap rules, some states obtained multiple waivers with similar provisions. For example, Wisconsin obtained three sets of waivers containing provisions dealing with two-parent families, all with somewhat different combinations of rules. Both its Work Not Welfare and Pay for Performance demonstrations eliminated only the 100-hour rule along with other welfare policy changes (time limits in the former case and changes in work requirements and supports in the latter). The Parental and Family Responsibility Initiative, in contrast, eliminated all three of the unemployed parent rules.

The majority of states simply eliminated the three specific rules, but a few made more complex policy changes. Florida's Family Transition Program eliminated all three rules, but also provided case-by-case exceptions to the 6-month time limit, during which the family's principal wage earner was supposed to complete an employability plan. Missouri's demonstration, the Missouri Families—Mutual Responsibility Plan, Phase I, eliminated the 100-hour rule and work history requirements only for families in which both parents were under 21 years of age. Hawaii's Families Are Better Together based its deprivation criteria on need rather than the unemployment of a parent and eliminated the 100-hour and 30-day rules and the work history requirements.

PERSPECTIVES ON THE REFORMS

Economic and social theories offer considerable support for these particular welfare reform policies, though empirical support is more suggestive than conclusive. According to these theories, individuals modify their behaviors in response to economic incentives and to social and cultural norms. The various reform initiatives impinge upon both incentives and norms in ways that lead social theorists to predict that reforms targeted at fertility and family structure may achieve at least some success.

Family Caps

The economic arguments that support instituting family caps as a means of reducing fertility among welfare recipients are quite clear. Relative to current policy, welfare recipients who bear additional children will be poorer. In economic terms, recipients will face a higher net economic cost of bearing additional children than under the former welfare policy—a cost equal to the benefit increments for additional children that were paid under the former policy. Economic theory predicts that, ceteris paribus, increasing the net cost of childbearing will encourage some to forgo additional childbearing. An extension of this reasoning would also predict that, at the margin, some women who are deciding whether to have a child at all and become dependent on welfare might postpone childbearing until they are able to support the child themselves. But, insofar as the caps apply to second and later children, childless women may substantially discount the nominal "cost" of the new policy in their current childbearing decisions.

In practice, it seems unlikely that the change in economic incentives associated with family caps will induce sizable changes in fertility patterns, for two reasons. First, the policy-induced changes in income associated with the future fertility decisions of welfare recipients tend to be relatively small—both in proportion to the cost of childrearing and in absolute terms.[7] Their small absolute size is partly a function of earlier benefit-increment policies, under which the monthly increase in benefits for additional children most often was quite nominal. Moreover, increases in Food Stamp and housing benefits typically will offset portions of the welfare benefit reduction, and Medicaid benefits are unaffected by family caps.

Second, economic factors are, at best, weakly related to fertility decisions, in large part, we suspect, because of strong mediating influences of noneconomic factors. Nationally, family sizes tend to be inversely correlated with income. Moreover, three-fourths of pregnancies to women who have incomes below the poverty line are unintended, as are 88 percent of the pregnancies to women who have never been married (Brown and Eisenberg, 1995). Twenty-eight percent of births among never-married women, who are heavily represented among welfare recipients, are the result of unintended pregnancies (Brown and Eisenberg, 1995; Kost and Forrest, 1995). This is consistent with the fact that over 70 percent of low-income women who report not wanting to become pregnant also report using some form of contraception.[8]

Advocates of family caps do not rely solely on the expectation of behavioral responses to support their views. The policy discussions about family caps also often invoke principles and values in addition to social and economic theories and research. For example, many of the arguments of legislators in New Jersey and Wisconsin for both the family caps and the suspension of the 100-hour rule were value based. It seemed to matter less that marriage rates rose and divorce and fertility rates fell as a result of the policy changes than it did that everyone understood that society favors marriage and is not willing to reward those having additional children when they cannot adequately support the ones they have already.

---

[7]Even prior to family caps, AFDC recipients received widely different benefit increments for individual children, ranging from $24 to $247 per child, depending on the state of residence and family size and structure (U.S. House of Representatives, 1993).

[8]Nearly 80 percent of first-time teen parents on welfare report using some form of contraception; nearly all report not wanting more children; yet over a 30-month follow-up period, over two-thirds became pregnant again, and half gave birth to a second child (Maynard and Rangarajan, 1994).

Unemployed Parent Provisions

Altering the unemployed parent provisions affects four groups of welfare recipients: (1) those with spouses working in low-wage jobs; (2) those living with spouses who are not working but who could work in low-wage jobs; (3) those with nonresident partners working in low-wage jobs for more than 100 hours per month; and (4) those at the margin of a marital decision. It also could affect those nonrecipients who, on moral or other grounds, have decided to marry and not participate in welfare, even though their spouses have limited earnings potential.

Eliminating the 100-hour rule means that, at the margin, some wage earners in two-parent families may increase their work effort beyond their current level, thereby increasing family welfare at the same time that reliance on public assistance declines. Some unemployed spouses of welfare recipients may be enticed to seek employment for similar reasons and with similar results. Some couples who previously bypassed marriage or divorced to preserve their welfare eligibility may elect to get or stay married, because the financial loss from doing so is diminished. On the other hand, some nonrecipients could be attracted to welfare as a result of the policy change, because welfare would offer an income supplement without jeopardizing the marriage option.

Suspension of the 100-hour rule sends two quite clear messages to recipients and nonrecipients: (1) work is valued and (2) so is marriage. Eliminating the "work test" and "waiting periods" is expected to have similar, though somewhat more complicated, effects.

EMPIRICAL EVIDENCE FROM PRIOR RESEARCH

The research basis for the welfare waiver demonstrations and the reform provisions under PRWORA is extremely limited, consisting of studies of family structure and of the determinants of fertility behavior. Many of these studies are discussed in chapters by Klerman and Moffitt that appear elsewhere in this volume. As noted below, more direct tests of the efficacy of the family cap and unemployed parent rules will be forthcoming from the various demonstrations and TANF programs over the next few years. There also is some research from prior welfare reform demonstrations, particularly those that targeted the AFDC-UP population and a handful of demonstration programs for teenage parents that are designed, in part, to modify fertility behavior.

Fertility Decisions

The decision making that leads to family formation and expansion is very complex. Major differences in fertility rates are associated with income class, cultural identity, age, and marital status. These relationships have been changing rapidly over time. Fertility rates are higher among low-income families than among middle- and higher-income families; they are higher among blacks and Hispanics than among whites and Asians; the mean age of first birth has risen to about 23 and the variance has been increasing; and roughly 30 percent of all births are out-of-wedlock, but vastly higher proportions of poor women and teenagers are unmarried when they give birth (U.S. Department of Health and Human Services, 1995).

Several studies that have examined the welfare incentives for childbearing have found a slight association between AFDC and increases in childbearing, but this association is not characteristic of all recipients (Plotnick, 1990; Lundberg and Plotnick, 1990; Gottschalk, 1990, 1992; Moffitt, 1992; Haveman and Wolfe, 1994; Plotnick and Lundberg, 1995). In fact, in 1995 Moffitt argued that we do not know enough to characterize these findings as evidence of an actual *effect* of AFDC on childbearing (Moffitt, 1995; but see Moffitt, Chapter 4, in this volume). Moreover, the research suggests that impacts on fertility decisions may have been mediated by funding for family planning.

Federal support for family planning and reproductive health issues offers real returns to taxpayers from a variety of sources, most notably lower rates of infant and neonatal death, lower fertility rates among low-income women who are at high risk of tightly spaced births, and fewer low-birthweight babies (Meier and McFarlane, 1994). Although there is limited evidence that these funds reduce teenage pregnancy rates (Haveman et al. 1997), they clearly reduce teenage birth rates through increasing abortions (Olsen and Weed, 1986; Moore et al., 1994).

The behavioral research on the effects of welfare on fertility is complemented by a limited body of demonstration research that tests various changes in welfare and social service policies designed to reduce fertility among teenage parents already on welfare or at high risk of going onto welfare. The eight such programs with strong evaluations represent four different strategies for addressing the needs of teenage parents, albeit with overlapping features: (1) employment and training programs serving significant numbers of teenage parents (Job Corps and Job Start); (2) comprehensive education and training programs targeted specifically at teen parents (New Chance and Project Redirection); (3) welfare-based education and employment programs that mandate education and job preparation services for teenage parent welfare recipients (Ohio Learnfare and the Teenage Parent Welfare Demonstration); and (4) health-focused programs targeted at first-time parents, many or all of whom are teenagers (the Teenage Parent Health Care Program and the Elmira Nurse Home Visiting program). The table in the appendix to this chapter provides references for the evaluations of these programs.

These demonstrations are relevant insofar as roughly half of all welfare recipients are current or former teenage parents, and the rates of repeat pregnancies and births are especially high among this group (Jacobson and Maynard,

1995). Recognizing that subsequent pregnancies and births would interfere with the central education and employment goals of these programs, all of the demonstration programs except the two youth employment programs devoted considerable resources to helping the young mothers control their fertility, offering family planning services and counseling as part of the basic intervention.

Still, repeat pregnancy rates were high—above 50 percent—in all programs except the teenage parent health care program (28 percent over 18 months). Only the two health-focused programs were successful in reducing the repeat pregnancy rates (Table 6-5). The Teenage Parent Health Care Demonstration, which involved home visitor services by trained social workers, reduced the repeat

TABLE 6-5   Impacts of Welfare-Related Demonstrations on Fertility Behavior of Teenage Parents

Program	Outcome Measure		
	Pregnancies	Abortions	Births
Estimated Program Impact (percent of control/comparison group mean)			
Job Start	12.7[a]	n.a.	17.1[a]
New Chance	7.5[b]	34.2[a]	8.4
Project Redirection	6.9	−41.5[b]	20.0[a]
Ohio Learnfare	n.a.	n.a.	4.3
Teen Parent Welfare Demonstration	0.1	−16.9	6.6[b]
Teen Parent Health Care	−57.1[a]	n.a.	n.a.
Elmira Nurse Home Visiting	−43.1[a]	n.a.	n.a.
Participant group mean			
Job Start	76.1%	n.a.	67.8%
New Chance	57.0%	14.9%	28.4%
Project Redirection	3.3[c]	0.3[c]	2.4[c]
Ohio Learnfare	n.a.	n.a.	26.7%
Teenage Parent Welfare Demonstration	1.0[c]	0.16[c]	0.64[c]
Teen Parent Health Care	28.0%	n.a.	n.a.
Elmira Nurse Home Visiting	0.7[c]	n.a.	n.a.

NOTE: Data for the Job Start evaluation pertain to 4 years after sample enrollment; for Job Corps 4 years after enrollment; for New Chance 18 months after enrollment; for Project Redirection 5 years after enrollment; for Ohio Learnfare 3 years following enrollment; for the Teenage Parent Welfare Demonstration 2 years after enrollment; for the Teen Parent Health Care Demonstration 18 months after enrollment; and for the Elmira Nurse Home Visiting Demonstration, 46 months after enrollment. n.a. = not available
[a]Significant at the 10% level.
[b]Significant at the 5% level.
[c]Mean number of occurrences.
SOURCE: Sources of data presented in this table are detailed in the appendix to this chapter.

pregnancy rate by an estimated 57 percent, and the Elmira Home Visiting Demonstration reduced the rate by 43 percent.

Pregnancy rates increased significantly among participants in both the Job Start and the New Chance demonstrations (by 13 percent and 8 percent respectively). One can only speculate as to why these programs would increase pregnancy rates. However, one possible explanation includes their role in increasing opportunities for the young women to meet men, their promotion of higher self-esteem, and their facilitation of independent living, while failing to improve contraceptive practices. Among New Chance participants, the abortion rate also increased sufficiently to offset the higher pregnancy rate, whereas in Project Redirection and the Teenage Parent Welfare Demonstrations, the abortion rate declined sufficiently to show increases in the birth rates among program participants, even though the repeat pregnancy rates had not increased significantly. These differential patterns of abortion likely reflect differences in the philosophies of program staff and in access to contraceptive services. The Teenage Parent Welfare Demonstration, for example, had an explicit policy of not making referrals for abortion.

The upcoming evaluation of the Job Opportunities and Basic Skills Training program, which is the employment support program introduced with the Family Support Act of 1988, will include measures of fertility effects. However, none of the intervening evaluations of welfare reforms for adult recipients has measured such effects, in part because fertility control was not a major goal of the interventions. Most of these evaluations relied on limited data collected from state welfare and Unemployment Insurance data systems.

Family Formation, Dissolution, and Single Parenthood

The overwhelming message from this research is that the various welfare reforms are likely to have modest impacts on family formation and fertility (see Chapter 4). In several studies using national databases, researchers have found weak or no relationships between the generosity of welfare benefits and marriage, divorce, and out-of-wedlock childbearing (Ellwood and Bane, 1985; Lundberg and Plotnick, 1990; Haveman and Wolfe, 1994; McLanahan and Sandefur, 1994; Moffitt, 1995; Plotnick and Lundberg, 1995). The effects that were observed are small in relation to the quite dramatic decreases in marriage, increases in divorce, and skyrocketing rates of out-of-wedlock childbearing observed in society (Moffitt, 1992; Brown and Eisenberg, 1995; Lichter, 1995). Given that the research has relied on analysis of time trends and cross-site variation in state-level data, we are cautioned that a "major ambiguity in the conclusion . . . is whether any observed relationship between welfare and nonmarital childbearing is real . . . or reflects the effects of other unmeasured cross-state differences in . . . environments. . . . [W]e are left with only the suggestion of an effect" (Moffitt, 1995:172).

Some researchers have begun to look at these issues with national longitudinal datasets, from different aspects. One study examines whether patterns of childbearing and marriage affect the earnings potential and general economic well-being of families (Brien and Willis, 1997). Finding relatively modest effects, the researchers speculate that one reason is that the current welfare system discourages men from marrying the mothers of their children.

An emerging literature suggests that welfare-dependent mothers, particularly young black mothers, are not especially interested in marrying the fathers of their children or, in most cases, even in pursuing a formal child support order (Polit, 1992; Maynard, 1993; Quint et al., 1994b). Historically, there has been little or no financial gain to formal child support for recipients of public assistance, which accounts for the father's diminished willingness to contribute formal support when under order to make regular payments. Edin and Lein (1997) report that many young unwed mothers receive informal child support from the fathers of their children. In these studies, young women gave various reasons for their lack of interest in marriage, which can be summarized as follows: Men are not reliable sources of economic and emotional support; welfare can at least be relied upon for economic support.

The best available evidence from the research suggests that rule changes may only minimally affect the likelihood that mothers in AFDC-UP families will end up as single parents. The experimental research on family formation and dissolution is limited to that from the negative income tax experiments of the late 1960s and 1970s. The somewhat controversial results from these demonstrations suggest that more generous income support offered under the experiments had, at most, modest impacts on family formation and stability (Cain, 1987; Hannan and Tuma, 1990; Cain and Wissoker, 1990). Using longitudinal state-level data, another study found no evidence that the AFDC-UP program destabilized two-parent families, and found some evidence suggesting that the program may have encouraged family stability (U.S. General Accounting Office, 1992). None of the welfare reform demonstration evaluations of the 1980s focusing specifically on the AFDC population has examined the effects on this set of outcomes, even though many of them included program provisions that, theoretically, could have affected family formation, stability, and fertility decisions. Moreover, none of the early evaluations of demonstrations coming out of the Family Support Act of 1988 focused on the family formation outcomes.[9]

We do know from the many welfare reform demonstrations of the 1980s, as well as from evaluations of many other employment and training programs targeted at disadvantaged young men, that they have modest or no effects on work behavior and earnings. The Job Training Partnership Act programs led to mod-

---

[9]There are ongoing demonstrations of the suspension of the 100-hour rule in California, Utah, and Wisconsin. Each of these projects has serious implementation and evaluation design flaws, as well as poor outcome measures (Birnbaum and Wiseman, 1996).

est, but statistically significant, gains in employment and earnings of disadvantaged men (Bloom et al., 1994). The subsidized employment demonstrations of the 1980s were only modestly successful in getting male AFDC recipients into low-wage jobs, but at high cost (Brock et al., 1993). And the mandatory welfare-to-work programs of the past decade, for example California's welfare reform demonstrations, have led to relatively modest changes in the employment behavior of men (Gueron and Pauly, 1991; Friedlander and Burtless, 1994).

We might infer from the modest changes in employment behavior that these policies have had little to no effect on decisions about family formation and dissolution. However, few of these studies have looked specifically at such outcomes. Two of the evaluations that have addressed them focused on teenage parents and service-oriented interventions rather than financial incentives for working—the Teenage Parent Welfare Demonstration and the New Chance demonstration. In both cases, the programs had no significant impact on family structure over a 2- to 3-year follow-up period (Maynard, 1993; Quint et al., 1994a, 1994b).

PROSPECTIVE FINDINGS FROM THE WAIVER DEMONSTRATIONS

In virtually all cases in which states received Section 1115 waiver authority to explore new welfare policies, they were required to commission rigorous evaluations of their reforms and to monitor their fiscal impacts to ensure that the innovations were cost neutral with respect to federal fiscal liability. In all but a handful of cases, these evaluations have entailed randomly assigning welfare recipients or prospective recipients to the old or new welfare provisions and monitoring their outcomes over several years. In most instances, the studies have been designed principally to assess the efficacy of the new welfare regime, often a package of reforms bundled together, relative to a counterfactual, usually consisting of the remains of the old AFDC program. These studies offered the federal government evidence to enforce the fiscal neutrality provisions required under the 1115 waivers. They also are relevant to individual state deliberations about whether to retain, modify, or abandon their waiver reforms.

The evaluations are much more limited in their ability to enhance our general understanding of the behavioral choices leading to and perpetuating dependency and/or poverty. Seldom were evaluation designs constructed that would isolate the effects of particular reform provisions, contrast alternative reform plans, or disaggregate the importance of particular components to any change in outcomes. The high degree of variation in the specific provisions related to a particular area of reform and the bundling of reforms complicate any such efforts to sort out the causal paths to outcomes (Table 6-6). For instance, only Wisconsin implemented demonstrations of family cap provisions by themselves and, even in Wisconsin, the caps were introduced in many sites as part of larger reforms.

TABLE 6-6 Elements of Reform Bundles: Examples of States with Waivers Including Family Cap Provisions: 1986-August 1996

State and Program Name	Exemptions for	Family Cap Provisions Time Limit Exclusion (months)
Number of states with provision		19
AZ Employing and Moving People Off Welfare and Encouraging Responsibility (EMPOWER)	Rape or incest/conceived when not on welfare	10
AR AFDC-M	Rape or incest/birth to minor[b]	10
CA Work Pays Demonstration Project (WPDP)	Rape or incest	10
Work Pays Demonstration Project Modified (CWPDP-M)	None	24
CT Reach Jobs 1st (Fair Chance)	Rape or incest; birth to minor, residence;[c] conceived when not on welfare	10
DE BETTER CHANCE	Rape or incest; birth to minor, residence; conceived when not on welfare	10
FL Family Responsibility Act	None	10
GA Personal Accountability and Responsibility Act	Rape or incest; birth to minor, residence; conceived when not on welfare	24
IL Work and Responsibility	None	10
IN IMPACT	Rape or incest; birth to minor, residence; conceived when not on welfare	10
IMPACT—M	None	
KS Actively Creating Tomorrow	None	10

Liberalized Treatment of Earnings and Child Support	Benefits Vary by Number of Children[a]	Other Major Reform Provisions (number)
8	3	
X		Income and asset disregards; time limits; Food Stamp cash-out; two-parent eligibility (4)
		Learnfare (1)
X		Income and asset disregards; transitional child care and Medicaid; Learnfare (3)
		Income and asset disregards; benefit reductions; time limits; work requirements (4)
	X	Income and asset disregards; transitional child care and Medicaid; child support pass-through; work requirements (4)
X		Income and asset disregards; time limits; two-parent eligibility; teens at home; parenting and family planning; child health; Learnfare (7)
X	X	Two-parent eligibility; work requirements; Learnfare (3)
		Work requirements; parenting and family planning (2)
		Time limits (1)
		Income and asset disregards; benefit reductions; time limits; two-parent eligibility; Food Stamp eligibility; child health; work requirements; Learnfare (8)
		Reduce transitional child care and Medicaid; cash-out Food Stamps; teens at home; child support; Learnfare (5)
		Income and asset disregards; time limits; transitional child care and Medicaid; Medicaid expansions; two-parent eligibility; teens at home; child support; Learnfare (8)

TABLE 6-6 Continued

State and Program Name		Exemptions for	Family Cap Provisions	
			Time Limit Exclusion (months)	
MD	Family Investment Program	Rape or incest	10
MA	Transitional AFDC Program (Welfare Reform '95)	None	
MS	New Direction—Modifications	Rape or incest	10
NE	Welfare Reform Demonstration Project	Rape or incest; birth to minor, residence	10
NJ	Family Development Program	Birth to minor; conceived when not on welfare	10
NC	WORK First	Rape or incest	10
OK	Mutual Agreement	None	
SC	Family Independence Program (FIP)[d]	Rape or incest	10
TN	Families First	Rape or incest; birth to minor	10
VA	Virginia Independence Program (VIP)	None	10

Liberalized Treatment of Earnings and Child Support	Benefits Vary by Number of Children[a]	Other Major Reform Provisions (number)
		Income and asset disregards; two-parent eligibility; teens at home; family planning and parenting; child health; work requirements (6)
X		Income and asset disregards; transitional child care and Medicaid; cash-out of Food Stamps; two-parent eligibility; teens at home; child health; child support; work requirements; Learnfare (9)
		Income and asset disregards; two-parent eligibility; child health; Learnfare (4)
X		Income and asset disregards; reduced benefits; time limits; transitional child care and Medicaid; two-parent eligibility; work requirements; Learnfare (7)
X		Two-parent eligibility; work requirements; employment training; child health
		Income and asset disregards; time limits; two-parent eligibility; teens at home; child health; child support (6)
		Income and asset disregards; time limits; transitional child care and Medicaid; two-parent eligibility (4)
		Income and asset disregards; two-parent eligibility; drug testing and counseling; family planning and parenting; child support; work requirements; Learnfare (7)
		Income and asset disregards; time limits; two-parent eligibility; child health; child support; work requirements; Learnfare (7)
X		Time limits; child support pass-through; teens at home; child health; work requirements; Learnfare (6)

TABLE 6-6 Continued

State and Program Name	Exemptions for	Family Cap Provisions Time Limit Exclusion (months)
WI Parental and Family Responsibility Act (PFR)[e]	None	10
Work Not Welfare (WNW)	Rape or incest; conceived when not on welfare	10
AFDC Benefit Cap Demonstration Project (ABC)[f]	Rape or incest; birth to minor; residence	10

NOTES: Twenty-one states have implemented a total of 25 demonstrations that include family cap provisions.
[a]Percentage of benefits changes as number of children increases.
[b]These provisions exempt first-born minors already receiving benefits.
[c]These provisions exempt children not living with the parent.

Since these various reforms are being implemented in particular contexts, evaluations typically will generate site- and context-specific findings. For example, the results of various reforms implemented in a high-benefit state with a strong economy cannot be assumed to apply to low-benefit states and/or states with weak economies; nor can the results of family caps with low-benefit increments for additional children be generalized to circumstances where there are large per capita benefit increments. However, over time it likely will be more feasible to tease out some more generalizable findings from the observed cross-site and cross-time results.[10]

Evaluation of New Jersey's Family Development Program

The preliminary results of the New Jersey Family Development Program illustrate both the complexities in carrying out meaningful evaluations of welfare reform and the limitations of findings produced even under the best of circumstances. Beginning in August 1993, most of the state's welfare applicants and recipients were converted to the new welfare policies and services, including mandatory work requirements, expanded job training, liberalized eligibility for two-parent families, the family cap, and decreased taxes on earnings for those

---

[10]See for example, Gueron and Pauly (1991), Friedlander and Burtless (1994), and Maynard (1997).

Liberalized Treatment of Earnings and Child Support	Benefits Vary by Number of Children[a]	Other Major Reform Provisions (number)
	X	None (0)
		Time limits; transitional child care and Medicaid; two-parent eligibility (3)
		None (0)

[d]Vouchers are given in lieu of cash benefits.
[e]This provision applies only to specific population groups, designated by age.
[f]Family cap is a single waiver and not part of the larger waiver request.
SOURCE: U.S. Department of Health and Human Services, Administration for Children and Families (various years). See also, U.S. Department of Health and Human Services (1997).

having additional children while on welfare. For evaluation purposes, several thousand applicants and recipients in selected counties were randomly assigned to remain on the old welfare policies and thereby serve as a control group or counterfactual. This control group is being compared with about 6,000 randomly selected welfare applicants and recipients participating in the Family Development Program.

For several reasons, however, the emerging results of the evaluations are not especially useful for guiding either state or national policy (O'Neill, 1994; Camasso, 1995; Myers, 1995; Donovan, 1995). First, they reflect the effects of a complex set of reforms, only one piece of which pertains to the treatment of additional children born to welfare recipients. Economic and social theories predict that changes in economic opportunities and net wages might affect fertility behavior as much as the reform-induced changes in welfare benefits and economic needs resulting from the birth of an additional child. Neither of the two evaluations conducted was designed to disentangle the impacts of these various elements.

Second, there was tremendous publicity concerning the development and introduction of the family cap. Not only was New Jersey the first state to implement the policy, but it also was the first state to take a public stand on the issue of whether welfare ought to hold families financially harmless for their decisions to bear additional children. As a result, many control group members believe they have been subject to the family cap provision, even though they have not. In the parlance of the evaluation literature, the control group may have been subjected to contamination bias.[11]

Third, the actual financial consequence of the policy change for families having additional children was quite small. This is because Food Stamp benefits were increased to account for the family size change. Because there was no increase in cash benefits for families having another child under the cap, their Food Stamp benefits increased sufficiently to fill half to two-thirds of the lower cash assistance resulting from the new family cap policy relative to the old AFDC benefit rules.

Fourth, there are problems with the measurement of outcomes in the New Jersey demonstration. The primary source of data on births has been the welfare records. Yet, those whose benefits are not increased as a result of a birth (those subject to the cap) are less likely to report the birth to welfare officials than are those in the control group, for whom the reporting of a birth will trigger a benefit increase.[12]

Finally, the evaluation design does not lend itself to the measurement of any entry or exit effects. That is, it will not measure any deterrent effect, in the form of either delayed parenting or increased abortion rates. Nor will it measure any possible program entry effects due, for example, to the more generous education and training services.

Similar Complexities in Other State Demonstration Evaluations

The prospects that state evaluations will sort out empirically any causal links between selected welfare reforms and family outcomes of interest are not favorable, for a variety of reasons:

• *There are very few tests of single policy changes or even of a limited number of changes.* As is clear from Table 6-6 and would be equally evident from a similar table for the unemployed parent reforms, there are very few pure tests of specific policy changes. For example, there was initial hope that the unemployed parent reforms in several states (California, Utah, and Wisconsin) would provide clear tests of the underlying economic theories. But closer examination of the project and evaluation designs tempered this optimism: "All three experiments with the 100-hour rule are flawed, and problems with both design and implementation reduce the usefulness of the experiment" (Birnbaum and Wiseman, 1996). Utah's 100-hour rule demonstration, implemented in 1992,

---

[11]A *Wall Street Journal* article reported survey results suggesting that the controls were as likely as the demonstration participants to believe that the family caps applied to them (Harwood, 1997).

[12]This differential propensity to report a birth to welfare officials may account for much of the large measured reduction in birth rates reported by the first two studies of fertility effects of New Jersey's reforms (O'Neill, 1994; New Jersey Department of Human Services, 1995). An attempt to collect better data through surveys has resulted in unusually low response rates.

initially eliminated only the 100-hour rule. In 1995, however, the demonstration was incorporated into the state's Single Parent Employment Demonstration Project (SPEDP), which contains at least 11 other major provisions, making it increasingly difficult to segregate the individual component effects.

• *There is increased churning and volatility within states.* For example, family caps have been introduced in Wisconsin in three different waivers. At least six states with waivers affecting two-parent provisions have modified their state plans. With the passage of PRWORA, we can expect another round of major reforms and policy changes. These planned variations in policy are sometimes in response to and other times overlaid on changes in the political, social, and economic climate in the states.

• *Future support for strong evaluations appears highly uncertain.* Under PRWORA, the federal government will not mandate evaluations of new reforms. Rather, it will encourage states to continue expanding their knowledge by providing financial support and sponsoring selected demonstrations. Serious empirical work likely will require investments of state resources or significant contributions from private sources.

• *There are very difficult technical and methodological challenges to estimating the behavioral responses to many of the new reforms.* For example, the new generation of reforms intends to change community and agency cultures. Classical experiments with random assignment of subjects is inappropriate when the purpose of the reform is to effect community change. But without an experimental design, how does one develop an appropriate counterfactual? How do we design an evaluation whose results can be generalized to other settings with different economic conditions, different complements of employment services, and different ground rules governing welfare participation?

The evaluations of the welfare reform demonstrations can best be thought of as laboratory studies of changes in a particular set of policies, being tested in particular economic, social, and political contexts. As such, they can be enormously valuable to the states sponsoring them as well as to states that share similar social and economic contexts. Moreover, they contribute to the general knowledge base by providing additional data regarding behavioral responses to particular "bundles" of policy changes.

States should be encouraged to continue their evaluation efforts, particularly if they have strong experimental designs in place to capture important aspects of their reforms. At the same time, it is important to capitalize on the great social experiment that is about to unfold as authority and responsibility for welfare policy devolve to the states. States may want to be "free riders," letting others do the empirical work upon which they can build future policy choices. But they must realize that they will bear the full fiscal risk of bad policy decisions and reap the benefits of wise ones, thus raising the stakes associated with formulating policy on the basis of either no research or flawed research.

EVALUATING THE GREAT SOCIAL EXPERIMENT

The next generation of welfare reforms could well have its largest effects by changing social norms—particularly by increasing the social stigma attached to childbearing out of wedlock and to childbearing among those unable to support their children or already dependent on welfare. From the parochial perspective of the states implementing the reforms, there is little reason to look beyond whether welfare rolls decline and fewer children are being reared out of wedlock. A broader social view, however, argues for adopting a more comprehensive and longer-range research and evaluation plan involving multiple goals and assessment strategies.

Ideally, the next wave of research on welfare reform will support the ability of states to simulate the likely response of target populations to various model welfare policies. In that ideal world, New Hampshire, as an example, would be able to simulate the change in caseloads and in the economic welfare of its low-income population that might be expected from continuing current policies, and to contrast these outcomes with what might happen if the state were to adopt policies more like those in Massachusetts or in Maine. And it would be able to conduct its simulations under alternative assumptions about the direction of its economy and demographic trends. Such simulations will result in a better understanding than we now have of why the expected results will occur.

At the same time, the next wave of research needs to look inside the "black box" of change much more carefully than have past studies. The reforms that are about to occur under PRWORA are simply too major in scope to assume there will be only marginal implications for family and child well-being. Meeting this objective suggests that the future research agenda related to welfare policy should address multiple, overlapping goals: (1) meet local program, policy monitoring, and assessment needs; (2) enhance basic knowledge of behavioral responses to various policies; (3) promote our understanding of contextual influences on human behavior; and (4) strengthen our understanding of program and policy outcomes. The first of these goals is best addressed through research such as that of the waiver demonstration evaluation projects. These projects can inform the remaining goals, but they fall far short of providing generalizable findings. For these, we need both to capitalize on the ongoing national experiment we are witnessing and to conduct some carefully planned subexperiments within this natural experiment.

State governors and legislatures, as well as local service deliverers, will need local monitoring and assessment strategies to address their own requirements for accountability and feedback. In order to meet these requirements, states should gather and analyze their program outcome measures on a regular basis, making certain those data are accurate and not subject to the types of reporting errors or delays that have plagued many of the waiver demonstration evaluations, such as the early assessments of New Jersey's family cap policy. States should pay close attention to defining the relevant population. For example, they should consider whether they need to track the rate and characteristics of case openings and closings as well as monitor the activities of the ongoing caseload.

Additionally, monitoring efforts should factor in demographic and contextual shifts. Economic change is demonstrably linked to welfare caseloads; changes in local labor market conditions can alter the likelihood that resident fathers will increase their hours of work and/or even find employment that will move them off welfare. Such conditions should be included in any monitoring of the consequences of suspending the 100-hour rule. Likewise, significant changes in the availability of family planning services are known to affect both fertility and pregnancy resolutions among low-income women, and these factors, not welfare policy changes, could drive apparent shifts in fertility outcomes among the welfare population.

Predicting Behavioral Responses to Welfare Policies

In the context of the broader mission of supporting extensive simulation results by states, research needs to focus more on the behavioral responses of individuals to *specific* welfare parameters. We need to know the expected change in the out-of-wedlock birth rate associated with particular income changes and needs resulting from an increase in family size. It also is important to know how marriage rates change as we vary the probability that individuals will be eligible for welfare and, conditional on their being eligible, vary their expected benefits. In both of these examples, we need to take into account the initial characteristics of the individual and other contextual factors. The change in the out-of-wedlock birth rate associated with various benefit increments likely will differ by the number of children one has already, the baseline benefit level (including whether the person is on welfare at all), and other social circumstances.

The particulars of the policy parameters that states have already changed or will modify under TANF are less important in themselves than are the consequences of these changes in terms of welfare eligibility and expected benefit levels for current and prospective welfare recipients. In general, the decisions of current and prospective recipients regarding future employment, family formation, child support, and childbearing are going to be determined less by the policies and policy language than by what actually happens to their family's welfare eligibility status and benefit levels if they make particular choices such as the choice to have another child, to marry the father of their child, to get a job, to cooperate with child support, or to get divorced.

Still, the specific formulation of certain policies itself may send important messages to the public regarding expectations and values, which could affect behavior. A prime example in which the message may be as powerful, or more powerful, than the financial consequences of the policy is the family cap. Family caps send a very clear message that taxpayers look down upon out-of-wedlock childbearing, especially if parents are unable to support their children.

The wave of welfare reforms offers an unparalleled opportunity to learn about behavioral responses to income incentives, economic uncertainty, and social support opportunities. We also can estimate the independent effect, if any, of the manner in which the economic consequences and support opportunities are packaged. For example, imagine that we collect and analyze longitudinal data on decisions that poor or near-poor people make and their consequences in terms of program eligibility and benefits for each welfare jurisdiction and for each year from 1992, when the flurry of welfare reform activity began, through the next 5 years. We could gather such information from a micro-level review of welfare applications and case records.[13]

That is, we could sample records from the welfare files for all those years in all 50 states and in some counties and construct a database that includes, for each case: (1) basic information, such as number of children, age of youngest child, marital status, employment status, time on welfare, child support status, area of residence, age, and race/ethnicity; (2) status changes, if any, reflecting major behavioral decisions (for example, the birth of another child, a marriage or divorce, the acquisition or loss of a job, and increasing or decreasing hours of employment); and (3) for those with a status change, the impact of this on their welfare eligibility and benefit levels. The resulting database will allow us to create measures of the expected welfare response a person in situation "X" might face if he or she makes particular decisions regarding family formation and status.

Once we have the hypothetical consequences for welfare eligibility and benefits of various behavioral choices that people make, we can use these data in statistical models designed to measure the strength of the behavioral response by current and prospective welfare recipients to particular welfare policy environments. For example, we can estimate the impact of a particular benefit change (such as the introduction of a family cap) on fertility decisions of individuals with particular baseline characteristics and facing a particular policy context prior to the change. In essence, however, we would translate the family cap into particular eligibility and benefit changes associated with fertility decisions that would result in the particular site and for particular individuals. Similarly, we could estimate the impact of a particular marriage penalty or reward on the likelihood of marriage, given the prevailing baseline context.

---

[13]Alternatively, we could simply gather welfare rules governing eligibility and benefit changes for individuals in various statuses and create rules-driven predictors of the policy response to behavioral choices facing individuals. Or we could survey a representative sample of low-income families and gather data on their reports of system responses to their behavioral changes. This has the problems of introducing recall and reporting bias and of being relatively costly.

Assuming we have sufficient variation from our natural experimental database, we should be able to generalize the results of particular policy shifts to other settings.[14] We could also incorporate into these behavioral models measures of possible "message" effects (for example, the effects of a family cap policy beyond its effect on the marginal benefit level associated with a decision to have another child). Doing this would require gathering data for analysis on the understanding and beliefs of poor and near-poor families as well as service deliverers.

Contextual and Ethnographic Analysis

Now more than ever, it is critical that trained social scientists conduct systematic, in-depth evaluations to further our understanding of the economic and social welfare of highly at-risk families; of the behavioral choices these families face and the decisions they make; and of the family, community, and social services they draw on to meet the challenges faced by those living near or in poverty. The most optimistic world under welfare devolution is likely to be one in which state and local welfare reforms succeed in trimming the welfare rolls by providing greater incentives for those with the greatest social capital and familial support to eschew welfare. It also will undoubtedly fail to meet the income security needs of a portion of the current and prospective recipient pool who simply enter parenthood and/or adulthood without the social capital to escape poverty through their own labor or that of their partners. Even with strong employment support interventions, some poor families will hit the time limits and will risk taking their families to homeless shelters or the streets.

The unfolding social experiment in welfare policy will enable us to identify and learn from these two very important subgroups of the poverty population. If we plan carefully, we can estimate the number and characteristics of those falling into each category. But, more important, we also could learn an enormous amount about the factors that contribute to family resilience under a "tougher" world vis à vis social welfare policy, and why some families need much more than offered by either the past welfare system or that which emerges under TANF. The results of such in-depth studies could provide the foundation for designing preventive and ameliorative policies directed at this the most needy group and at moving other families more quickly through transition dependency.

One subset of such research could build on more routine longitudinal surveys of near-poor and poor families to track their movements on and off welfare; in and out of the labor market; through family formations and dissolutions; and

---

[14]The analytic models would operate rather like Mathematica Policy Research's STEWARD (Simulation of Trends in Employment, Welfare, and Related Dynamics) microsimulation model (Beebout et al., 1995).

through fertility decisions. Researchers could then carefully select families fitting various profiles of special interest—for example, seemingly low-resource families who succeed under various welfare support settings, their counterparts who "fail," and high-resource families who fail under various welfare support options—and conduct an in-depth study of a sample of such families over a period of time to reconstruct the factors that contributed to varying degrees and in varying combinations to the successes or failures of the families.

Another subset of this strand of research would entail intensive ethnographic research with at-risk families.[15] The focus of these studies will be on understanding the interactions among a broad set of contextual factors in determining behavioral choices of families and their short- and long-run implications. Such research would, for example, contribute to our understanding of the issues that poor and near-poor families consider in deciding whether to subsist on a low-wage job rather than apply for welfare or whether to place their child in poor-quality care in order to avoid welfare time limits. This research could then also follow the families to inform us of how the various decisions these families make play out for themselves and their children.

Targeted Experimental Evaluations

Some areas of reform are so different from past policy and practice that prudence argues for conducting targeted experimental evaluations as part of a phased implementation plan. Despite their limitations in terms of generalizability of findings and their inability to address systemic reform, we should not abandon experimental evaluations. They are unquestionably the best means of judging the efficacy of targeted interventions, particularly in cases where there is not yet sufficient evidence to support universal implementation of the policy.

The strategies for conducting these types of evaluations are well documented, and there are dozens of models to draw on (Bell et al., 1995; Gordon et al., 1997; Boruch, 1997). These types of evaluations are especially valuable in cases where policy makers are interested in comparing the status quo with proposed new policies or interventions designed to achieve specific improvements in outcomes. The researchers then design an efficient experimental evaluation with the primary goal of testing the hypothesis that the new policy or intervention does have the intended consequences. To the extent feasible, such studies should also be accompanied by qualitative evaluations of the intervention or policy change and in-depth studies of purposefully selected subsets of the demonstration participants for the purpose of understanding the contents of the so-called black box and, further, of helping to understand and interpret the impact analysis findings

---

[15]We are only recently beginning to constructively integrate the results of such analyses with the statistical research to identify behavioral models and to assess the efficacy of particular program models (e.g., see Polit, 1992; Quint et al., 1994a, 1994b; Luker, 1996; and Herr et al., 1996).

and translate them into more general conclusions for the benefit of the broader research and policy community.

CONCLUSION

State and local governments are being called upon to handle some of society's most vexing and intractable social problems. The empirical evidence available to support prudent policy making at the subfederal level is not as extensive as one might expect, given the amount of recent demonstration and evaluation activity.

The basic research needed to guide future policy improvement entails aggressive study of the innovation and experimentation associated with PRWORA. We should be proactive in addressing evaluation issues and challenges. Surprisingly little was learned about how past welfare reforms have affected those behaviors considered most important to the current reforms. We must learn from that history and do a better job of exploiting the knowledge development opportunities arising from the devolution of responsibility for welfare from the federal government to the states and even to local governments. Whatever social and economic challenges PRWORA creates, it also opens up an enormous opportunity to study behavioral responses to quite major shifts in the incentives created by various types of welfare policies.

ACKNOWLEDGMENTS

The authors are most appreciative of comments provided by Isabel V. Sawhill on the conference version of the paper and of comments provided by Robert Moffitt and two anonymous referees on an interim draft.

REFERENCES

Beebout, H., R. Cohen, J. Czajka, J. DiCarlo, M. Dynarski, J. Jacobson, and R. Moffitt
    1995   Simulation of Trends in Employment, Welfare, and Related Dynamics (STEWARD). Report submitted to the U.S. Department of Health and Human Services, Assistant Secretary for Planning and Evaluation. Washington, D.C.: Mathematica Policy Research, Inc.
Bell, S., L. Orr, J. Blomquist, and G. Cain
    1995   *Program Applicants as a Comparison Group in Evaluating Training Programs: Theory and a Test.* Kalamazoo, Mich.: The Upjohn Institute.
Birnbaum, M., and M. Wiseman
    1996   Extending assistance to intact families: State experiments with the 100 hour rule. *FOCUS* 18(1, Special Issue):38-41.
Bloom, D., V. Fellerath, D. Long, and R. Wood
    1993   *LEAP: Interim Findings on a Welfare Initiative to Improve School Attendance Among Teenage Parents.* New York: Manpower Demonstration Research Corporation, May.
Bloom, H., L. Orr, G. Cave, S. Bell, F. Doolittle, and W. Lin
    1994   *The National JTPA Study: Overview of the Impacts, Benefits, and Cost of Title IIA.* Bethesda, Md.: Abt Associates, January.

Boruch, R.
  1997   *Randomized Experiments for Planning and Evaluation: A Practical Guide.* Thousand
          Oaks, Calif.: Sage Publications.
Brien, M., and R. Willis
  1997   Costs and consequences for the fathers. In R. Maynard, ed., *Kids Having Kids: Costs and
          Social Consequences of Teenage Pregnancy.* Washington, D.C.: Urban Institute Press.
Brock, T., D. Butler, and D. Long
  1993   *Unpaid Work Experience for Welfare Recipients: Findings and Lessons from MDRC
          Research.* New York: Manpower Demonstration Research Corporation, September.
Brown, S., and L. Eisenberg, eds.
  1995   *The Best Intentions: Unintended Pregnancy and the Well-Being of Children and Fami-
          lies.* Washington, D.C.: National Academy Press.
Cain, G.
  1987   Negative income tax experiments and the issues of marital stability and family composi-
          tion. In Alicia Munnell, ed., *Lessons from the Negative Income Tax Experiments.* Boston,
          Mass.: Federal Reserve Bank of Boston.
Cain, G., and D. Wissoker
  1990   A reanalysis of marital stability in the Seattle-Denver income-maintenance experiment.
          American Journal of Sociology 95(5):1235-1269.
Camasso, M.J.
  1995   New Jersey's evaluation. In *Addressing Illegitimacy: Welfare Reform Options for Con-
          gress.* Washington, D.C.: American Enterprise Institute, September.
Cave, G., H. Bos, F. Doolittle, and C. Toussaint
  1993   *JOB START: Final Report on a Program for School Dropouts.* New York: Manpower
          Demonstration Research Corporation, October.
Center for Law and Social Policy
  1995   *CLASP Guide to Welfare Waivers: 1992-1995.* Washington, D.C.: Center for Law and
          Social Policy, May.
Donovan, P.
  1995   The 'family cap': A popular but unproven method of welfare reform. *Family Planning
          Perspectives* 27(4):166-171.
Edin, K., and L. Lein
  1997   *Making Ends Meet: How Single Mothers Survive Welfare and Low-Wage Work.* New
          York: Russell Sage Foundation.
Ellwood, D., and M. Bane
  1985   The impact of AFDC on family structure and living arrangements. In R. Ehrengerg, ed.
          Research in Labor Economics. Greenwich, Conn.: JAI Press.
Friedlander, D., and G. Burtless
  1994   *Five Years After: The Long-Term Effects of Welfare-to-Work Programs.* New York:
          Russell Sage Foundation.
Gordon, A., J. Jacobson, and T. Fraker
  1997   *How to Evaluate Welfare Reform: Guidance for States.* Princeton, N.J.: Mathematica
          Policy Research, Inc., March.
Gottschalk, P.
  1990   AFDC participation across generations. *American Economic Review* 2(May):367-371.
  1992   Is the correlation between AFDC participation across generations spurious? Department
          of Economics, Boston College.
Gueron, J.M., and E. Pauly
  1991   *From Welfare to Work.* New York: Russell Sage Foundation.

Hannan, M., and N. Tuma
  1990   A reassessment of the effect of income maintenance on marital dissolution in the Seattle
          and Denver experiment. *American Journal of Sociology* 95(5):1270-1298.
Harwood, J.
  1997   *Wall Street Journal* (January 30):1.
Haveman, R., and B. Wolfe
  1994   *Succeeding Generations: On the Effects of Investments in Children.* New York: Russell
          Sage Foundation.
Haveman, R., B. Wolfe, and E. Peterson
  1997   Children of early childbearers as young adults. Pp. 257-284 in R. Maynard, ed., *Kids
          Having Kids: Economic Costs and Social Consequences of Teen Pregnancy.* Washing-
          ton, D.C.: Urban Institute Press.
Herr, T., S. Wagner, and R. Halpern
  1996   *Making the Shoe Fit: Creating a Work-Prep System for a Large and Diverse Welfare
          Population.* Chicago, Ill.: Project Match, Erikson Institute.
Hershey, Alan, and M. Silverberg
  1993   *Program Cost of the Teenage Parent Demonstration.* Princeton, N.J.: Mathematica Policy
          Research, Inc.
Jacobson, J. and R. Maynard
  1995   Unwed mothers and long-term welfare dependency. In *Addressing Illegitimacy: Welfare
          Reform Options for Congress.* Washington, D.C.: American Enterprise Institute, Septem-
          ber.
Kost, K., and J. Forrest
  1995   Intention status of U.S. births in 1988: Differences by mothers' socioeconomic and
          demographic characteristics. *Family Planning Perspectives* 27(1):23-27.
Lichter, D.
  1995   The retreat from marriage and the rise in nonmarital fertility. In *Report to Congress on
          Out-of-Wedlock Childbearing.* U.S. Department of Health and Human Services, National
          Center for Health Statistics. Washington, D.C.: U.S. Government Printing Office.
Long, D., J.M. Gueron, R.G. Wood, R. Fisher, and V. Fellerath
  1996   *LEAP: Three-Year Impacts of Ohio's Welfare Initiative to Improve School Attendance
          Among Teenage Parents.* New York: Manpower Demonstration Research Corporation,
          April.
Luker, K.
  1996   *Dubious Conceptions: The Politics of Teenage Pregnancy.* Cambridge, Mass.: Harvard
          University Press.
Lundberg, S., and R. Plotnick
  1990   Effects of state welfare, abortion and family planning policies on premarital childbearing
          among white adolescents. *Family Planning Perspectives* 22:246-251.
Maynard, R., ed.
  1993   *Building Self-Sufficiency Among Welfare-Dependent Teenage Parents.* Princeton, N.J.:
          Mathematica Policy Research, Inc., June.
Maynard, R.
  1997   The role for paternalism in teen pregnancy prevention and teen parent services. In L.
          Mead, ed., *The New Paternalism.* Washington, D.C.: Brookings Institution.
Maynard, R., and A. Rangarajan
  1994   Contraceptive use and repeat pregnancies among welfare-dependent teenage mothers.
          Family Planning Perspectives 26(5):198-205.

Maynard, R., W. Nicholson, and A. Rangarajan
    1993   Breaking the Cycle of Poverty: The Effectiveness of Mandatory Services for Welfare-Dependent Teenage Parents. Princeton, N.J.: Mathematica Policy Research, Inc., December.
McLanahan, S., and G. Sandefur
    1994   Growing Up with a Single Parent. Cambridge, Mass.: Harvard University Press.
Meier, K.J., and D.R. McFarlane
    1994   State family planning and abortion expenditures: Their effect on public health. American Journal of Public Health 84:1468-1472.
Moffitt, R.
    1992   Incentive effects of the U.S. welfare system: A review. Journal of Economic Literature 30:1-61.
    1995   The effect of the welfare system on nonmarital childbearing. In Report to Congress on Out-of-Wedlock Childbearing. U.S. Department of Health and Human Services, National Center for Health Statistics. Washington, D.C.: U.S. Government Printing Office.
Moore, K., C. Blumenthal, B. Sugland, B. Hyatt, N. Snyder, and D. Morrison
    1994   State Variation in Rates of Adolescent Pregnancy and Childbearing. Washington, D.C.: Child Trends, Inc.
Myers, R.
    1995   New Jersey's 'family cap.' In Addressing Illegitimacy: Welfare Reform Options for Congress. Washington, D.C.: American Enterprise Institute, September.
New Jersey Department of Human Services, Office of Public Affairs
    1995   News release, May 16.
Olds, D., C. Henderson, Jr., and R. Tatelbaum
    1988   Improving the life-course development of socially disadvantaged mothers: A randomized trial of nurse home visitation. American Journal of Public Health 78(11):1436-1145.
Olsen, J., and S. Weed
    1986   Effects of family-planning programs for teenagers on adolescent birth and pregnancy rates. Family Planning Perspectives 20:153-170.
O'Neill, J.
    1994   Expert testimony in C.K. vs. Shalala, USDC, D. NJ, Civil Action No. 93-5354.
O'Sullivan, A., and B. Jacobsen
    1992   A randomized trial of a health care program for first-time adolescent mothers and their infants. Nursing Research 41(4):210-215.
Plotnick, R.
    1990   Welfare and out-of-wedlock childbearing: Evidence from the 1980s. Journal of Marriage and the Family 52:735-746.
Plotnick, R., and S. Lundberg
    1995   Adolescent and premarital childbearing: Do economic incentives matter? Journal of Labor Economics 13:177-200.
Polit, D.
    1992   Barriers to Self-Sufficiency and Avenues to Success Among Teenage Mothers. Princeton, N.J.: Mathematica Policy Research, Inc.
Quint, J., D. Polit, H. Bos, and G. Cave
    1994a   New Chance: Interim Findings on a Comprehensive Program for Disadvantaged Young Mothers and Their Children. New York: Manpower Demonstration Research Corporation, September.
Quint, J., J. Musick, and J. Ladner
    1994b   Lives of Promise, Lives of Pain: Young Mothers After New Chance. New York: Manpower Demonstration Research Corporation, January.

U.S. Department of Health and Human Services, Administration for Children and Families
 Various   Terms and conditions of waiver provisions for [state].
 years
U.S. Department of Health and Human Services
   1995   *Out-of-Wedlock Childbearing in the U.S.* Washington, D.C.: U.S. Government Printing
            Office.
   1997   *Setting the Baseline: A Report on State Welfare Waivers.* June. Washington, D.C.: U.S.
            Government Printing Office. Http://aspe.os.dhhs.gov/hsp/isp /waiver2.
U.S. General Accounting Office
   1992   *Unemployed Parents: An Evaluation of the Effects of Welfare Benefits on Family Stabil-
            ity.* GAO/PRMD-92-19BR. Washington, D.C.: U.S. Government Printing Office.
U.S. House of Representatives, Committee on Ways and Means
   1993   *1993 Green Book: Background Material and Data on Programs Within the Jurisdiction
            of the Committee on Ways and Means.* WMCP-103-18. Washington, D.C.: U.S. Govern-
            ment Printing Office.
   1996a   *1996 Green Book: Background Material and Data on Programs Within the Jurisdiction
            of the Committee on Ways and Means.* Washington, D.C.: U.S. Government Printing
            Office.
   1996b   Personal responsibility and Work Opportunity Reconciliation Act of 1996:   Conference
            Report to accompany H.R. 3734. Section 401, Purpose (p. 9), July 30.

APPENDIX 6A   Sources of Data on Impacts of Welfare-Related Demonstrations on Fertility Behavior of Teenage Parents

Program	Source(s) of Information on the Research Findings
Job Start	Cave, G., H. Bos, F. Doolittle, and C. Toussaint. October. "JOB START: Final report on a program for school dropouts." New York: Manpower Demonstration Research Corporation, 1993.
New Chance	Quint, J., D. Polit, H. Bos, and G. Cave. "New Chance: Interim findings on a comprehensive program for disadvantaged young mothers and their children." New York: Manpower Demonstration Research Corporation, June 1994.
Project Redirection	Polit, D. and C. White. "The lives of young, disadvantaged mothers: the five year follow-up of the Project Redirection Sample." Saratoga Springs, NY: Humanalysis, Inc., May 1988.
Ohio Learnfare	Long, D., J. Gueron, R. Wood, R. Fisher, and V. Fellerath. "LEAP: Three-year impacts of Ohio's welfare initiative to improve school attendance among teenage parents." New York: Manpower Demonstration Research Corporation, 1996.
	Bloom, D., V. Fellerath, D. Long, and R. Wood. "LEAP: Interim findings on a welfare initiative to improve school attendance among teenage parents: Ohio's Learning, Earning, and Parenting Program." New York: Manpower Demonstration Research Corporation, May 1993.
Teen Parent Welfare Demonstration	Maynard, R. (ed.). "Building self-sufficiency among welfare-dependent teenage parents." Princeton, N.J.: Mathematica Policy Research, Inc., June 1993.
	Maynard, R., W. Nicholson, and A. Rangarajan. "Breaking the cycle of poverty: The effectiveness of mandatory services for welfare-dependent teenage parents." Princeton, N.J.: Mathematica Policy Research, Inc., December 1993.
	Hershey, A., and M. Silverberg. "Program cost of the teenage parent demonstration." Princeton, N.J.: Mathematica Policy Research, Inc., 1993.
	Maynard, R. and A. Rangarajan. "Contraceptive use and repeat pregnancies among welfare-dependent teenage mothers." *Family Planning Perspectives* Vol. 26(5):198-205.
Teen Parent Health Care Program	O'Sullivan, A., and B. Jacobsen. "A randomized trial of a health care program for first-time adolescent mothers and their infants." *Nursing Research* Vol. 41(4):210-215.
Elmira Nurse Home Visiting Program	Olds, D., C.S. Henderson, R. Tatelbaum, and R. Chamberlin. "Improving the life-course development of socially disadvantaged mothers: A randomized trial of nurse home visitation." *American Journal of Public Health,* Vol. 78(11):1436-1445.

7

The Effect of Welfare on Child Outcomes

Janet Currie

There is broad support for the idea that welfare should benefit poor children. Yet most research on welfare programs, as well as much of the debate about welfare reform, has focused on the way that parents respond to incentives created by welfare, rather than on its effects on children. Less work has been devoted to the fundamental question of whether any of the web of programs supporting poor families benefit children.

If it can be shown that they do, then there are many other questions to be addressed: First, are the benefits short or long term? Second, which types of programs or combinations of programs are most effective; for example, do cash or in-kind programs produce bigger benefits for children? Third, do welfare programs have different effects on different groups, and if so why? Fourth, how exactly do successful programs work? And finally, can efficacious programs pass the more stringent test of cost-effectiveness?

This review focuses on the eight large federal programs shown in Table 7-1: Aid to Families with Dependent Children (AFDC), which has been replaced with the new Temporary Aid for Needy Families program (TANF); the Earned Income Tax Credit (EITC); housing assistance; Food Stamps; the Supplemental Feeding Program for Women, Infants, and Children (WIC); school nutrition programs; Medicaid; and Head Start. The programs are evaluated with respect to their effects on the health and educational achievement of children. Where possible, documented effects on long-term outcomes are noted. The first section of this chapter is a brief discussion of how we know what we know about these programs. The evidence regarding the effects of cash programs and in-kind programs, respectively, is then reviewed in the next two sections.

TABLE 7-1 Trends in Program Expenditures (billion 1995 $)

	1975	1980	1990	1995
Cash Transfers				
AFDC				
Total	23.8	21.8	21.8	22.0
Federal only	13.1	11.8	11.9	12.0
Earned Income Tax Credit				
Total	3.4	3.7	8.1	22.2
Refunded portion of credit	2.5	2.6	6.2	19.0
In-Kind Transfers[a]				
Housing assistance	7.0	10.0	18.2	23.7
Food Stamps	13.5	17.4	19.4	25.7
WIC	0.7	1.4	2.5	3.5
School nutrition				
School lunch	5.4	5.8	4.3	5.3
School breakfast	0.4	0.5	0.7	1.2
Medicaid				
Total[b]	35.1	46.3	76.3	111.2
Federal only	20.1	27.0	47.8	86.6
To dependent children	6.3	6.0	10.7	17.8
To adults in families with				
dependent children	5.9	6.4	10.1	14.0
Head Start	1.1	1.3	1.9	3.5

[a]All but the Food Stamps figure for 1975 are actually from 1972.
[b]The Medicaid figures for 1980 are actually from 1981.
SOURCE: U.S. House of Representatives (1993, 1994, 1996).

The evidence indicates that contrary to much current publicity, the system is not entirely "broken" when judged using the metric of child well-being: there are specific programs that produce important benefits for children. Nevertheless, not all programs are equally effective, and benefits are not equally distributed across children. Hence, a review of what we know about these programs can provide a useful starting point for welfare reform, as well as highlighting gaps in what we need to know in order to carry out intelligent reform. The last section of the paper discusses fruitful directions for future research and the importance of enhanced data collection efforts.

HOW WE KNOW WHAT WE KNOW

A comprehensive review of the program evaluation literature is far beyond the scope of this chapter. However, since several different methods are used in the studies discussed here, some comment on methodology is in order. A somewhat fuller, nontechnical discussion can be found in Currie (1995a) or Heckman (1990).

The fundamental problem facing researchers and policy makers is that the children of welfare recipients may have bad outcomes for reasons that have nothing to do with the receipt of assistance per se. It is possible that a program could have substantial benefits for poor children and still leave many children disadvantaged relative to better-off peers.

Evidently, parents of children on welfare are worse off than other parents in observable ways: they are poorer, likely to have less education, and may also have health problems. Many datasets available to researchers contain at least crude measures of these observable variables so that observed differences between parents on welfare and other parents can be accounted for using standard regression models.

To take a simple example, suppose that children of high school dropouts have lower scores on standardized tests than children of college graduates. Then if mothers on welfare are more likely to be high school dropouts than college graduates, a simple comparison of the two group's average scores might tell you more about the effects of maternal education than about the effects of welfare. A simple way to "control" for the effects of education in order to focus on the effects of welfare might involve drawing a sample of high school dropouts and comparing children of welfare mothers to other children within this group. Any differences between the welfare children and the others could then be attributed to welfare use and not to maternal education. Multiple regression techniques simply allow one to control for the effects of several observable variables at the same time.

The problem becomes much more difficult however if parents on welfare also differ from other parents in ways that are not observed. For example, they may lack motivation or be discouraged by previous misfortune. Failure to properly control for these differences could lead one to incorrectly infer that it was being on welfare that was associated with negative child outcomes, rather than these underlying conditions. Some underlying problem, such as maternal depression, might cause *both* welfare dependence and negative child outcomes.

There are basically two approaches to this issue of unobserved characteristics. First, one may design a social experiment, randomly assigning eligibles to a "treatment" group and a "control" group. Random assignment ensures that, on average, the two groups will have the same observed and unobserved characteristics. In principle, one can then assess the effect of the treatment simply by comparing mean outcomes for the two groups, just as one would do in a drug trial. The key advantage of an experimental evaluation is its transparency.

One disadvantage of social experiments is that they may be very expensive. But there are several disadvantages in addition to high cost (Heckman, 1990). These include differential attrition between treatments and controls (which causes the treatment group to become less and less like the comparison group over time); the fact that subjects assigned to the control group may not accept their fate passively (for example, subjects denied training in a government program might sign up for an alternative program); and the fact that it may be difficult to use the experiment to examine differential effects of the treatment on different groups.

Nonexperimental evaluations attempt to control statistically for unobserved variables associated both with participation in the program and with the outcome of interest. One method of doing this is to find a third set of variables, called "instruments," that are associated with participation in the program but not with the important unobserved variables. For example, a researcher interested in the effects of participation in Medicaid on child health might argue that the generosity of state AFDC benefits is associated with participation in Medicaid because of the link between AFDC recipiency and Medicaid eligibility, but that the level of AFDC benefits does not have any effect on child health other than through its effect on participation in Medicaid. If this assumption were true, then the level of AFDC benefits would qualify as an "instrumental variable."

This instrument would be used (along with other observable characteristics of the mother) to predict Medicaid participation, and predicted participation would be substituted for actual participation in the model explaining child health. The idea is that predicted participation will depend only on observable characteristics and differences in state AFDC benefit levels, and not on the unobserved characteristics of the mother. The procedure is analogous to an experiment in which AFDC benefit levels are varied across states, Medicaid participation responds, and only this source of variation in participation rates is used to identify the effects of Medicaid on health.

The difficulty with instrumental variables techniques is that the key assumptions may not be satisfied. Suppose that states with more generous AFDC benefits also have higher-income populations and that higher incomes are associated with better child health. Then unless one takes account of this relationship, one will tend to find a spurious positive relationship between participation in Medicaid and child health. Alternatively, suppose that states raise AFDC benefit levels in response to poor child health. Then one might observe a spurious negative relationship between predicted Medicaid participation and child health.

An alternative approach involves assuming that the relevant omitted characteristics are fixed within a family or for the same child over time. Suppose for example that the relevant unobserved variable is maternal attitudes towards education and that this remains fixed over some period of time. Suppose further that one sibling participated in Head Start and one did not. Then comparing the sibling who participated to the one that did not provides a measure of the effect of Head Start that is not affected by the fact that, on average, mothers of Head Start children may have more positive (or negative?) views of education than other similarly situated mothers. Of course, the problem with this approach is that the relevant variable may not be fixed within households or over time.

The studies discussed below all rely on one of these methodological approaches. Their conclusions are only as valid as the assumptions underlying the chosen approach. It is in cases where the same result has been obtained using different assumptions and data sources that we can be most confident of the conclusions.

WHAT WE KNOW ABOUT CASH PROGRAMS

Aid to Families with Dependent Children

The term "welfare" has usually been identified with the Aid to Families with Dependent Children program. This oldest and largest of the federal welfare programs provided cash transfers to (predominantly female-headed) families with children. This is the program that recent welfare reforms (the Personal Responsibility and Work Opportunity Reconciliation Act of 1996 [PRWORA]) effectively ended, replacing it with the new Temporary Aid for Needy Families program. TANF differs from AFDC because it ends the "entitlement" of all needy families to welfare benefits, because it introduces time limits on welfare benefits and because it provides states with much more latitude in developing their own welfare programs. Nevertheless, since most of what we know about cash welfare programs comes from studies of AFDC, and because many states will respond to TANF by only gradually altering their AFDC programs, it is of interest to summarize this literature here.

Like TANF, AFDC was administered at the state level within federal guidelines. As a result, program characteristics varied widely from state to state. For example, as of January 1993, the maximum monthly AFDC grant for a one-parent family of four persons varied from $164 in Alabama to $923 in Alaska (U.S. House of Representatives, 1993). On average the federal government pays 54 percent of benefit costs, as shown in Table 7-1. The continuous erosion of real AFDC benefit levels over the past 15 years provides compelling evidence of the unpopularity of this program: the average monthly AFDC benefit declined from $483 (1993 dollars) in 1980 to $373 in 1993, even though the average family size remained constant at three persons (U.S. House of Representatives, 1994).

One of the problems involved in evaluating the effects of AFDC on children is that the benefits of a cash transfer program can be expected to be diffuse. Small increases in household expenditures on a wide range of items may produce overall benefits for children without affecting any one indicator a great deal. A second problem is that although income is often used as a shorthand summary of a household's socioeconomic status, it is in practice extremely difficult to separate the effects of income from the effects of other family background characteristics including neighborhoods (Mayer, 1996).

Most research about the effects of AFDC on children focuses on the fact that daughters of women who participate in AFDC are themselves more likely to participate (cf. Gottschalk, 1990; Murray, 1984). What is less clear is whether the relationship is causal or whether it merely reflects the fact that the children of the poor are more likely to be poor—older studies tended to conclude that the relationship was not causal, but studies using more recent data have questioned this conclusion. See Moffitt (1992) for a fuller discussion of this issue.

There has been comparatively little research linking maternal AFDC participation to other child outcomes, but the empirical issues are the same. First, it is necessary to control for some measure of income as well as for AFDC status since otherwise the estimated effects of participation are likely to reflect the relative poverty of AFDC mothers. Second, within the group of poor women, one would like to control for the fact that women choose whether or not to go onto AFDC. Blank and Ruggles (1996) show that only 60 percent of eligible women actually take up welfare benefits. Those who do are likely to differ from those who do not in many unobservable respects.

Hill and O'Neill (1994) find that, when instrumental variables methods are used to take account of unobserved variables that might be correlated with AFDC status, AFDC participation has no effect on children's scores on a standardized test of vocabulary, given income. Currie (1995a) confirms that their results hold up even when sibling comparisons are used to account for unobserved maternal background characteristics. Currie and Cole (1993) use data from the 1979 to 1988 waves of the National Longitudinal Survey of Youth (NLSY) to examine the effect of AFDC participation during pregnancy on the utilization of prenatal care and birthweight. They use both sibling comparisons and instrumental variables methods to take account of unobserved variables that might be correlated with both participation in the AFDC program and outcomes,[1] and find that AFDC participation has no additional significant effect on birthweight given income. Together, these studies suggest that income from AFDC has much the same effect on children as family income from any other source.

The Earned Income Tax Credit:
A Comparison to the Negative Income Tax

The slack in the growth of AFDC payments over time has been taken up by the growth in expenditures on the Earned Income Tax Credit, which doubled between 1975 and 1990. The EITC was introduced in 1975 as a means of granting tax relief to low-income tax payers. Because it is administered through the tax system, the EITC is not always viewed as a welfare program. However, unlike most tax credits, the EITC is "refundable," that is, if the amount of the credit exceeds the taxpayer's federal income tax liability, then the difference is refunded. Table 7-1 shows that, in fact, most EITC expenditures are outlays of this kind rather than forgone tax dollars. The EITC differs from traditional cash welfare programs primarily because the majority of recipients work and benefits are available to all kinds of families. Thus, it creates fewer perverse incentives than AFDC.

---

[1]They instrument AFDC participation using state-level variation in program characteristics.

If it is difficult to identify the effects of cash transfers under AFDC, the problems involved in identifying the effects of the EITC are even more formidable. The fundamental problem is that the amount of the credit depends on the parents' earnings, and earnings are likely to reflect many unobserved factors relevant to child well-being. However, the EITC is in many respects similar to the negative income tax (NIT), an income guarantee program that was subjected to exhaustive scrutiny through four large-scale social experiments, although it was never implemented.[2] The four experiments were conducted in New Jersey and Pennsylvania; Seattle and Denver; Gary, Indiana; and rural areas of North Carolina and Iowa. It is important to note that the North Carolina and Gary samples were much poorer than the others.

The income guarantees paid out under the NIT program were large relative to cash transfers that have been made under the EITC. The average payments in the Seattle-Denver experiment, for example, ranged from $919 to $2,031 (1972 dollars), depending on the treatment group. By way of comparison, the poverty line for a family of three persons was $3,099 in 1972. In 1992, the maximum EITC was $1,384 and the poverty line $11,280. Since NIT participants were randomly assigned to "treatment" and "control" groups, the NIT experiments provide a unique opportunity to assess the effects of income transfers per se on the well-being of children in poor families.

Despite the large transfers, findings about the effects of the NIT are inconsistent across studies and experimental populations. In addition, econometric estimates are sometimes at odds with those derived from simple comparisons of treatments and controls. For example, Kehrer and Wolin (1979) find that the mean birthweight of infants born to the treatment group in the Gary experiment was actually lower than the birthweight of the controls. Yet estimates from their structural model suggest that the infants of treatments had higher birthweights in 9 out of 12 maternal age groups.

O'Conner et al. (1976) examine the effect of the NIT on child nutrition using data from the rural experiment. Among subjects in North Carolina, they found positive and significant treatment effects on nutrient intakes. However, the treatment did not appear to have any significant effect in Iowa, a finding that the authors attribute to the relative poverty of the North Carolina sample.

---

[2]Under a NIT, a family that earns no income is guaranteed a minimum income G. Families with earnings Y receive a payment D, where $D = G - t_1 Y$. The quantity $B = G/t_1$ is referred to as the break-even level of income since workers who earn more than B receive no payments. If income is equal to the wage multiplied by hours worked, and workers face a tax rate t, then workers on the NIT earn w $(1 - t - t_1)$ for every hour of work, whereas workers with incomes above B earn $w(1 - t)$. That is, workers on the NIT face a higher tax rate. The EITC differs from the NIT in that the EITC has no income guarantee. Also, since at first the size of the credit increases with earnings, the EITC lowers effective marginal tax rates for the poorest rather than raising them. After a certain level of income, the credit begins to be phased out, creating a higher implicit tax rate.

Maynard and Crawford (1976) found that elementary school children from NIT families in North Carolina showed statistically significant improvements in attendance, standardized tests, and grades. However, there were no effects for elementary school children in Iowa. Once again, this pattern of results is attributed to the fact that the children in North Carolina were more disadvantaged than those in Iowa. Maynard and Murnane (1979) found that in the Gary experiment the NIT treatment had positive effects on reading scores of young children but that these effects were statistically significant only among children whose families had been in the program for 3 or more years.

Finally, in an analysis of data from the New Jersey experiment, Mallar (1977) found that teenagers whose parents were enrolled in NIT were 20 percent to 90 percent more likely to complete high school depending on the NIT plan. However, Venti (1984) found only an 11 percent increase in the probability of completing high school for youth in the Seattle-Denver experiment. This lower estimate seems more probable in view of the relatively short duration of the experiments and the many long-term factors (such as achievement in early grades) that have been linked to educational attainment. These results may also be related to the fact that, in all four experiments, youths in treatment households were less likely to be employed than controls (Robins, 1985).

These studies suggest that the relatively large income transfers made to families under the NIT had a positive effect on the nutritional status and educational attainment of children in the poorest families. However, the magnitudes vary greatly from study to study. Perhaps unsurprisingly, studies of the effects of the NIT on consumption also show that families spent much of the subsidy on goods that may not have been directly related to the well-being of their children. For example, the NIT appears to have had a negative effect on the labor supply of married women,[3] and positive effects on housing expenditures and purchases of consumer durables (Robins, 1985; Michael, 1978).[4]

WHAT WE KNOW ABOUT IN-KIND PROGRAMS

A parallel "in-kind" welfare system has grown up alongside the cash system. This system aims to directly provide for a child's "basic needs": decent housing, food, medical care, and quality early education. Table 7-1 shows that expenditures on virtually all of these programs have shown steady growth over time (the exception being the School Lunch Program). Table 7-2 indicates that in contrast to stagnant AFDC caseloads, caseloads for most in-kind programs have been increasing.

---

[3]No convincing evidence of a link between maternal employment and children's well-being has been found. See Blau and Grossberg (1990) and Desai et al. (1989).

[4]The NIT may also have increased the probability of marital dissolution, although this finding remains controversial (cf. Cain and Wissoker, 1990; Hannan and Tuma, 1990).

TABLE 7-2 Trends in Caseloads (millions)

	1975	1980	1990	1995
Cash Transfers				
AFDC				
Total recipients	11.1	10.6	11.5	13.6
Child recipients	7.8	7.2	7.8	9.3
Earned Income Tax Credit				
No. of families	6.2	7.0	12.6	17.4
In-Kind Transfers				
Housing Assistance				
No. of households	3.2[a]	4.0	5.4	5.8
Food Stamps				
Total recipients	16.3	19.2	20.0	26.6
WIC				
No. of women	0.2[a]	0.4	1.0	1.6
No. of infants	0.2[a]	0.5	1.4	1.8
No. of children	0.5[a]	1.0	2.1	3.5
School nutrition				
School lunch				
No. any meals	26.3[a]	26.6	24.1	25.6
No. free meals	10.5[a]	10.0	10.3	12.4
School Breakfast	2.5[a]	3.6	4.0	6.3
No. free meals	2.0[a]	2.8	3.3	5.1
Medicaid				
Total recipients	22.0	21.6	25.3	35.1
Child recipients	9.6	9.3	11.2	17.2
Head Start	0.3	0.4	0.5	0.7

[a]These figures are for 1977.
SOURCE: U.S. House of Representatives (1993, 1994, 1996).

Initial evaluation of these in-kind programs is more straightforward than the evaluation of cash transfer programs because we can ask whether the program has an impact on the specific child outcome it was designed to affect. For example, we can ask whether receipt of housing assistance is associated with improvements in housing or whether household participation in the Food Stamps program improves a child's diet.

We might then wish to ask whether the program has additional effects on related child outcomes. For example, better nutrition could influence a child's cognitive abilities. Also, subsidies to food and housing may influence child outcomes more generally by relaxing the family's budget constraint (see Moffitt, 1989, and Citro and Michael, 1995, for discussions of the valuation of in-kind benefits).[5] However, since the effects of income transfers are discussed above,

---

[5]The National Research Council (Citro and Michael, 1995) concludes that for simplicity's sake, "near-cash" benefits such as Food Stamps and housing assistance should be counted at their dollar

the focus in this section is on any effects of participation in in-kind programs on the specific outcomes that the programs were designed to affect. In practice, this restriction eliminates very few studies from consideration.[6]

Housing Assistance

In contrast to AFDC and Food Stamps, housing assistance is not an entitlement: when funds allocated to the program run out, people who are eligible must be wait-listed. It is estimated that about half of federal expenditures on housing assistance directly benefit children, while the elderly are the other large group of beneficiaries.

Most expenditures are on rental assistance programs rather than on low-rent public housing (which is what many people think of as "public housing"). And since 1982, most new authorizations for rental housing assistance have been for Section 8 programs (Pedone, 1988). The Section 8 existing housing program provides rent subsidies to families who find an apartment of their own choosing, as long as the rent is below the "Fair Market Rent" established by the Department of Housing and Urban Development (HUD) and the unit meets minimum quality standards. Rental assistance typically reduces a family's rental payments to 30 percent of its income, after deductions for certain expenses are taken into account.

Deficient housing is hazardous to children. For example, lead poisoning is three times more common among poor children than among nonpoor children and is directly related to housing conditions. The risk of accidental death is also three times higher for poor children, and some of this increased risk may be due to hazards in the home (Starfield, 1985). In 1989, 18 percent of poor households (2.2 million households) lived in housing with severe or moderate physical problems compared to 7 percent of nonpoor households.[7]

It is not known whether, in general, housing assistance enables families in deficient housing to move to adequate housing. A 1988 HUD study found that more than half of public housing households lived in projects that needed moderate to substantial rehabilitation just to meet HUD's own standards. The estimated cost of bringing these units up to standard would have exceeded $20 billion 1986 dollars (Lazere et al., 1991).

---

value when comparing the resources available to different households, and various procedures for valuing housing benefits are discussed. However, the panel also recommends that health insurance be excluded from these comparisons because it is too hard to come up with a meaningful estimate of its value to households in different circumstances.

[6]An exception that deserves mention is Meyers et al. (1993) who found that in a sample of poor children in Boston, those who received housing assistance were less likely to be anemic. The study did not control for selection into public housing.

[7]Problems that HUD classifies as severe include lack of basic plumbing facilities, serious heating breakdowns, and rat infestations. An example of a moderate deficiency is the use of unvented gas, oil, or kerosene heaters as primary heating equipment.

Section 8 programs require families to locate a landlord willing to participate and to arrange with the landlord for inspections and repairs within a fixed period of time. One case study of 56 single mothers in eastern Massachusetts in 1985 and 1986 found that after waiting an average of 2 years to receive a certificate, 24 women returned them unused because they were unable to find housing that met program requirements within the allotted time (Mulroy, 1988). On the other hand, there is some evidence that recipients of vouchers pay higher rent (Kennedy and Finkel, 1987; Apgar, 1990) and move to better neighborhoods (Johnson, 1986). The often dismal social conditions in many public housing projects must be weighed against any improvements in the physical housing stock. However, it is very difficult to identify the effects of neighborhoods and schools because any relationship we observe between neighborhood characteristics and individual outcomes could reflect the characteristics of the individual or of his or her family that placed them in these neighborhoods in the first place.

The Gautreaux program sheds light on this issue. Under the program, residents in public housing projects can apply for Section 8 housing certificates and move to private apartments. Some apartments are in predominantly white suburbs, while others are in the inner city. Although the persons admitted to the program are not a random sample of public housing residents,[8] Rosenbaum (Rosenbaum et al., 1986; Rosenbaum, 1992) asserts that the program assigns apartments in an approximately random manner, since people get whatever is available when they reach the top of the waiting list. He finds that 7 years after their move, children who had moved to the suburbs were 15 percent less likely to have dropped out of school, 16 percent more likely to be in a college-track program, and 34 percent more likely to be employed than those who had moved within the inner city. All of these differences are statistically significant at the 90 percent level of confidence.

These findings suggest that voucher programs can have a positive effect on the life chances of children if they enable families to find housing in better neighborhoods. On the other hand, they suggest that the disamenities associated with large public housing projects may have significant negative effects. However, the study is marred by high rates of attrition from the sample. HUD is currently conducting an experimental evaluation of a program similar to Gautreaux in four cities.[9] An experimental evaluation that took care to minimize attrition could shed great light on the possible beneficial effects of housing vouchers, and on the issue of the effects of neighborhoods more generally.

Despite their bad reputations, housing projects may be better than much of

---

[8]Applicants are screened to make sure that they have paid their rent regularly and that they have adequate housekeeping abilities. The program does not serve families with more than four children because few large housing units are available in the suburbs. In addition, the act of applying for an apartment in an unknown location may indicate that a person is strongly motivated to improve his or her circumstances.

[9]Personal communication, Lawrence Katz, Department of Economics, Harvard University, 1997.

the housing available to poor families who do not have access to voucher programs. By combining data from the 1990 Census and the Current Population Surveys, Currie and Yelowitz (1997) are able to examine the effects of residence in public housing projects on housing quality as measured by the extent of overcrowding and the density of the housing complex. They also examine the effect on the probability that a child has been retained in grade, an important index of educational attainment. They find significant positive effects on all three outcomes.

The Food Stamp Program

Food Stamps are issued in the form of booklets of coupons that may be used to purchase all foods except alcohol, tobacco, and hot foods "intended for immediate consumption." In contrast to AFDC, Food Stamps are available to all families who meet federally determined income-eligibility requirements, though AFDC recipients are automatically eligible.

The value of a family's Food Stamp allocation is typically much less than what the family spends on food. Hence, it is likely that the increase in the family's food expenditures will be less than the value of the Food Stamps because families can spend the same amount on food that they would have in the absence of the program and use the "freed-up" money for something else. In fact, economic theory suggests that Food Stamp families may spend a little more on food because they feel wealthier, but that there should be no difference between the effects of Food Stamps and the effects of cash transfers to the family. However, recent experimental studies of Food Stamp "cash-outs" conclude that families spend more than the expected amount of their Food Stamp income on food.[10]

In these cash-outs, Food Stamp Program (FSP) participants were randomly selected to receive the cash value of their Food Stamps rather than the coupons. Fraker et al. (1995) summarize the results of four of these demonstrations. In three of the four, reductions in food expenditures ranged from 7 percent to 22 percent. In one site, there was no effect on food expenditures. However, in this site, the change was introduced with little publicity, and recipients continued to receive separate checks from AFDC and the FSP, rather than one combined check. Fraker et al. argue that these differences can explain the fact that the switch to cash had little impact at this site.

Two intriguing hypotheses have been advanced to explain why Food Stamp income might have a different effect on food expenditures than cash income. First, it is possible that households view FSP benefits as a more permanent source of income than other sources—thus they are more likely to spend the money rather than saving it for a "rainy day." Second, women with children may be

---

[10]Nonexperimental studies of this issue have proved inconclusive. See Fraker (1990a, 1990b) and Korenman and Miller (1992) for examples, and Currie (1995a) for a discussion.

more likely to spend a given amount of income on food than men, and the female head of household may have more control of Food Stamp coupons (which are likely to be issued in her name) than she has over the household's cash income.[11] Neither theory has been subjected to an empirical test.

Supplemental Feeding Program for Women, Infants, and Children

In addition to the Food Stamp Program, the federal government offers several feeding programs that give food directly to needy children and their mothers. The WIC program provides nutritional counseling and food supplements to pregnant and lactating mothers and their infants as well as to low-income children up to age 5. All participants must be certified to be nutritionally "at risk." WIC is funded by appropriation, and the size of each year's appropriation limits the number of people that can be served. WIC is currently operated out of some 8,330 sites and serves approximately 60 percent of those eligible (Jones, 1992). The law requires that the WIC program provide foods containing protein, iron, calcium, vitamin A, and vitamin C. Food packages must be appropriately tailored to meet the needs of each category of recipient.[12] In fiscal year 1991, the average monthly WIC package was valued at $31.67.

Many studies find that WIC has positive effects on the utilization of prenatal care and on measures of infant health including birthweight, the incidence of low birthweight, gestational age, and infant mortality.[13] Schramm (1985) and Devaney et al. (1990) examine the effects of WIC on the Medicaid costs of newborns. The results are of particular interest because they can be used to compare the costs and benefits of the WIC program. Schramm found that in 1980, a dollar spent on WIC reduced Medicaid costs in Missouri by approximately 80 cents in the first 30 to 45 days after birth. Devaney et al. examined Medicaid costs in the first 60 days after birth in five states and found that reductions in Medicaid costs over this period more than offset the costs of providing WIC.

Unfortunately, only two WIC studies, by Metcoff et al. (1985) and Caan et al. (1987), have used random assignment to generate a comparison group. If WIC participants are worse off than nonparticipants because places are scarce and only the neediest are admitted into the program, then studies that compare

---

[11]Some circumstantial evidence pertinent to this hypothesis comes from the Washington State Welfare Reform Demonstration Program. AFDC recipients in demonstration counties had the option of choosing to receive their AFDC and Food Stamp benefits in the form of a single consolidated check rather than continuing to receive Food Stamp coupons. Over 20 percent of these women opted to continue receiving the coupons.

[12]The categories are children 0 to 3 months of age, children 4 to 12 months, women and children with special dietary needs, children from 1 to 5, pregnant and nursing mothers, and postpartum nonnursing mothers.

[13]See Devaney et al. (1990) for a review.

WIC participants and nonparticipants will underestimate the effects of the program. Conversely, if WIC participants are more highly motivated or better informed than nonparticipants, then studies of this type may overestimate the program's effects. Without knowing more about the selection mechanism underlying participation, it is difficult to assess the probable direction of this bias.

Still, given that the program is locally administered, the factors governing selection into the WIC program are likely to differ considerably over time and across sites. Hence, the fact that estimated effects are remarkably constant across states and over time suggests that the positive results are not entirely driven by selection. This conclusion is reinforced by a recent study by Brien and Swann (1997) who use both instrumental variables and sibling comparison methods to analyze data from the 1988 National Maternal and Infant Health Survey. They find significant effects of WIC on birth outcomes and on maternal behaviors (such as reductions in drinking while pregnant) among blacks, but they are unable to detect any effect among whites.

Studies of the effects of WIC on the nutrient intakes of children generally find positive effects (cf. Fraker, 1990a), but these studies are also plagued by possible selection bias. One way to control for bias is to follow the same child over time. The Centers for Disease Control reported the results of a study that followed child WIC participants in six states over a 2-year interval (United States Department of Health and Human Services, 1978). The study found that after three WIC visits the percentage of children who were anemic fell by more than half. In addition, the fraction of 6- to 23-month-old children below the tenth percentile of length-for-age fell from 21 percent to 15 percent after three WIC visits.

Hicks et al. (1982) focus on 21 pairs of siblings from rural Louisiana. Because of the design of the WIC program in that state, the younger child in each pair was eligible for supplementation beginning in the third trimester of pregnancy, while the older child became eligible for WIC only after the first year. The results show that the "early supplementation" group had significantly higher scores on a range of cognitive tests.

School Nutrition Programs

The federal government supports six other programs that provide meals or monthly food supplements to low-income children. The largest is the National School Lunch Program (NSLP). The NSLP is an entitlement that operates by reimbursing schools for each meal served. School lunches are provided free to children with family incomes less than 130 percent of the federal poverty line and are subsidized if the family income falls between 130 and 185 percent of the poverty line. In 1990, lunches were served to approximately 12.8 million students, and 10.3 million students received free lunches. The School Breakfast Program (SBP) serves fewer, typically needier, students.

The effects of school nutrition programs are controversial. Older studies found that participants had higher 24-hour nutrient intakes than nonparticipants and that SBP participants were more likely to eat breakfast than nonparticipants (Hanes et al., 1984). However, more recent studies show higher intakes of some nutrients, but also higher intakes of fat and cholesterol (Gordon et al., 1995).

Surprisingly, there have been few attempts to evaluate the effects of school nutrition programs on cognitive outcomes. In one of the more compelling studies, Meyers et al. (1989) examined 1,092 third to sixth grade children in Lawrence, Massachusetts, before and after the SBP was introduced at their school in 1987. They found that the Breakfast Program participants showed greater improvements on the Comprehensive Test of Basic Skills, relative to their initial scores, than nonparticipant children. SBP participation also reduced tardiness.

Medicaid

Medicaid is the main system of public health insurance for poor women and children. It is a federal-state matching entitlement program, administered at the state level. Table 7-1 shows that expenditures on children account for a relatively small share of total Medicaid expenditures: The average expenditure on an AFDC child is $891 (1992 dollars) compared to $3,778 for an aged person (U.S. House of Representatives, 1994). Still, both expenditures and caseloads continue to grow as shown in Tables 7-1 and 7-2.

States were required to offer Medicaid coverage to AFDC recipients, and until recent extensions of coverage to other groups, there was a very close link between AFDC recipiency and Medicaid eligibility. However, evidence that many children and pregnant women were not receiving adequate preventive care led Congress to expand Medicaid coverage for pregnant women and children beginning in 1984. States are now required to cover all pregnant women and children under 6 with family incomes less than 133 percent of the federal poverty line, regardless of family structure.[14] Beginning on July 1, 1991, states have been required to cover all children born after September 30, 1983, whose family incomes are less than 100 percent of the federal poverty line.

The recent 1997 Budget Reconciliation Act allocates $47 billion over the next 10 years to allow states to expand health insurance coverage to an even larger group of uninsured children, either through the Medicaid program or through separate state initiatives. States must contribute 70 percent of what the state would have contributed under the matching provisions of the Medicaid program—that is, states can get federal money to expand health insurance coverage at a very favorable match rate. These new provisions make it more pressing than ever to determine the effects of public health insurance on children.

Currie and Thomas (1995a) use panel data that follow the same child over time and show that, when children are covered by Medicaid, they are more likely

---

[14] The coverage of pregnant women is limited to services related to the pregnancy.

to have had *any* doctor visits in the past 6 months. Moreover, the effect of being covered by Medicaid is larger than the effect of being covered by private health insurance, which probably reflects the fact that Medicaid has no copayments or deductibles. This effect is the same for black and white children. However, white children also receive more visits for illness when they are covered by Medicaid than when they are uninsured, and this is not true for African Americans. Thus, equivalent insurance coverage does not guarantee equal care.

Currie and Gruber (1996a) look at the effect of becoming *eligible* for Medicaid on the utilization of medical care and on child health. The effects of Medicaid eligibility are identified using the recent federally mandated expansions of the Medicaid program to pregnant women and children described above. They find that expansions of eligibility to pregnant women increased the fraction of women eligible from 12 to 43 percent. This increase was associated with an 8.5 percent decline in the infant mortality rate.

However, earlier extensions of Medicaid eligibility to very poor women who were already income-eligible for AFDC were much more cost-effective than later expansions to higher-income women. The reason is that higher-income women were less likely to become covered early in their pregnancies. Hence, they did not avail themselves of free preventive prenatal care available under the Medicaid program. There is evidence, however, that hospitals enrolled eligible women in Medicaid at delivery so that costly services received by unhealthy newborns were paid for by the program. These results suggest that outreach programs designed to improve take-up could increase the cost-effectiveness of the Medicaid extensions to pregnant women.

Currie and Gruber (1996b) use the same methodology to look at the effects of extending eligibility to additional groups of low-income children. They find that, although many newly eligible children did not take up coverage, becoming eligible for Medicaid reduced the probability that a child went without a doctor's visit in the past year and also improved the quality of care as measured by the fraction of these visits that took place in doctor's offices rather than hospital outpatient clinics or emergency rooms. These changes were linked to significant reductions in child mortality from internal causes and had no effect on mortality from external causes (e.g., accidents). This is the pattern one might anticipate if the changes in mortality were linked to increases in the use of preventive care.

The complex relationship between formal take-up and benefits received is further explored by Currie (1995b) in a study that focuses on differences between children of immigrants and children of the native born. She shows that recent expansions of Medicaid eligibility had smaller effects on Medicaid coverage among immigrant children but increased the utilization of basic services by at least as much among immigrants as among nonimmigrants.

The differences in patterns of take-up and utilization by race and natality are consistent with evidence from other countries that extensions of insurance coverage alone will not eliminate socioeconomic differences in health care utilization or health (Currie, 1995c). It is unlikely that lack of information alone can explain the differences, since black and immigrant parents are as likely as other parents to bring their children in for free preventive care when they become eligible for Medicaid. Similarly, purely cultural explanations that posit that some groups value medical care less than others are difficult to reconcile with this evidence.

Disparities in the availability of private health insurance, in the transaction costs associated with enrolling in the Medicaid program, or in access to providers willing to accept Medicaid payments may all be important determinants of group differences. Currie et al. (1995) examine the last of these three factors and show, using state-level data, that increases in Medicaid fee ratios for obstetricians/ gynecologists are associated with significant declines in infant mortality, presumably because of increases in either effective physician supply or the quality of services provided.

The fraction of children with private health insurance fell over the period of the Medicaid expansions to such an extent that there was actually a small decrease in the fraction of children with any health insurance coverage. These trends lead one to suspect that public health insurance may have "crowded out" private insurance coverage. Cutler and Gruber (1996) estimate that as many as 50 percent of the people who became covered by the Medicaid expansions may previously have had private health insurance. While a switch from private to public insurance does not raise the fraction of children covered, the Currie and Thomas (1995a) results suggest that it may still improve the health of children by encouraging the utilization of preventive care.

Other analysts (see Dubay and Kenney, 1997) point out that private health insurance coverage was declining even among groups such as single men whom one would not expect to be affected by the expansions. If one asks what fraction of the total decline in private health insurance coverage is a result of substitution towards Medicaid, the answer is approximately 15 percent. Clearly, much research remains to be done on the causes and consequences of the decline in private health insurance coverage.

Head Start

Head Start is a federal-local matching grant program that aims to improve the skills of poor preschoolers so that they can begin schooling on a more equal footing with their more advantaged peers. Unlike Medicaid, it is not an entitlement program, and only about a third of eligible children are served (Stewart, 1992). Head Start has enjoyed widespread bipartisan support over a long period, although evidence regarding long-term effects is inconclusive. Experimental studies that focus primarily on inner-city African-American children typically find an initial positive effect on children's cognitive achievement that fades out in 2 or 3 years.

Supporters of the program argue that a narrow focus on cognitive test scores is inappropriate, given that Head Start is intended to affect a range of outcomes (see McKey et al., 1985). Evidence from the Perry Preschool Project, which found that program children were less likely to drop out of high school, engage in crime, or become pregnant as teenagers, is often cited. However, since the project included only 58 treatments and 65 controls, was funded at about twice the rate of a typical Head Start program, and did not involve a national sample, it is not clear that the findings generalize.

Currie and Thomas (1995b) examine sibling comparisons from a national sample and find that children who were in Head Start have higher test scores at the end of the program than either stay-at-home siblings or siblings who went to other preschools. The effects are of the same magnitude for both black and white children and indicate that Head Start closes one-third of the gap between these children and others. But consistent with the experimental studies, they find that the effects on black children fade out rapidly. These results suggest that the positive effects of Head Start may be undermined by subsequent deprivation among these children.

In contrast, the effects on the test scores of white children do not fade out. Moreover, white children 10 and over are significantly less likely to have repeated a grade if they attended Head Start and are thus less likely to have experienced the age/grade delay that often leads to high school noncompletion. Both black and white children who attended Head Start were more likely to be immunized than stay-at-home siblings, although there was no effect on height-for-age, a measure of long-term nutritional status.

In related work, Currie and Thomas (1996a) find that Head Start has large and lasting effects on the test scores of Latino students. A closer inspection of the data reveals that these positive effects are largest for Mexican-origin children and smallest for Puerto Rican children. However, due to sample size limitations it is not possible to sort out the effects of ethnicity and the effects of region. It is possible, for example, that the ethnic differences reflect differences in the programs available in New York, where Puerto Rican children tend to be located, and California and Texas, where Mexican-origin children are concentrated, rather than any independent effect of ethnicity per se.

Currie and Thomas (1996b) ask whether differences in school quality can explain differences in the pattern of "fadeout" in test scores between whites and blacks. Specifically, the initial positive effects of the Head Start program may be undermined if Head Start children were subsequently exposed to inferior schools. And since we see fadeout for blacks but not for whites, it would have to be the case that black Head Start children are attending worse schools than other black children but that the same was not true among whites.

Currie and Thomas test this hypothesis using a sample of eighth graders from the National Educational Longitudinal Study of 1988 (NELS). Their work builds on earlier research by Lee and Loeb (1995) who showed, using these data, that the schools attended by Head Start children are of worse quality in some observable dimensions than the schools attended by other children. Even if family income and parent's education are controlled for, children who attended Head Start have lower test scores than other children. This result is to be expected if Head Start does not entirely compensate for early disadvantages.

However, among black children, the gap between Head Start children and other children is virtually eliminated when we compare children within the same school. That is, within schools, black Head Start children do no worse than other black children. But since they perform more poorly than other children on average, they must be attending schools in which all black children do badly. If a "quality" school is defined as one in which children do well, then these results suggests that black children who attend Head Start go on to attend schools of significantly worse quality than other black children. In contrast, among non-Hispanic white children there appears to be little difference in the schools attended by Head Start and other children.

WHAT WE NEED TO KNOW

The preceding discussion is summarized in Table 7-3. The table presents a matrix of programs and effects. Differences in the effects of programs across groups have been suppressed, although one theme that has emerged from the discussion so far is that they are important. The most striking feature of Table 7-3 is that there are many empty cells—we clearly need to learn a great deal more about the effects of welfare before we can make informed public policy. In some cases, research has been limited by lack of appropriate data. In others, existing information has not yet been fully exploited. This section highlights some unanswered research questions and discusses the extent to which better data collection efforts could help.

Effects of Welfare on Long-Run Outcomes

Ultimately, what many people care about is whether investments in children today will produce productive, well-socialized adults tomorrow. However, Table 7-3 highlights the fact that little is known about the effects of welfare on long-term outcomes. Lack of data places major limitations on this type of research. Many important outcomes can only be examined 10 to 15 years after childhood participation in welfare programs. There are few existing datasets that combine information about childhood participation in welfare, other family background characteristics, and the outcomes of interest.

One exception is the National Longitudinal Survey's Child-Mother file (NLSCM). The NLSCM contains information about the children of a sample of approximately 6,300 women who were between the ages of 14 and 21 in 1978. Information about childhood participation in AFDC, the Food Stamp Program, Medicaid, Head Start, and WIC is available. By the time the 1994 wave is

196

TABLE 7-3 Summary of Effects of Welfare Programs on Measures of Child Well-Being

Measure	AFDC	EITC/ NIT	Food Stamps	Housing	Medicaid	WIC	School Nutrition	Head Start
Health								
Infant mortality or birthweight	0					+	+	
Nutrition/food exp.		+?/?	?/+			+	?/?	
Preventive care					+	+		+
Primary Education								
Test scores	0	+?				+	+	+
Schooling attainment		+		+?				+
Long-Run Measures								
Welfare dependence	0							
Teen pregnancy	0							?
Employment		−		+?				
High school graduation								?
Crime								?

NOTE: 0 = no effect; + = positive effect; − = negative effect; ? = effect indeterminate.

released, there will be more than 800 children over 16. Of course, since these children will have been born to young mothers, they will not be a nationally representative sample of 16 year olds. Still, this sample is a valuable resource. If future waves of the survey continue to be funded, it will grow in size and in representativeness and allow us to address many questions about the relationship between welfare and long-term outcomes such as schooling attainment, teen parenthood, and crime.

A second exception is a special supplement to the Panel Study of Income Dynamic (PSID) that was fielded in 1995. This module contains retrospective information about early childhood education and criminal activity that can be linked to data about welfare participation from the original PSID file. The PSID is currently undertaking an even more ambitious data collection effort, the 1997 Child Development Supplement. The survey of 3,500 0 to 12-year-old children will have assessments of cognitive, behavioral, and health status. Data are being collected from the mother, a second caregiver, the absent parent (if relevant), teachers, school administrators, and the children themselves. The survey will also include time diaries for caregivers, children, and teachers, to examine inputs into child development. Finally, other inputs such as resources in the home and neighborhood will also be measured. Once again, this information can be linked to data about welfare participation from the main files, and follow-up on these children may help to identify long-term effects of participation. Fielding this type of supplement to existing data sources promises to be a cost-effective method of providing information on the link between the current outcomes of young adults and their participation in various programs as children.

An additional issue that can be addressed is whether there are links between the short-term outcomes that have been examined in previous research and longer-term outcomes. If it is found that particular short-term outcomes are reliable "markers" for longer-term outcomes, then future evaluations of welfare programs may not require as much costly long-term follow-up of the participants.

Why Do Effects Appear to Vary with Race, Ethnicity, and Natality?

The PSID and NLSCM datasets will both support analyses stratified by race, ethnicity, and natality. However, in many cases the sample sizes are very small. In order to properly document differences in outcomes, or even in utilization, it will be necessary to add questions to existing large-scale datasets. For example, the Census asks questions only about the use of cash welfare, even though expenditures on in-kind programs constitute the largest and fastest-growing share of the welfare bill.

A second problem is that large-scale, individual-level datasets typically lack information about neighborhoods and administrative procedures that could be used to test specific hypotheses about group differences. For example, one might believe that black children on Medicaid receive fewer visits for illness than white children because the providers that serve them are overcrowded and it is more difficult to get additional appointments. It would be very useful to know the extent to which group differences are associated with the administration of welfare programs, rather than with differences in parental tastes or circumstances.

It is unlikely that many detailed questions of this type will be added to large-scale surveys, but it would be possible to match data from other sources to the surveys if finer geographical information were made available to researchers. While issues of confidentiality are important, the amount of information that could be gained if it were routinely possible to match survey data to, say, zip-code-level data from other sources can hardly be underestimated.

This type of matching is also greatly facilitated by the existence of a central agency that collects program information (and is willing to give it to researchers). There is a real danger that further devolution of responsibility for welfare to the states will result in a loss of information about the administration of programs, making it more difficult to identify program effects using state-level variation in the programs.

How Do Programs Interact?

One glaring omission from this survey is that there has been no discussion of multiple program participation. Many children are covered by more than one program. For example, AFDC participants are covered by Medicaid and are automatically eligible for Food Stamps. As of 1990, half of AFDC children received free school lunches, 35 percent lived in public or subsidized rental housing, and 19 percent participated in WIC. Conversely, half of all Food Stamp recipients, 42 percent of Medicaid recipients, 38 percent of WIC recipients, and 24 percent of those in public housing also received AFDC. Moffitt (1992) estimates that in 1984, 26.4 percent of nonelderly single-parent families received AFDC, Medicaid, and Food Stamps, and 11 percent received at least one benefit in addition to AFDC.

It is impossible to say how multiple program participation affects the child outcomes discussed above since there has been little research on this topic. Some programs may be duplicative, while others may interact to produce more positive outcomes. For example, Currie and Thomas (1995b) found that children in Head Start were more likely to be immunized than other children, even though many Head Start children would have been eligible for free vaccinations under the Medicaid program in any case. Head Start may help families to enroll in Medicaid, may help them locate a Medicaid provider, or may bypass Medicaid altogether by arranging for children to be immunized at the Head Start center.

An analysis of multiple program participation would assist us in answering the question of whether the current patchwork system of programs is an efficient way to provide welfare. The proliferation of programs increases possibilities for fraud, waste, and mismanagement. On the other hand, the evidence surveyed here suggests that targeting specific benefits directly to individual children has advantages in terms of ensuring that specific benefits are received. We need to know more about the balance between these benefits and costs.

How Do Successful Programs Work?

Data limitations place severe restrictions on our ability to look inside the "black box" of welfare programs. For example, we can show that expansions in Medicaid eligibility have been related to reductions in child mortality rates at the state level, but we do not know why. It could be due either to increased use of preventive care or to more intensive palliative care for sick children. The two possibilities have quite different implications for child well-being as well as for efficiency and program costs. Better information about what goes on during doctor visits and about objective measures of child health status (short of mortality statistics) could help us to address this question. It might be possible, for example, to add questions about anemia, lead poisoning, and anthropometrics (e.g., height-for-age, weight-for height) to the next National Health Interview Survey.

Still, the most likely scenario is one in which we chip away at these questions using an interactive, multidisciplinary approach: analysis of large-scale surveys can be used to develop broad hypotheses, which can then be tested using case studies. The case studies can then be used to develop more precise hypotheses about the survey data and to suggest supplemental survey questions.

Cost-Effectiveness

Evidently, if a program has no effect at all on a desired outcome, then it cannot be considered cost-effective. Many of the programs discussed above have passed this initial test—they can be shown to have positive effects. The question remains however, of whether they are cost-effective, that is, whether the benefits outweigh the costs. The figures discussed above for WIC are quite impressive in this regard. Cost-effectiveness studies exist for other small-scale early intervention programs (not reviewed here) but have not generally been conducted for large-scale federal programs. Although it is unlikely that there will be agreement on all of the costs and benefits that should be included in such an analysis, some rough calculations under varying assumptions would no doubt be useful to policy makers.

CONCLUSIONS

This survey chapter discusses eight large federal welfare programs that affect children. The available evidence is incomplete but suggests a consistent story: programs that target services directly to children have the largest measured effects, while unrestricted cash transfer programs have the smallest, perhaps because their benefits are more diffuse or because the amounts of money involved are typically quite small.

There are also striking and largely unexplained differences in the effects of some programs by race, ethnicity, and/or natality. These differences could reflect nonlinearities in the effects of programs—that is, one might expect larger effects for poorer than for richer children, and children from some groups are more likely to be poor. Alternatively they may reflect differences in the programs available to children of different origins or unobserved differences between participants from different groups that have not been adequately accounted for.

This survey concludes with five questions for future research: (1) Do welfare programs have long-term effects on children? (2) Why do programs have differential effects by race, ethnicity, and natality? (3) How do programs interact? (4) How exactly do successful programs work? (5) Are programs cost-effective? These questions indicate that though we know much more than we did even 5 years ago about the effects of welfare on children, there is still much work to be done if we are to make informed decisions about public policy.

ACKNOWLEDGMENTS

The author is grateful to Lindsay Chase-Lansdale, Greg Duncan, Bentley MacLeod, and Robert Moffitt for helpful comments. Support from the Alfred P. Sloan Foundation, the National Science Foundation under grant #SBR-9512670, and the National Institute of Child Health and Human Development under grant #R01HD31722-01A2 is gratefully acknowledged. The author is solely responsible for the opinions expressed.

REFERENCES

Apgar, W.
   1990   Which housing policy is best? *Housing Policy Debate* 1(1):1-32.
Blank, R., and P. Ruggles
   1996   When do women use AFDC and food stamps? The dynamics of eligibility vs. participation. *Journal of Human Resources* (Winter).
Blau, F., and A. Grossberg
   1990   Maternal Labor Supply and Children's Cognitive Development. NBER Working Paper No. 3536. Cambridge Mass.: National Bureau of Economic Research.
Bloom, B.
   1990   Health insurance and medical care. In *Advance data from vital and health statistics of the National Center for Health Statistics* No. 188. October. Washington D.C.: U.S. Public Health Service.
Brien, M., and C. Swann
   1997   Prenatal WIC Participation and Infant Health: Selection and Maternal Fixed Effects. University of Virginia Department of Economics. Discussion Paper 295. June.

Caan, B., D. Horgen, S. Margen, et al.
  1987 Benefits associated with WIC supplemental feeding during the interpregnancy interval. *The American Journal of Clinical Nutrition* 45:29-41.
Cain, G., and D. Wissoker
  1990 A reanalysis of marital stability in the Seattle-Denver income-maintenance experiment. *American Journal of Sociology* 95:1235-1269.
Citro, C.F., and R.T. Michael, eds.
  1995 *Measuring Poverty: A New Approach.* Washington, D.C.: National Academy Press.
Clarkson, K.
  1975. *Food Stamps and Nutrition.* Washington, D.C.: American Enterprise Institute.
Currie, J.
  1995a *Welfare and the Well-Being of Children.* Fundamentals of Pure and Applied Economics No. 59. Chur, Switzerland: Harwood Academic Publishers.
  1995b Do Children of Immigrants Make Differential Use of Public Health Insurance? NBER Working Paper No. 5388, December. Cambridge, Mass.: National Bureau of Economic Research.
  1995c Socio-economic status and health: Does universal eligibility for health care reduce the gaps? *Scandinavian Journal of Economics* 4
Currie, J. and N. Cole
  1993 Welfare and child health: The link between AFDC participation and birth weight. *American Economic Review* 283(3).
Currie, J., and J. Gruber
  1996a Saving babies: The efficacy and cost of recent expansions of Medicaid eligibility for pregnant women. *Journal of Political Economy* (December).
  1996b Health insurance eligibility, utilization of medical care, and child health. *Quarterly Journal of Economics* (May).
Currie, J., and D. Thomas
  1995a Medical care for children: Public insurance, private insurance, and racial differences in utilization. *Journal of Human Resources* (Winter).
  1995b Does head start make a difference? *American Economic Review* (June).
  1996a Head Start and Cognition Among Latino Children. NBER Working Paper No. 5805. Cambridge, Mass.: National Bureau of Economic Research, December.
  1996b Could Subsequent School Quality Affect the Long Term Gains from Head Start. Cambridge, Mass.: National Bureau of Economic Research, December.
Currie, J., and A. Yelowitz
  1997 Are Public Housing Projects Good for Kids? NBER Working Paper, October. Cambridge, Mass.: National Bureau of Economic Research.
Currie, J., J. Gruber, and M. Fischer
  1995 Physician payments and infant mortality: Evidence from Medicaid fee policy. *American Economic Review* (May).
Cutler, D., and J. Gruber
  1996 Does public insurance crowd out private insurance? *Quarterly Journal of Economics* 111(2):391-430.
Desai, S., L. Chase-Lansdale, and R. Michael
  1989 Mother or market? Effects of maternal employment on the intellectual ability of 4-year-old children. *Demography* 26(4):545-561.
Devaney, B., P. Haines, and R. Moffitt
  1989 *Assessing the Dietary Effects of the Food Stamp Program, Volume 2: Empirical Results.* Washington, D.C.: Mathematica Policy Research Inc.
Devaney, B., L. Bilheimer, and J. Schore
  1990 *The Savings in Medicaid Costs for Newborns and Their Mothers from Prenatal Participation in the WIC Program.* Washington, D.C.: Mathematica Policy Research Inc.

Dubay, L., and G. Kenney
  1997   Did Medicaid expansions for pregnant women crowd out private coverage? *Health Af-
          fairs* (Jan./Feb.):185-193.
Ellwood, D., and M. Bane
  1985   The impact of AFDC on family structure and living arrangements. Pp. 137-207 in R.
          Ehrenberg, ed., *Research in Labor Economics*, Greenwich, Conn.: JAI Press.
Ensminger, M., and A. Slusarcick
  1992   Paths to high school graduation or dropout: A longitudinal study of a 1st grade cohort.
          Sociology of Education 65(April):95-113.
Fraker, T.
  1990a   *The Effects of Food Stamps on Food Consumption: A Review of the Literature.* Washing-
          ton, D.C.: USDA Food and Nutrition Service.
  1990b   *Analyses of the 1985 Continuing Survey of Food Intakes by Individuals, Volume II—
          Estimating the Effects of the WIC and Food Stamp Programs on Dietary Intake by Women
          and Young Children.* Washington, D.C.: USDA Food and Nutrition Service.
Fraker, T., A. Martini, and J. Ohls
  1995   The effect of food stamp cashout on food expenditures. *Journal of Human Resources*
          30(4):633-649.
Gordon, A.R., B.L. Devaney, and J.A. Burghardt
  1995   Dietary effects of the national school lunch program and the school breakfast program.
          American Journal of Clinical Nutrition 61(January):221-232.
Gottschalk, P.
  1990   AFDC participation across generations. *The American Economic Review* 80(2):367-371.
Hannan, M., and N. Tuma
  1990   A reassessment of the effect of income maintenance on marital dissolution in the Seattle-
          Denver experiment. *American Journal of Sociology* 95(5):1270-1298.
Hanes, S., J. Vermeersch, and S. Gale
  1984   The national evaluation of school nutrition programs: Program impact on dietary intake.
          American Journal of Clinical Nutrition 40(August):390-413.
Heckman, J.
  1990   Alternative approaches to the evaluation of social programs: Econometric and experimen-
          tal methods. Address to the World Econometric Society Meetings, Barcelona, Spain.
Hicks, L., R. Langham, and J. Takenaka
  1982   Cognitive and health measures following early nutritional supplementation: A sibling
          study. *American Journal of Public Health* 72:1110-1118.
Hill, A., and J. O'Neill
  1994   The transmission of cognitive achievement across three generations. *Journal of Human
          Resources* 29(4).
Johnson, G.
  1986   Rent paying ability and racial settlement patterns: A review and analysis of recent
          housing allowance evidence. *American Journal of Economics and Sociology*
          45(1):17-26.
Jones, J.
  1992   The WIC program: Eligibility, coverage, and funding. Washington, D.C.: Congressional
          Research Service, January 10.
Kehrer, B., and C. Wolin
  1979   Impact of income maintenance on low birth weight: Evidence from the Gary experiment.
          Journal of Human Resources 14(4):434-462.
Kennedy, S., and M. Finkel
  1987   *Report of First Year Findings for the Freestanding Housing Voucher Demonstration.*
          Cambridge, Mass: ABT Associates, Inc.

Korenman, S., and J. Miller
   1992   Food stamp program participation and maternal and child health. Draft Report to the Food
          and Nutrition Service of the U.S. Department of Agriculture, May.
Lazere, E., P. Leanard, C. Dolbeare, and B. Zigas
   1991   *A Place to Call Home: The Low Income Housing Crisis Continues.* Washington, D.C.:
          The Center on Budget and Policy Priorities.
Lee, V. and S. Loeb
   1995   Where do Head Start attendees end up? One reason why preschool effects fade out.
          Educational Evaluation and Policy Analysis 17(1):62-82.
Mallar, C.
   1977   The educational and labor supply responses of young adults on the urban graduated work
          incentive experiment. In Harold Watts and Albert Rees, eds., *New Jersey Income Mainte-
          nance Experiments*, New York: Academic Press.
Mayer, S.
   1996   *Can More Money Buy Better Kids?* Cambridge, Mass.: Harvard University Press.
Maynard, R., and D. Crawford
   1976   School performance. *Rural Income Maintenance Experiment: Final Report.* Madison,
          WI: Institute for Research on Poverty.
Maynard, R., and R. Murnane
   1979   The effects of a negative income tax on school performance: Results of an experiment.
          Journal of Human Resources 14(4).
McKey, R., L. Condell, H. Ganson, B. Barrett, C. McConkey, and M. Planz
   1985   *The Impact of Head Start on Children, Families and Communities: Final Report of the
          Head Start Evaluation, Synthesis and Utilization Project.* Washington, D.C.: CSR, Inc.
Metcoff, J., D. Rubin, M. Napoleone, and K. Nichols
   1985   Effect of food supplementation (WIC) during pregnancy on birth weight. *American Jour-
          nal of Clinical Nutrition* 41(May).
Meyers, A., A. Sampson, M. Weitzman, and H. Kayne
   1989   School breakfast program and school performance. *American Journal of Diseases of Chil-
          dren* 143(10):1234-1239.
Meyers, A., D. Rubin, M. Napoleone, and K. Nichols
   1993   Public housing subsidies may improve poor children's nutrition. *American Journal of
          Public Health* 83(1).
Michael, R.
   1978   The consumption studies. In John Palmer and Joseph Pechman, eds., *Welfare in Rural
          Areas: The Iowa Income Maintenance Experiment.* Washington, D.C.: The Brookings
          Institution.
Mitchell J., and R. Shurman
   1984   Access to private obstetrics/gynecology services under Medicaid. *Medical Care* 22(No-
          vember):1026-1037.
Moffitt, R.
   1992   Incentive effects of the U.S. welfare system: A review. *Journal of Economic Literature*
          30(March):1-61.
   1989   Estimating the value of an in-kind transfer: The case of food stamps. *Econometrica*
          57(2):385-410.
Moore, K. and S. Caldwell
          The effect of government policies on out-of-wedlock sex and pregnancy. *Family Plan-
          ning Perspectives* 9(4):164-169.
Mulroy, E.
   1988   The search for affordable housing. In E. Mulroy, ed., *Women as Single Parents: Con-
          fronting the Institutional Barriers in the Courts, the Workplace and the Housing Market.*
          New York: Auburn House.

Murray, C.
   1984   *Losing Ground.* New York: Basic Books.
O'Conner, F., P. Madden, and A. Prindle
   1976   Nutrition. *Rural Income Maintenance Experiment: Final Report.* Madison, Wisc.: Insti-
           tute for Research on Poverty.
Pedone, C.
   1988   *Current Housing Problems and Possible Federal Responses.* Washington, D.C.: Congres-
           sional Budget Office. 1988.
Robins, Philip
   1985   A comparison of the labor supply findings from the four negative income tax experi-
           ments. *Journal of Human Resources* 20(4):567-582.
Rosenbaum, J., L.S. Rubinowitz, and M.J. Kulieke
   1986   *Low Income African-American Children in White Suburban Schools.* Evanston, Ill.: Cen-
           ter for Urban Affairs and Policy Research.
Rosenbaum, J.
   1992   Black pioneers—Do their moves to the suburbs increase economic opportunity for moth-
           ers and children? *Housing Policy Debate* 2(4):1179-1213.
Schramm, W.
   1985   WIC prenatal participation and its relationship to newborn Medicaid costs in Missouri: A
           cost/benefit analysis. *American Journal of Public Health* 75(8).
Starfield, B.
   1985   *Effectiveness of Medical Care: Validating Clinical Wisdom.* Baltimore, Md.: Johns
           Hopkins University Press.
Stewart, A.
   1992   *Head Start: Funding Eligibility, and Participation.* Report for Congress. Washington,
           D.C.: Congressional Research Service. July 22.
U.S. Department of Health and Human Services
   Various *Vital Statistics of the United States: Natality.* Washington, D.C.: Government Printing
   years   Office.
U.S. Department of Health and Human Services, Centers for Disease Control, Public Health Service
   1978   *CDC Analysis of Nutritional Indices for Selected WIC Participants.* FNS-176, June.
U.S. House of Representatives, Committee on Ways and Means
   1993   *1993 Green Book: Background Material and Data on Programs Within the Jurisdiction
           of the Committee on Ways and Means.* WMCP-103-18. Washington, D.C.: U.S. Govern-
           ment Printing Office.
   1994   *1994 Green Book: Background Material and Data on Programs Within the Jurisdiction
           of the Committee on Ways and Means.* WMCP-103-27. Washington, D.C.: U.S. Govern-
           ment Printing Office.
   1996   *1996 Green Book: Background Material and Data on Programs Within the Jurisdiction
           of the Committee on Ways and Means.* Washington, D.C.: U.S. Government Printing
           Office.
Venti, S.
   1984   The effects of income maintenance on work, schooling, and non-market activities of
           youth. *Review of Economics and Statistics* 66(1):16-25.